ARTISTS AND WRITERS COLONIES

RETREATS, RESIDENCIES, AND RESPITES FOR THE CREATIVE MIND

Blue Heron Publishing, Inc. • Hillsboro, Oregon

Artists and Writers Colonies:
Retreats, Residencies, and Respites for the Creative Mind

Copyright © 1995 by Gail Hellund Bowler.

Printed and bound in the United States of America.

Published by
Blue Heron Publishing, Inc.
24450 Northwest Hansen Road
Hillsboro, Oregon 97124
503.621.3911

First edition.

ISBN 0-936085-34-7
Library of Congress Catalog Card Number 95-79449

Publisher's Cataloging-in-Publication Data

Bowler, Gail Hellund.
    Artists and Writers Colonies/ by
        Gail Hellund Bowler. — 1st ed.
        p.   cm.
    Includes appendices and index.
    ISBN 0-936085-34-7
    1. How-to. 2. Artists and writers colonies.
3. Reference   I. Title

Contents

For my parents

June and Willie Hellund

Acknowledgments

First and foremost, I'd like to thank Dennis and Linny Stovall for enthusiastically supporting this project.

Words cannot express my gratitude to Nancy Nordhoff, Linda Bowers, Denise Anderson, and the entire staff at *Cottages at Hedgebrook* for providing me with two months of uninterrupted time, fabulous gourmet meals, a new cadre of wild and insane friends, and continuing support and friendship.

No writer makes her way alone, so for critiques, friendship, and advice along the way, I'd like to thank Barbarajene Williams, Tracy Robert, Tina Welling, Irene Wanner, Paul Sinor, Leslie Adkins, Eve Phillips, Linda Smith, Judi Raebel, Providence Cicero, Jeryl Phillips Stanton, Issabel Martinez, and Karen Thomas.

I'd also like to thank the *Edmonds Arts Commission* for inviting me to lecture on writers' colonies at their 1993 *Write on the Sound* conference. The research for that lecture led to the writing of this book.

And I must, of course, thank each and every one of the arts organizations listed in this book for providing artists with the unfettered gift of time and for supplying me with the information, application forms, brochures, and photographs that made this book a reality.

Last but not least, many thanks to my husband Michael for giving me a stable, loving, and supportive home environment and for encouraging me in my literary pursuits. And thanks also to my children, Shasta Turner and Bret Turner, for bringing purpose some twenty-odd years ago to my formerly eccentric and somewhat whimsical lifestyle.

A Note on the Data

Most of the information for this book was culled from brochures, flyers, and letters sent to me by the facilities listed. Another level of detail is provided to each applicant upon acceptance. All information was checked for accuracy at one point in time, but the research for this book began in 1992 and ended in mid-1995, so some information may need minor updating. I did my best to contact by letter, telephone, facsimile, or e-mail each of the facilities whose information was sent to me before 1995. Many responded with great alacrity, others did not. Therefore, I urge you to confirm offerings with the administrators of any facility in which you have an interest. People move. Programs lose funding. Area codes get reassigned. And rates change.

This book is meant to guide you in your search for a meaningful creative experience. It is not the bible of offerings and no facility is bound by what I've written. Please be sure to ask for the most recent guidelines when requesting your application forms, and always, I mean always, include a SASE with your request. Most of these organizations are nonprofit groups and their money would be better spent enhancing their facilities and programs than mailing out brochures.

Finally, please read each listing carefully before sending for information. If you meet all the qualifications, are capable of disengaging from your everyday life for the length of time they provide, and are able to finance the amenities not included with the award, then by all means, write or call and request an application form and brochure. Give yourself enough time to do justice to the application procedure — otherwise, you're wasting both your time and theirs. Good luck in your search for the experience of a lifetime.

Introduction

I know a man who took an Amtrak train from Seattle to Chicago and back so he could finish his manuscript before deadline. He was desperate. He bought the ticket, paid extra for one of those little sleeper compartments, and holed up in the train for six days. Later, he told his wife it was the only place he could think of where he knew he wouldn't be disturbed — where he would receive no telephone calls, no mail, no visitors — where he could stroll to the dining car when he wanted to eat and fold down his bed when he wanted to sleep. I thought he was brilliant until I found out how much the trip cost.

By contrast, I know a woman who took a one-year sabbatical from her teaching job, loaded all that mattered into her car, stored her furniture, broke-up with her boyfriend, and headed for the Pacific Northwest. She successfully piggybacked four writing residencies into free room and board for nine consecutive months, then returned to her hometown richer for the experience and clinging to a draft of her newly completed first novel. The woman had done her homework.

Artists' and writers' colonies are a well-kept secret. The colonies themselves don't advertise because the ratio of applicants to residencies is already quite high. And while most artists have a vague knowledge of the existence of colonies, either from magazine articles or from citations on the Acknowledgment page of a best seller, detailed information on colonies is so scarce, they're perceived as inaccessible — only for the elite. This is simply not true.

Opportunities exist for all types of artists from all walks of life. Across the board, each of the juried selection committees in this book is looking for one important thing: quality in the work. Some hosts prefer the innovative, experimental artist, while others want well-honed traditionalists. If your work doesn't appeal to one colony, it might appeal to another. Don't give up. Perseverance furthers.

Remember, just because some colonies charge a fee or request donations, don't rule them out. Imagine what it would cost you to hole-up in a cabin or motel for a month; or if you're a visual artist, what it would cost you to rent a studio or loft big enough to accommodate you and your work and to outfit it with all the tools you need. Can you find a place as reasonable in cost as a colony? A place that provides state-of-the-art equipment, low-cost (or free) materials, and the technical expertise of experienced professionals? A place that provides interaction with other artists and valuable professional contacts? Think about it. Then consider my friend who was willing to spend $864 to ride Amtrak's *Empire Builder* across the United States in a room no bigger than a closet just so he could concentrate on his work.

How to Use This Book

Artists and Writers Colonies includes residency, retreat, and fellowship opportunities for all types of artists and writers. There are many other opportunities available, such as grants, academic fellowships, and competition awards, but this book is focused on opportunities that provide either the time, the space, or the money for you to attempt new creative projects you would not otherwise be able to attempt in your everyday life.

There's a big difference between what counts as a residency for artists and what counts as a residency for writers. In the end, though, both artists and writers are seeking a place to work — without too much interference from the outside world, and without too much hassle from bill collectors. Luckily, there are people who understand us and do their best to support our efforts. Some provide studio space, equipment, and materials for visual artists; others offer theaters, sets, and audiences for performers; still others provide quaint little cottages for writers; and many offer funds to buy time or supplies.

This guide is arranged alphabetically in a simple-to-read format that allows you to scan the 175 comprehensive domestic listings with various personal considerations in mind, then to delve deeper as selection criteria are met and interest in a listing is piqued. Each listing provides the colony's name, address, and telephone number along with other pertinent data divided into eleven categories to help you make your decision. Start with listings in your area (use the appendix in the rear of the book to view listings by state); many facilities restrict their awards to people who live in their geographic region. Then study the other items of importance to you — cost, housing, equipment, etc. Look at the whole picture before you make your choice.

There are five types of listings in this book (and some variations on those). These definitions are general, not literal and sometimes seem to overlap:

Residencies: Residencies are a specific allotment of time awarded to an applicant to complete a specific project, which was probably predefined during the application process. Most residencies are served on the campus or grounds of a colony, foundation, university, art center, museum, or estate. Residencies provide various levels of physical and financial support for the artist. Some charge minimal fees for food, housing, materials, or studio space — some are free.

Retreats: Retreats are various commercial and noncommercial enterprises who cater to artists. They range from bed & breakfast houses and private lakeside cabins to monasteries and villas. Most retreats offer artists a private room with a private (or shared) bath. Some offer access to communal kitchens and/or studios, others send you out into the world to eat. All charge a fee, but because they house artists for long periods, most offer substantial discounts for long-term guests, especially during the winter. Some retreats have an application/selection process so they can screen candidates and assure residents of the atmosphere, privacy, and quiet they have a right to expect — others are booked on a first-come, first-served basis with no application necessary. Retreats are good for those who face deadlines and do not have time to go through the application, selection, notification, acceptance, and scheduling processes of colonies. Some retreats cost less than colonies and residencies.

Fellowships (and Grants): Fellowships are awards to artists, usually in the form of a combination of a residency and stipend. Most fellowships require Fellows to participate in the promotional activities of the sponsors, to interact with staff, community, and/or students, and to either teach classes, donate works of art, or allow the sponsors to advertise their affiliation with the artist. The amount of support for the artist varies and can be substantial. In some cases, it is based upon the recipient's pre-award earnings — other times it's a flat subsistence. Some fellowships provide housing and meals — some just give you a stipend. Many are nonresidential.

Opportunities for Playwrights: Because the structure of playwriting programs is a bit different from other programs, I have included those that offer full production, staged readings, and/or participation in developmental workshops, rehearsals, or playwriting festivals in this book. They do not provide undisturbed time as such, but they do provide playwrights with a valuable look at other aspects of their craft — the production experience — and the opportunity to see their work come alive on stage.

Artist-in-Residence Programs: These programs provide studio space, use of the center's equipment, materials, and sometimes room and board for free or at greatly reduced rates for selected artists. Residencies in these programs are usually long-term (from six months to three years). Since few of us have twelve to fifteen foot ceilings, overhead cranes, kilns, printing presses, or any of the other highly specialized tools these centers may provide, it's safe to say the work could not have been accomplished without the residency. Those who do not provide a stipend or living accommodations for the artists realize the artist must usually work (at least part-time) in order to survive. Some allow the artist to work at the center (either for a wage or for even exchange), others allow the artist to work outside the center as long as they spend a certain number of hours each week in their studios developing their art.

In the course of my research, I learned several things: Every state has an arts commission or an arts council. So do many cities and towns. Check the government listings in your telephone directory and call the arts commissions or councils in your area. Ask to be added to their mailing lists. See if any of their programs are suitable for you.

In light of the funding cuts to the National Endowment for the Arts, I decided not to list their programs in this book. That doesn't mean these programs aren't valuable; they are. But because the government has so many provisos to their awards, it would take another 300 pages to accurately describe their offerings. Besides, the likelihood of these programs surviving the current wave of budget cuts intact is slim, so I'm reluctant to describe programs that may undergo drastic restructuring. If you are interested in any N.E.A. programs, write for current offerings to the following address:

National Endowment for the Arts
Nancy Hanks Center
1100 Pennsylvania Avenue, N.W.
Washington, D.C. 20506-0001

If you know the name of the program, tell them. If you don't, do a little research at the library, at a university, or at an artist's resource organization in your area. If you have no luck, write the N.E.A. and tell them what you do. They'll send the appropriate booklets.

Another valuable booklet is *Internships and Fellowships* put out by the Smithsonian Institution (see my listing for the Smithsonian/Renwick Gallery). This booklet contains several opportunities for scholars and a few for writers and artists. Write to the address below to request their booklet:

Smithsonian Institution
Visitor Information and Associates' Reception Center
SI Building, Room 153, Stop 010
Washington, D.C. 20560

Another great place for writers is the public library. Libraries in the large metropolitan areas often offer little cubicles (and sometimes enclosed rooms) where writers can work. Some are free — some charge a modest fee. Some allow you to set up shop by bringing in your own computer, books, and materials, thereby establishing the area as your own. Some do not — they don't want the responsibility should your things mystically disappear. Besides space to work, libraries often sponsor readings, literary salons, and book signings, especially by local authors. Contact your librarian regarding these opportunities.

Here's another recommendation: check out the *Sanctuaries* books (there are two of them) by Jack and Marcia Kelly. One is for Monasteries, Abbeys, and Retreats in the Northeast and the other is for Monasteries, Abbeys, and Retreats in the Southwest. The Northeast volume was published in 1991 and has been remaindered. You can't order it from bookstores (although some still have copies on their shelves). The Southwest volume was published in 1993 and is still available through retail outlets. Many sanctuaries have programs for artists and writers, though this is not noted in their listings. (See my *Zen Mountain Monastery* listing.) If there is a monastery or abbey near you, you might give them a call and see if they have extended-stay programs. You'll be shocked at how inexpensive they are, considering most provide you with a private room and three meals a day, as well as a quiet environment in which to do your work.

Also, if you send for a brochure and don't receive anything back, don't fret. Many facilities deal with their application/selection processes only once or twice a year. If you catch them off cycle, you won't hear from them until they start preparing for their next batch of residents. You may have to wait months.

Okay, that's it. I've done all I can do for you now. It's your turn. Get out your highlighter pens, your Post-it Flags, or your Book Darts. Start searching. If you don't have any marking materials, grab a handful of paperclips, or limber up your thumb and forefinger — dog-ear the pages that interest you. Then sit down and request a few brochures. The opportunities are as varied as the listings themselves. There's no telling what may come from all this.

A simple glossary:

> SASE = Self-addressed, stamped envelope
> SASP = Self-addressed, stamped postcard
> SASB = Self-addressed, stamped box
> AIR = Artist-in-Residence
> Rolling application process = Apply anytime

Academy of Motion Picture Arts & Sciences
THE NICHOLL FELLOWSHIPS   CA

Academy of Motion Picture Arts & Sciences
Academy Foundation
The Nicholl Fellowships in Screenwriting
8949 Wilshire Boulevard
Beverly Hills, California 90211-1972

Attention: Julian Blaustein, Chair
(310) 247-3035

Type of Facility/Award
Fellowship.

Who Can Apply
Screenwriters.

Provisos
Screenwriters who have not earned money or other consideration as a screenwriter for theatrical films or television, or for the sale of (or sale of an option to) any original story, treatment, screenplay or teleplay for more than $1,000 are eligible. Applicants may not have received a screenwriting fellowship that includes a "first look" clause, an option, or any other *quid pro quo* involving the writer's work. No students.

Dates of Operation
Fellowship year begins in mid-November.

Location
This is a nonresidential fellowship.

History
No history or background provided.

What They Offer
Up to five awards of $25,000 each payable in five installments over a one-year period may be awarded each year. Winners are expected to complete at least one original screenplay (100 to 130 pages in length) during the fellowship year. Installment payments are made quarterly, subject to the Committee's satisfaction with the recipient's progress and work. Schedule and nature of fellow's progress will be established at the time of the initial fellowship payment (November 11 for 1995). Nicholls Fellowships may not be held concurrently with other fellowships or any other similar award or while completing a formal course of study. The fellowship year may be deferred to allow a student winner to complete his or her education.

Facility Description
This is a nonresidential fellowship.

How to Apply
Send a SASE for an application form and brochure. Return the completed application, a $30 entry fee, and a single copy of your original screenplay (in screenplay format standard to the United States motion picture industry) to the Academy. Screenplays must have been originally written in English — no translations. No collaborative works. Scripts will not be returned. Those who make it to the final judging round will be asked to submit a letter to the Nicholl Committee giving the Committee some idea of the writer's personal and professional interests as they relate to the fellowship should he or she receive one.

Deadline
May 1 (postmarked). Notification in mid-October.

Approximate Cost of a Four-week Residency
$30, plus transportation, housing, meals, materials, and incidentals offset by stipend.

ACADIA NATIONAL PARK   ME

Acadia National Park
Artist-in-Residence Program
P.O. Box 177
Bar Harbor, Maine 04609

Attention: Coordinator
(207) 288-5459 or (207) 288-5507 Fax

Type of Facility/Award
Artist-in-Residency Program.

Who Can Apply
Professional writers, musicians, composers, dancers, and all visual and performing artists.

Provisos
None listed.

Dates of Operation
Spring and Fall.

Location
Bar Harbor, Maine.

History

"In the mid 1800's, landscape painters, including Thomas Cole and Frederic Church, came to Mount Desert Island and captured its beauty on canvas. Their work inspired writers, composers, naturalists, and folks from far away to seek the natural splendor of the island. Those who followed were known as rusticators because they ate and lived with the local fisherman and farmers during their summer stay. The rusticators returned each summer to delight in the tranquillity of Mount Desert Island, and for some, to practice their craft. Villagers' cottages and fishermen's huts soon overflowed and by 1880, thirty hotels competed for vacationers' dollars. Ballet, opera, musical festivals, and readings flourished each summer on Mount Desert Island. Over the years accommodations have increased, but the heart of what first drew people here remains as Acadia National Park."

What They Offer

Acadia provides housing to artists for two-week periods of time in the Spring and the Fall. There is no stipend for living expenses. In return, artists are asked to donate a piece of work to the Park's collection. Works will be displayed or shared with the public through appropriate means. Artists are also asked to share an offering with the public in the form of a demonstration of skills, a talk, an exploratory hike, or a performance requiring only a few hours of the artist's time.

Facility Description

Acadia National Park offers a perfect setting for artists to practice and pursue their craft. With its dramatic cliffs stretching to the sea, its balsam scented forests, and spring warbler serenades, the area offers artists the age-old inspiration of nature. No description of artist's housing was provided.

How to Apply

Send a SASE for brochure. Submit six copies of the following: a one- to two-page résumé and summary of creative works, and a one-page statement describing what you hope to achieve while in residency at the park. Submit an appropriate sample of your recent work and an adequate SASE for its return. *Visual artists:* send six slides. *Musicians* and composers: send a cassette recording. *Dancers and performing artists:* send a ¹/₂" VHS video tape. *Writers and poets:* send a brief manuscript excerpt, a short story, an article, and/or some poems (maximum six pages).

Deadline

January 10. Notification by March 1.

Approximate Cost of a Four-week Residency

Transportation, meals, materials, and incidentals.

ACTS Institute
ACT 1 CREATIVITY CENTER   MO

Act 1 Creativity Center
Box 278
Lake Ozark, Missouri 65049

Attention: Charlotte Plotsky, Administrator
(314) 365-4404

Notice: All attempts to contact the administrator of Act 1 Creativity Center failed. All mail was returned marked "Moved. Not Forwardable." The Center's residency program had converted to "by invitation only" several years ago and information on them after that became sketchy. The above telephone number is not disconnected, but no one answers. Inquire at your own risk.

The Adamant Community Cultural Foundation
THE ADAMANT PROGRAM   VT

The Adamant Program
P.O. Box 73
Adamant, Vermont 05640-0073

Attention: Patricia Hutchinson, Assistant Resident Manager
(802) 223-2324 or (802) 223-0915 Fax

Administration and Winter Address:
The Adamant Program
P.O. Box 1515
7055 N.E. Crawford Drive
Kingston, Washington 98346

Attention: Magdalena Herreshoff, Resident Manager
(360) 297-7220

Type of Facility/Award
Residency.

Who Can Apply
Visual artists, writers, poets, playwrights, and screenwriters.

Provisos
The program seeks applicants with professional standing in their field, but will consider emerging artists of recognized ability. Couples and collaborators must apply individually. Collaborators should submit a joint description of their project. It benefits The Program if collaborators share one studio.

Dates of Operation
September and October (eight weeks). Dates vary from year to year.

Location
The Village of Adamant is near Montpelier, Vermont.

History
"The goal of The Program is to provide an opportunity for participants to work with optimum freedom and privacy in a non-competitive atmosphere. A diverse cluster of approximately fifteen artists in different fields attend The Program resulting in rich personal and artistic interchanges."

What They Offer
The Adamant program offers residency terms of three weeks to eight weeks each year in early Fall. Housing is provided. All meals are provided: lunch and dinner are prepared; breakfast materials are supplied. (Residents are asked to have their evening meals together.) No cleaning services are supplied, so everyone must cooperate in keeping the buildings clean and comfortable. The residency fee is $25 per day. This includes housing, all three meals, and your studio space. One or two full grants are available for artists of special talent who can demonstrate need, and limited fee reductions ($10 or $15 per day) are available (with additional documentation) to those who are unable to pay the full cost. (Federal Tax Returns must be submitted with your request for a fee reduction or grant.) Residents are encouraged to share their work with one another at informal evening get-togethers. A mini-exhibition in town is organized for artists and the community. The *Quarry Works Program* consists of a "Month of Sundays" of original play readings, Wednesday night playwriting classes, and the *Granite Series* — intensive workshops on selected plays-in-progress or finished plays. Indicate on your application if you'd like to participate in the *Quarry Works Program*. No pets are allowed.

Facility Description
Visual artists' studios have northern light and are equipped with an easel, tabouret, and work table. The writing studios have tables with desk lights. Because all studios are separate, residents work in undisturbed quiet and privacy. Studios are simply furnished. The Phillips Experimental Theatre, a professionally designed space for intimate performances, is at the Quarry site, a fifteen minute walk from the main house. Costume changes and other related theater activities take place in a small building next to the theater. Also at the Quarry is a lounge overlooking the pond where artists and writers can relax and think.

How to Apply
Send a SASE for an application form and brochure. (Information in this listing is from their 1994 brochure. Request current guidelines when inquiring.) Return completed application with a $10 nonrefundable application fee, a résumé, a history of your recent achievements, three references who know you and your work (first-time

applicants only), and a work sample. Enclose an adequate SASE if you want your sample returned. Send applications and inquiries to the Resident Manager in Kingston, Washington. *Writers:* Send a sample of work representative of the genre in which you intend to work at Adamant. If you submit a work-in-progress, you must also submit a sample of a finished work. Submit three copies of six to ten poems, three copies of up to three short stories, three copies of a book (or one book and three sets of photocopies of the first chapter or first ten pages), or two copies of a complete script for playwrights or screenwriters. *Visual artists:* Send five color slides of recent work (packaged and labeled according to instructions) with accompanying descriptive sheet. *Photographers:* Send five actual examples of work in a suitable mailer. *Printmakers:* Send five unmatted, original prints in a suitable mailer. If you are accepted, you may pick up your work samples when you arrive for your residency.

Deadline

May 31 (received). Notification in June.

Approximate Cost of a Four-week Residency

$710, plus transportation, materials, and incidentals. One or two full grants are available. Limited fee reductions are available.

The Edward F. Albee Foundation, Inc.
THE WILLIAM FLANAGAN MEMORIAL
CREATIVE PERSONS CENTER   NY

The William Flanagan Memorial Creative Persons Center
Fairview Avenue
Montauk, New York 11954
(516) 668-5435

Administration/Information/Applications

The Edward F. Albee Foundation, Inc.
14 Harrison Street
New York, New York 10013

Attention: Artist's Residency Program
(212) 226-2020

Type of Facility/Award

Residency.

Who Can Apply

Writers, painters, sculptors, and composers.

Provisos

The Foundation encourages qualified artists of all backgrounds to apply. It does not discriminate against anyone on any basis whatsoever other than artistic merit and need. It is the policy of the Foundation that no one with the AIDS virus, ARC, or HIV shall be denied admission as long as he or she is qualified. The Foundation expects all those who are accepted to work seriously and to aid fellow artists in their endeavors.

Dates of Operation
June 1 to October 1.

Location
The Center is on Long Island, two miles from the center of Montauk.

History
The Foundation was established in 1968.

What They Offer
The Edward F. Albee Foundation offers one-month residencies at the William Flanagan Memorial Creative Persons Center on Long Island. Specify which month you would prefer, but include second and third choices. The Center can comfortably accommodate four or five people at a time. Standards for admission are talent and need. Writers and composers are offered a room. Visual artists are offered a room and studio space. Residents are responsible for their own food, travel, and other expenses. Residents are expected to do their share of work to maintain the condition of "The Barn."

Facility Description
"The Barn," as the Center is known, rests on a secluded knoll, offering residents a quiet, private, and peaceful atmosphere.

How to Apply
Send a SASE for an application form and guidelines. Return the completed application form and the Personal Information Form with a résumé, two letters of recommendation, a letter of intent (outlining your proposed project), two mailing labels (last name first), and some samples of your work (with an adequate SASE for their return). *Painters or sculptors:* Send six to twelve slides of your work. *Playwrights or screenwriters:* Send a manuscript. *Poets:* Send twelve poems. *Fiction writers:* Send one short story or two chapters from a novel. *Nonfiction writers:* Send three essays or articles. *Composers:* Send a recording of at least two original compositions. Application materials must be sent to the Harrison Street address by regular mail only. No hand deliveries. No mail deliveries that require extra postage or signed receipts.

Deadline
April 1 (postmarked). Applications will only be accepted between January 1 and April 1 each year. Fellowships announced by May 15.

Approximate Cost of a Four-week Residency
Transportation, meals, materials, and incidentals.

Alternate Visions
c/o Alternate Roots
1083 Austin Avenue, N.E.
Atlanta, Georgia 30307

Attention: Lisa Grady-Willis
(404) 577-1079

Type of Facility/Award
Fellowship/Grant.

Who Can Apply
All artists — all disciplines — individuals and collaborators.

Provisos
Individuals and teams of collaborators who have resided for more than one year in Georgia, Kentucky, Tennessee, North Carolina, or South Carolina. High school students, or students enrolled full-time in a degree-granting program are not eligible. Nor are grant recipients from the most recent year. Staff and Executive Committee members of Alternate Roots are ineligible.

Dates of Operation
Open year-round.

Location
This is a nonresidential grant.

History
The Alternate Visions Grant Program seeks to support new artistic projects from individual artists and groups of collaborating artists who: extend or explore new definitions or boundaries of traditions and cultures, such as exploring ancestral approaches in a contemporary format; push the limits of artistic expression through experimentation with new forms; explore different artistic disciplines, resulting in interdisciplinary work (using two or more art forms); and take risks by challenging values, beliefs, stereotypes, and cultural limits. This program is supported by the National Endowment for the Arts Presenting Program, The Rockefeller Foundation, The Andy Warhol Foundation for the Visual Arts, the North Carolina Arts Council, the Kentucky Arts Council, the South Carolina Arts Council, the Tennessee Arts Commission, and Alternate Roots.

"Alternate Roots is a regional membership organization that supports the creation and presentation of original, community-based performing arts in the Southeast. Services including communication, networking, artistic development, audience/community development, and regional and national liaisons."

What They Offer

Ten to twelve grants, ranging from $2,000 to $5,000, will be awarded each year for projects that reflect the cultural and aesthetic diversity of our country. Intercultural projects are particularly encouraged. Work should begin in October and take no longer than one year to complete. Grants will not fund: projects that are already completed; work used toward the completion of a degree program, or conceived primarily as an educational project or student production; travel to other countries; or projects that consist solely of documentation of work (for example, a video of previously produced work).

Facility Description

No facility or studio description is provided.

How to Apply

Send a SASE for an application and brochure. Return the original and nine additional copies of the completed application form and the Project Budget Proposal Form, typed or printed neatly. Include ten copies of each of the following: a one-page résumé, career summary, or bio for applicant and collaborators (if any), then: a one-page Collaborators' Statement, describing the relationship between the artists (ownership of completed work, division of responsibilities) and the role of each in the creative process, signed by all collaborators. Also send a sample of your work (collaborators must provide a work sample from each collaborator). Include no more than two of the following forms: a ¹/₂" VHS Video tape cued to a continuous five minute sample; a cued audio tape (each work on a separate tape); ten collated copies of five typed pages of a manuscript; up to ten slides (labeled according to instructions) per artist and accompanied by a descriptive sheet; compact discs (with track number indicated); or clearly labeled sketches, photos, site maps, etc. No long-playing record albums accepted with proposal. Do not include original artwork or slides. Optional inclusions with your submission are: a SASE adequate for return of your support materials; one copy each of up to three examples of other support materials such as past reviews, press coverage, letters of support, etc.; and a SASP if you want Alternate Visions to acknowledge receipt of your proposal.

Deadline

1995 dates:
June 1 (postmarked) for proposals. Announcement of Awards: October 1. Dispersal of Funds: October 15. Interim Report due: April 1. Final Project Report Due: Upon completion (no later than October 1 the following year).

Approximate Cost of a Four-week Residency

Transportation, housing, meals, and incidentals.

MARY ANDERSON CENTER FOR THE ARTS   IN

The Mary Anderson Center for the Arts
101 St. Francis Drive
Mount St. Francis, Indiana 47146

Attention: Sarah Roberson Yates, Director or Susan G. Fey, Assistant Director
(812) 923-8602

Type of Facility/Award
Residency with or without fellowship.

Who Can Apply
Writers, musicians, visual artists, artisans, composers, and scholars.

Provisos
None listed. Center is handicapped-accessible.

Dates of Operation
Open year-round.

Location
The Center is located in rural southern Indiana, ten minutes from downtown Louisville, Kentucky. It shares 400 wooded acres with the Mount St. Francis Friary and Retreat Center, but is not affiliated with the Franciscan Order or the Catholic Church.

History
The program for artists' residencies was established in 1989. It began as a secular outgrowth of the Conventual Franciscan Friars to continue their 700-year heritage of fostering spiritual, cultural, and educational expressions. The name and inspiration for the Center came from the 19th century Louisville actress, Mary Anderson, who originally owned the 400 acres that became Mount St. Francis. By giving the land to the stewardship of the Friars, she hoped to preserve its natural environment. The setting provides calm and beauty for body and mind.

What They Offer
The Center has a year-round residency and retreat program. Residency terms are from one week to three months. Retreats are from one to six days. Residencies are by application. Retreats are by reservation. The fee for either is $50 per day. This includes your room, studio space (if necessary), and all meals. There are no fee abatements available for retreats. Reduced fee residencies are available by application. Applicants are asked to pay what they can afford, but the suggested minimum is $25 per day. The Center also requests those attending on a reduced fee basis to donate a work of art to be used in Loftus House or the Center's library, or as a tool for fund raising. In the case of published authors or recorded audio artists, they request a donation of autographed copies of at least one work. For visual artists, they request one work in any medium. Additionally, the Center offers a few par-

tially- and fully-subsidized fellowships. Fellowship information is included in every application packet.

The Center also has three continuing fellowship programs. Eight *Mary Anderson Fellowships* are awarded annually. Four fellowships are offered to writers in any genre, three are offered to visual artists and artisans, and one is offered to a musician or composer. This fellowship awards artists at mid-career the opportunity to spend one month in residency. The *Senior Fellows Program* recognizes artistic excellence in writers and visual artists and artisans who are fifty years old or older. Four awards are made annually, two to artists from Indiana and two to artists from Kentucky. *Mentoring Fellowships for Emerging Artists* are designed to recognize talent and potential in artists who do not yet have a significant publication or show record. Other fellowship opportunities provided by various endowments (but not necessarily on an annual basis) are also available each year. Interested artists should contact the Center for details on those programs.

Artists and scholars who are accepted are offered a residency that includes a private room, use of studio space (visual artists), and all meals except Sunday and Monday night dinners. If you go out to dinner on Sundays or Mondays, the Center will reimburse you up to $6 toward your meal if you provide them with a receipt. Breakfast foods are provided, but not prepared. Residents must provide their own transportation to the Center. No visitors. No children. No pets. No phones in rooms.

Facility Description

The Center is located on 400 acres in Indiana. It is a wildlife refuge with trails to hike and a lake to fish in or just sit beside and contemplate. The Loftus House, which is handicapped-accessible, contains the Center's offices, resident's sleeping rooms, and some studios. Each resident is provided with a sleeping room (with wash basin and mirror), which doubles as their studio for writers and scholar. There are six rooms available, three on each floor. Each floor has one bathroom for residents' shared use. The Visual Arts Studio, which is near the Great Barn, has two to four studio spaces. The top floor has two Vandercook letter presses; the lower level has a potter's wheel and kiln. The Center does not have any radios, televisions, or stereo equipment, nor do they subscribe to a daily newspaper. If you want these things, you must bring them.

How to Apply

Send SASE for brochure and application. Submit the $15 nonrefundable application fee and two copies of everything, including: completed application form; description of project; list of publications, performances, exhibitions, or presentation credits; two references who have professional knowledge of your work and who are professionally active in your creative area; and a work sample (with SASE). *Writers and scholars:* Two copies of a maximum of thirty pages of prose or twenty pages of poetry. *Visual artists and artisans:* One set of ten slides (labeled according to instructions) with accompanying descriptive sheet. *Musicians, composers, and performers:* One audio or video tape (VHS only) with accompanying narrative sheet.

Deadline

Rolling application process. Decisions within one month of application. Mary Anderson Fellowships: Visual Arts — July 1; Writing — August 1; Music — November 1. Senior Fellowships: September 1. Mentoring Fellowships: Variable.

Be sure to call about various other offerings provided during the year. Sometimes the center receives one-time gifts to fund residencies.

Approximate Cost of a Four-week Residency

$1,415 for the retreat, plus transportation, materials, and incidentals. $715 for a reduced-fee residency, plus transportation, materials, and incidentals. Some fellowships are free except for transportation, materials, and incidentals. Call the Center for details on financial aid and one-time fellowship gifts.

ANDERSON RANCH ARTS CENTER   CO

Anderson Ranch Arts Center
P.O. Box 5598
5263 Owl Creek Road
Snowmass Village, Colorado 81615

Attention: Artists Residency Program
(303) 923-3181, (800) 525-2722, or (303) 923-3871

Type of Facility/Award

Residency.

Who Can Apply

Visual artists (woodworkers, furniture makers, photographers, painters, sculptors, ceramists, printmakers, book artists, etc.)

Provisos

Anderson Ranch Arts Center seeks artists who are eager to learn and to share and who have a commitment to exploration in the studio and a willingness to communicate formally and informally with other artists in a broad range of media.

Dates of Operation

October 1 through April 30.

Location

Anderson Ranch Arts Center is ten miles west of Aspen in Snowmass Village. United Airlines serves Aspen airport, which is seven miles from the ranch. Taxi or bus service is available to Snowmass Village. Denver airport is a four hour drive (200 miles) away. Limousine service is available through Aspen Limo. Travel discounts are available if you book your ticket through Aspen Travel.

History

Anderson Ranch Arts Center is a nonprofit educational organization with top national artists providing instruction in a variety of disciplines throughout the summer to artists of all ages and levels.

What They Offer

In exchange for twenty hours of work each month, Anderson Ranch offers each resident studio space, studio utilities (excluding kiln firings), technical consultations/discussions, and a spring show in the Dow's Gallery. They also provide a single-occupancy dorm room, ten meals weekly (delicious, healthy, fresh), and a monthly materials stipend of $200. The six-month residencies are for self-motivated artists — no formal instruction is involved. Anderson Ranch Arts Center also has a summer program for visiting professional and emerging artists who want to lead workshops. Call or write for information and an application if you are interested in that program.

Facility Description

The facility is spread out over four acres. Old West farm buildings house state-of-the-art studios and workshops. Hay lofts, barns, and outdoor patios serve as work places, too. There is a volleyball court and a big white tent for slide shows and gatherings.

How to Apply

Write or call for brochure and application form. Return completed application with ten to twenty 35 mm slides of your work, a descriptive sheet of the slides, a résumé, a brief statement of your career goals and reason for applying, three references who can be reached by phone and your relationship to each, and a SASE for return of your slides.

Deadline

5 p.m. on May 1. Notification by telephone — no time frame stipulated.

Approximate Cost of a Four-week Residency

Transportation, some meals, incidentals, and materials — offset by stipend.

APOSTLE ISLANDS NATIONAL LAKESHORE   WI

Apostle Islands National Lakeshore
Route 1, Box 4
Bayfield, Wisconsin 54814

Attention: Kate Miller, Artist-in-Residence Program
(715) 779-339 or (715) 779-3049 Fax

Type of Facility/Award

Artist-in-Residence Program.

Who Can Apply

All artists and writers.

Provisos

Applicants must be residents of the United States. Artist should be self-sufficient and in good health as the accommodations provided are somewhat primitive and remote. Selection committee will consider all forms of art except those that manipulate or disturb the park's environment. Selections are made without regard to race, religion, marital status, sex, age, or national origin. The Wellish Cabin is not handicapped-accessible.

Dates of Operation

Late June through mid-September.

Location

The Apostle Islands are located in Western Lake Superior, off Wisconsin's Bayfield Peninsula. The Park is ninety miles east of Duluth, Minnesota, 217 miles north of the Minneapolis/St. Paul area, and 352 miles north of Milwaukee, Wisconsin. Access is by private or concession-operated boat.

History

The Apostle Islands Artist-in-Residence program began in 1994. It's part of a continuing tradition by the National Park Service to support professional artists. Painters, photographers, writers, journalists, musicians, and composers (among others) have helped to stimulate interest in the national parks and foster an appreciation of them through artistic expression.

What They Offer

Artists are housed in the Wellish Cabin, located on the southeast shore of Sand Island about three miles by boat from the Little Sand Bay Ranger Station. The residency is a minimum of two weeks with no maximum stated. While basic cooking utensils and fuel are provided, the artist must bring bedding, personal gear, food, and art supplies — all of which need to be purchased before the residency begins. The cabin is about a half-mile from the boat dock; whatever you bring with you must be carried that distance. The artist is asked to donate a finished piece of work inspired during the island stay to the program.

Facility Description

Apostle Islands National Lakeshore is spread out over a 750-square mile area. Twenty-one of the twenty-two Apostle Islands and a twelve-mile stretch of the mainland shoreline make up the National Lakeshore.

Wellish Cabin is simple but roomy, with a large living room, three bedrooms, and a screened porch. The cabin has a vault toilet, no electricity, and no running water. Expect cool temperatures, muddy trail conditions, and insects. A forest trail connects the Wellish Cabin with the Sand Island Lighthouse, established in 1881 and now staffed by volunteers. "Along the way are old farmstead clearings, towering white pines that escaped the logger's axe, and stones for skipping over Justice Bay. Early summer's brilliant wildflowers give way to the lush blueberry patches in August. Storms roll in and retreat, leaving rainbows over the low green profiles of neighboring York and Raspberry Islands. The interplay of the land and lake, the song of wood thrushes, and lingering stories of shipwrecks and lightkeepers are among the many sources of inspiration for an artist's creative endeavors."

How to Apply

Send a SASE for an entry form and brochure. Return the completed form with a one-to-two page résumé and summary of your creative work, a statement describing your ability to meet the selection criteria and what you hope to achieve from a wilderness residency, your preference of dates, and samples of your work (with an adequate SASE for return). *Visual Artists:* send no more than six 35 mm slides. *Musicians and composers:* send a cassette. *Dancers and performing artists:* send a video cassette. *Writers and journalists:* send a brief manuscript excerpt, short story, article, etc.

Deadline

December 31 (postmarked).

Approximate Cost of a Four-week Residency

Transportation, meals, materials, and incidentals.

ARROWMONT SCHOOL OF ARTS AND CRAFTS   TN

Arrowmont School of Arts and Crafts
P.O. Box 567
556 Parkway
Gatlinburg, Tennessee 37738-0567

Attention: Artist-in-Residence Program
(615) 436-5860 or (615) 430-4101 Fax

Type of Facility/Award

Residency.

Who Can Apply

Visual artists.

Provisos

Arrowmont is looking for pre-professional, self-directed visual artists with "team spirit" who enjoy working independently as well as with staff, visiting faculty, and other residents. Interaction with community, conferences, children's programs, high-school programs, and Elderhostel art classes is encouraged.

Dates of Operation

Residencies begin in mid-September.

Location

The School is located just three miles from the entrance to the Great Smoky Mountains National Park in eastern Tennessee. Knoxville, Tennessee, and Asheville, North

---

Carolina, are within easy driving distance. Atlanta and Nashville are approximately four hours by car.

History

Arrowmont School, an internationally known visual arts complex, was established in 1945.

What They Offer

Three to five artists are selected annually for residencies lasting from nine to eleven months. Participation in Arrowmont's other programs is encouraged. Artists live on campus in the Watson House (a shared home) and have private studios in the resident artist studio complex for a modest monthly fee of $175 (covers housing and studio space). Access to Arrowmont's main studio (with specialized equipment) is available for a nominal fee. There is also an opportunity to work with visiting artists of national/international reputation. At the end of the residency, a group exhibition at the Arrowmont Atrium Gallery features work made by the artists during their residencies. In addition to pursuing their own work, residents are required to work for Arrowmont eight hours each week in one of the following capacities: community outreach (Artists in Schools), studio maintenance, gallery installation, instructing for other Arrowmont programs, food service, book/supply store, photography, or office/computer. Work assignments are established according to the resident's skill and interests before the residency begins. A scholarship for women in need (*Trabue Professional Arts Program for Women*) is available.

Facility Description

Situated on seventy acres of wooded hillside, the setting alone is a source of visual stimulation and inspiration. Arrowmont has large, well-equipped studio facilities for ceramics, jewelry, metalworking, textiles, weaving, papermaking, book arts, painting, drawing, photography, and woodturning. Arrowmont's resource center includes a wide assortment of books and periodicals for residents to use.

How to Apply

Send a SASE for application and brochure. Return the completed application with a $10 nonrefundable application fee, twenty slides of your most recent work (with an adequate SASE for their return), two letters of recommendation, and a personal statement of your present and future goals and what you expect to gain from a residency at Arrowmont. If you are applying for the *Trabue* scholarship (women only), include a letter explaining your financial need, plus a letter of support.

Deadline

April 30.

Approximate Cost of a Four-week Residency

$175 per month, plus $10 application fee, transportation, meals, incidentals, and materials.

Art Awareness, Inc.
Route 42, Box 177
Lexington, New York 12452-0177

Attention: Artists Residencies Director
(518) 989-6433

Type of Facility/Award
Residency.

Who Can Apply
Artists in the fields of dance, theater, performance art, and artists collaborating on interdisciplinary projects that include at least one of the above disciplines.

Provisos
Art Awareness is especially interested in providing a supportive environment, time, and funds for the development of new works. Students will not be considered for residencies, but may inquire about summer internships.

Dates of Operation
June through August.

Location
Lexington, New York, is three hours north of New York City and an hour and a half west of Albany, New York, in the northern Catskill Mountains.

History
Art Awareness is a nonprofit, multidisciplinary development-center for visual and performing artists. The center is located on the grounds of the Lexington House Resort, a turn-of-the-century Victorian hotel, now a center for the development of new works of art and for the presentation of new and established works by contemporary professional artists.

What They Offer
Residencies from two weeks to three months offer artists time to work on their projects, after which time they either mount an exhibition of their work or create an installation indoors in the galleries or outdoors on the grounds of Art Awareness. All works created belong to the artist. A stipend of up to $125 per week, a minimum travel allowance of $100, and up to $3,000 to cover artist's fees, materials, and supplies is available. (Average amount provided is $750 for fees and supplies.) Artists in residence are provided a combination living/studio space (private bedroom) and use of a shared kitchen and bath.

The Center also has a print studio and invites sculptors, painters, and other visual artists wishing to explore the printmaking process to submit proposals for two-week residencies in the silkscreen print studio. This program offers $125 weekly stipends plus all materials, supplies, and instruction.

Facility Description

Lodging and cooking facilities are provided for groups up to 20 in number. Additional lodging is available for larger groups at nearby facilities at prevailing rates.

How to Apply

Send a SASE for brochure. Then send a proposal with a budget and appropriate supporting materials (slides/minimum 20, video/audio tapes, résumé, reviews, etc.). Enclose an adequate SASE for return of your support materials.

Deadline

May 30 (for current year). October 30 (for residencies the following year).

Approximate Cost of a Four-week Residency

Limited transportation costs, meals, and incidentals according to approved budget, and offset by honorarium.

ART FARM   NE

Art Farm
1306 West 21st Road
Marquette, Nebraska 68854-2112

Attention: Ed Dadey and Janet Williams, Co-directors
(402) 854-3120 Voice and fax

Type of Facility/Award

Artist-in-Residence Program.

Who Can Apply

All artists.

Provisos

Artists must be self-motivated and resourceful. Those skilled with tools will find it a plus.

Dates of Operation

May 1 to October 31.

Location

Located in South Central Nebraska, Art Farm is about 130 miles west of Omaha.

History

Art Farm is a nonprofit organization providing a rural worksite for artists. Art Farm is set up to provide artists with a worksite, resources, support, and time to experiment with new ideas or projects. The Artist-in-Residence program at Art Farm began in 1993, though ground work began twenty years ago when Ed Dadey, after graduating from college, moved back to his family's farm near Marquette. In a search for studio space, he noticed a number of barns in the area and, over a seven year period, began moving them to his parent's farm. The work at Art Farm of restoring, repairing, and converting barns for studio space continues today.

What They Offer

Art Farm offers living accommodations and studio space for up to three artists at a time in exchange for fifteen hours of labor each week (three hours each day five days a week). Labor can be any of the following: general construction, deconstruction and carpentry (renovating barns, roofing, concrete pouring, etc.); maintenance (upkeep of grounds, mowing, tending the vegetable garden, fixing equipment and machinery, running errands, etc.); or office work. A residency of two months is recommended since it takes a while to adjust to the environment. Bring your own bed linens and towels. Artists must be able to cover their own daily expenses and telephone charges. Residencies are available from May 1 to October 31.

Facility Description

Art Farm is a working farm, growing everything from hybrid corn to eighty species of prairie grass. The environs are part of a drainage basin forming the headwaters of the Big Blue River. The landscape, mainly cornfields, varies from flat to gently rolling to shallow wetlands. Two miles northwest of the farm is the Platte River, where the flat landscape changes into clay bluffs. Besides the twenty outdoor acres, there are three farm buildings (each with approximately 750-square feet of floor space) used for studios. Other buildings will be converted in the future. The renovation plan includes a ceramics studio as well as additional studio and living space in what was once a rural schoolhouse. Additionally, there is a 12,000-square foot building being renovated for woodworking, metalworking, printing, photography, and computers. Artists must arrange to use this facility. A granary has been converted to a gallery. There are tractors and other farm equipment that can be used for loading, heavy lifting, and earthmoving.

Artists stay in a 100-year old white clapboard house. It accommodates three and is equipped with pots, pans, kitchen utensils, and laundry facilities.

How to Apply

Send a SASE for an application and brochure. Return completed application form with a current résumé, ten slides of your recent work (labeled according to instructions and with an adequate SASE for their return). The application asks for a brief statement of why you would like a residency at Art Farm, a description of your work-exchange skills, and the names and addresses of three references.

Deadline

March 1 for residencies beginning in May. June 1 for residencies beginning in August. Apply two months before desired residency period.

Approximate Cost of a Four-week Residency

Transportation, meals, materials, and incidentals.

ART/OMI
55 Fifth Avenue, 15th Floor
New York, New York 10003

Attention: Linda Cross, Executive Director
(212) 206-6060

Type of Facility/Award

Residency.

Who Can Apply

Visual artists.

Provisos

Artists worldwide are welcome to apply. Some artists are invited to apply because of referrals from arts professionals, others are selected through the application process. Emphasis is on painting and sculpture, but other media are invited to apply.

Dates of Operation

Three weeks in July. (Dates vary from year to year.)

Location

Omi is located in Columbia County, New York, in the Hudson River Valley.

History

ART/OMI's principal focus is "an international residency program to which artists from around the world are invited. The goal is to provide a supportive and stimulating community with uninterrupted time to create. The residencies offer participants a unique opportunity to interact with other artists representing a variety of cultures and backgrounds."

What They Offer

ART/OMI offers twelve to twenty people an intensive three-week residency. Held each year in July, residents receive housing, food, and studio space at no cost. At the end of the residency, there is an exhibition of the artists' work that receives considerable audience and publicity. Since ART/OMI is a nonprofit organization, they ask each artist to donate a piece of work created during the residency to the organization for inclusion in a fundraising project.

In August of 1995, ART/OMI sponsored a ten-day residency for arts professionals (critics, curators, etc.). This may have been a special program for 1995 only. Write or call if you are interested in attending a program of this nature in the future.

Facility Description

Residents are housed in the surrounding community. Meals and other group activities take place in one central location. A large, modern two-story barn, sitting on fifteen acres of rural farmland, is used for studios. There are several sheds that lend themselves well to large sculpture projects, while the grounds provide room for site-specific installations.

How to Apply

Send a SASE for application guidelines. Submit six 35 mm slides (packaged and labeled according to instructions) accompanied by a descriptive sheet and a curriculum vitae listing your education, exhibitions, name, address, telephone number, age, sex, and language spoken. Include a SASE for return of your slides.

Deadline

March 1.

Approximate Cost of a Four-week Residency

Transportation, materials, and incidentals.

ASIAN AMERICAN ARTS CENTRE   NY

Asian American Arts Centre
26 Bowery
New York, New York 1003

Attention: Artist-in-Residence Program
(212) 233-2154 or (212) 766-1287

Type of Facility/Award

Artist-in-Residence

Who Can Apply

Visual artists.

Provisos

Applicants must be Asian Americans under thirty years of age, must be residents of the state of New York, and must have recently graduated from a BFA or MFA program. (Artists who do not meet this criteria would need to present an exceptional case in their application materials.)

Dates of Operation

September through May.

Location

New York.

History

This program is funded by the New York Community Trust Van Lier Fund. "The goals for this Artist-in-Residence Program are: to support emerging artists whose work involves multicultural/Asian American issues; to support artists with financial need; to support artists who have a strong interest in the Asian American Arts

Centre and its resources (i.e., archival slide collection, library of catalogs, and other Asian American Artists materials) to further investigate these issues in their own work; and to support artwork of a high standard. Standard of quality is one of the key issues in a multicultural arts environment."

What They Offer

Three artists will be selected each year. Artists receive $1,200 per month for eight months ($9,600 total). Artists spend six days each month on their residencies, thirteen days each month in their studio working on their art, and one day each month meeting with the staff of the Arts Centre and/or with guest speakers to share information and discuss issues and progress. Residents are expected to work cooperatively. Questions, issues, and resources they wish to investigate and share with one another will be decided upon collectively. There will be a follow-up meeting one year after the residencies are completed.

The Asian American Arts Centre is anticipating changes in their program and funding. Under the new program, the Centre will host an introductory event with about six invited professional artists. Residency applicants must attend this presentation and choose one of the artists as a mentor. Selected artists will work with their mentoring professional one-on-one. The artist will work as an assistant to the professional for a portion of his or her time during the residency. The balance of time will be spent on the artist's own creative projects. Once a month, the mentor will visit the artist's studio and critique his or her work. At the conclusion of the program, the Asian American Arts Centre will sponsor an exhibition of the resident's work.

Facility Description

No facilities are provided.

How to Apply

Send a SASE for information and application guidelines. Submit twenty slides (packaged and labeled according to instructions) with an accompanying descriptive sheet, proof of your New York residency, identification showing your date of birth, and a statement about your work and artistic direction (include interests in multicultural/Asian American issues, what you want to pursue in your residency, and what you hope to accomplish). You may also submit some original art work (on a limited basis) for the committee's evaluation, but the Centre cannot be responsible for the work(s). If you are chosen, you may be asked to provide citizen status papers and to submit financial information that demonstrates need. Slides will be entered into the Asian American Artists Archive and will not be returned.

Deadline

Late June for AIR program. Date may change for Mentoring Program. (Dates vary from year to year.)

Approximate Cost of a Four-week Residency

Transportation, housing, meals, materials, and incidentals — offset by stipend.

Atlantic Center for the Arts
1414 Art Center Avenue
New Smyrna Beach, Florida 32168

Attention: Residency Program
(904) 427-6975 or (904) 427-5669 Fax

Type of Facility/Award

Artist-in-Residence Program.

Who Can Apply

Artists, musicians, and composers — Associates-in-Residence. Distinguished contemporary artists — Masters-in-Residence (by invitation).

Provisos

Associates are described as "mid-career."

Dates of Operation

January 9 to 15. March 6 to 26. May 15 to June 4. November 27 to December 17. (1994 dates.)

Location

The Center is located on the east coast of central Florida.

History

This interdisciplinary arts facility was chartered in 1979 to bring together mid-career writers, artists, musicians, and composers (Associates) with Master Artists (distinguished contemporary artists) in an informal interdisciplinary residency where they have the opportunity to interact, work, and perhaps collaborate with one another.

What They Offer

The Center offers four to six three-week residency sessions each year. Three Master Artists of different disciplines each choose ten Associate Artists through his or her own selection process. During the residency period, Associates spend half their time on weekdays working with the Masters in different ways: meetings, workshops, casual conversations, and occasionally participating in recreational activities. The rest of their time is free to spend pursuing their own projects. Session fee of $600 includes tuition, and an on-site private room and bath. No meals are provided. Nonresident tuition is $200. (1994 rates.) Some scholarships are available. Contact the Center for scholarship information and updated fees.

Facility Description

The Center includes an administration/gallery complex, a multipurpose workshop, a fieldhouse/commons building, three cottages for the resident Master Artists, Associate housing, and an outdoor amphitheater. Associates are provided a private room with bath with bath and small refrigerator, and communal living and kitchen space. The Center has a pay phone and laundry facilities for residents' use. Originally a ten-acre site, the facility acquired the surrounding fifty-seven acres, which are being developed to include an arts resource center and additional workshop space. The Center is air-conditioned and handicapped accessible.

How to Apply

Send a SASE for brochure. Choose the session you'd like to attend, then send for an application form and submittal guidelines. Each Master Artist in Residence selects his or her own Associates and sets the selection criteria. Applications should be submitted at least four months prior to residency period desired.

Deadline

October 15 for January session. November 15 for March session. January 15 for May session. April 15 for November session. (1993/94 dates.)

Approximate Cost of a Four-week Residency

$200, plus transportation, housing, meals, materials, and incidentals (per session). $600, plus transportation, meals, materials, and incidentals (per session).

BALTIMORE CLAYWORKS   MD

Baltimore Clayworks
Lormina Salter Fellowship
5706 Smith Avenue
Baltimore, Maryland 21209

Attention: Donna Lansman, Assistant Director
(410) 578-1919

Type of Facility/Award

Artist-in-Residence Program.

Who Can Apply

Ceramic artists.

Provisos

None listed.

Dates of Operation

September 1 to August 30.

Location

In the Mt. Washington neighborhood of northwest Baltimore City.

History

"Baltimore Clayworks was founded in 1978 by nine potters and sculptors to provide both facilities and a stimulating environment for ceramic artists. Our facilities permit experimentation with a variety of clay bodies and methods of glazing and firing. Our members have many approaches to clay, from production work to sculptural pieces. Clayworks enables the artist to work in a supportive, communal environment which also facilitates his/her individual growth."

What They Offer

Each year one person is awarded a one-year residency with a $100 monthly stipend for materials and firing, an individual work area (approximately 100 square feet), use of the common area (2000 square feet, including storage), access to telephone/ trash collection, receptionist services, administration services, a consignment gallery, use of the kilns and other equipment, storage, teaching and networking opportunities, the opportunity to take various workshops, co-op purchases of supplies, and use of equipment. Fellow must spend at least twenty-four hours each week on the premises (doing his or her own work) and up to ten hours annually on community outreach (slide lectures or demonstrations). Residents must participate in the collective life of the studio, be willing to abide by environmental concerns, and mount a solo exhibition. An in-person interview is required of finalists.

Facility Description

The facility is a renovated library, offering studio and exhibition spaces, classes, workshops, and ceramic supplies. Equipment available includes: Brent slab roller, Bailey slab roller, Bailey extruder, Alpine spray booth with 1 hp compressor, and a Ball mill. Kilns available for use include: 60-cubic-foot and 40-cubic-foot downdraft natural-gas car kilns, a 30-cubic-foot propane kiln, 10-cubic-foot high-fire/ raku propane kiln, flexible outdoor kiln area, six electric kilns, and an electric test kiln.

How to Apply

Send a SASE for an application and guidelines. Return completed application with a $10 nonrefundable processing fee, telling of your formal art education and any residencies, workshops or other school experience you may have had. Include a brief description of your experience with ceramics; mention any artistic interests other than clay; and tell them how a residency at the Clayworks might benefit your work as a clay artist and how your particular talents and abilities might benefit the collective studio environment at the Clayworks. Also mention any other residencies, fellowships, or opportunities you are applying for and whether or not you'd be interested in renting studio space from them if you do not get the fellowship. Include the following with your application: references (their affiliations and telephone numbers), your statement; your résumé, and ten slides of your work.

Deadline

July 1.

Approximate Cost of a Four-week Residency

$10, plus transportation, housing, meals, materials, and incidentals — offset by stipend.

The Banff Centre
LEIGHTON STUDIOS

Banff, Alberta
CANADA

The Banff Centre for the Arts
Box 1020, Station 28
107 Tunnel Mountain Drive
Banff, Alberta T0L 0C0 Canada

Attention: Registrar
(403) 762-6180, (800) 565-9989 (U.S. and Canada toll free), (403) 762-6345 Fax

Type of Facility/Award
Residency.

Who Can Apply
Writers, composers, musicians, visual artists, choreographers, theatre directors, and curators.

Provisos
Established artists of all nationalities are encouraged to apply. Applicants must be able to "demonstrate a sustained contribution to their discipline and show evidence of significant achievement."

Dates of Operation
Open year-round.

Location
Banff is 120 kilometers west of Calgary, where bus service is available from the airport.

History
"The Banff Centre for the Arts is a place for artists, and is dedicated to lifelong learning and professional career development in the arts, acting as site and catalyst for creative activity and experience. Located in the mountains of Canada's first national park, the Banff Centre for Continuing Education is a unique Canadian institution playing a special role in the advancement of cultural and professional life, internationally recognized for its leadership in arts and management, and for developing and hosting conferences on contemporary issues."

What They Offer
Leighton Studios provides residencies for artists for up to three months. Each resident is provided a private room with a bath and a telephone in the Centre's main residence. Studio residents may use the Banff Centre's dining room facilities and other food outlets on campus, and have full access to the Centre's library and its fitness and recreation equipment. Housekeeping services are provided three days a week in the living quarters and the studios. Children may be accommodated if arrangements are made in advance. Visitors are allowed only by appointment. No pets are allowed. Occasionally, periods of one to three weeks become available at

short notice. Be sure to call or write the Centre to check availability if you have an immediate need for space. Fees for residencies are: $273 per week for a studio residency; $182 per week for a single room; and $91.70 per week for the Flex meal plan (which provides ten full meals or your choice of individually priced cafeteria items). The meal plan is optional. Food can also be purchased on a cash basis. These prices are from March 1995. Dollar amounts are Canadian dollars. Taxes are additional. Discounts on the above fees may be awarded based on financial need. The Centre suggests applicants seek funding from outside sources as well.

Facility Description

Banff was Canada's first National Park. At 1,383 meters and surrounded by mountains, the town of Banff (pop. 7000) is a major tourist destination. The Banff Centre has performance theatres, recital halls, art galleries, an extensive library, a well-equipped recreation and fitness complex, and a campus store. The Leighton Studios, part of the Centre's complex, are set in a mountainside pine grove slightly apart from the main buildings. There are eight studios specially designed as workspaces for composers, writers, and artists. A ninth, for potters, is in the Visual Arts building. Studios are accessible twenty-four hours a day. Each comfortably furnished studio has a private view, a kitchenette, and a washroom. Studios have large windows, a skylight, and a large open space that allows for work on the walls or floors. They are equipped with adjustable track lighting, studio sinks, large work tables, and movable equipment trolleys. Easels are available. Leighton's ceramics space (in Glyde Hall) provides potter's wheels, kilns (electric, gas, wood, soda, and raku), a slab roller, an extruder, a sandblaster, an outdoor working pad, a plaster room, a clay mixing room, and a glaze room. The music studios are equipped with pianos. The writing studios have ample desk space, and typewriters and drafting boards are available.

How to Apply

Send a SASE for an application and brochure. Return completed application with a résumé, the names and addresses of three references (authorities in your field who are familiar with you and your work), a description of your proposed project, a list of your most important achievements in the last five years, a sample of your work, and press releases, reviews, etc. Appropriate work samples are: *Composers:* two or three scores and audio cassette or CD recordings of your work. *Visual artists:* eight slides representative of your recent work, plus catalogs and/or reviews. *Writers:* a selection of published work or manuscripts-in-progress. *Other artists:* an appropriate sample of your recent work. All materials will be returned.

Deadline

Rolling application process. Apply at least six months in advance of desired dates.

Approximate Cost of a Four-week Residency

$1,092 tuition (add $728 for a single room), plus transportation, meals, materials, and incidentals. Meal plans are available for $91.70 per week. Discounts are available (based on need). Dollar amounts are Canadian.

The Banff Centre
PLAYWRIGHTS' COLONY

Banff, Alberta
CANADA

The Banff Centre for the Arts
Box 1020, Station 28
107 Tunnel Mountain Drive
Banff, Alberta T0L 0C0 Canada

Attention: Registrar
(403) 762-6180, (800) 565-9989 (U.S. and Canada toll free), (403) 762-6345 Fax

Type of Facility/Award
Residency.

Who Can Apply
Playwrights.

Provisos
Applicants must be Canadian. The Banff Centre encourages applications from artists of all backgrounds. Full length plays, one-act plays, and plays for young audiences are eligible.

Dates of Operation
Late May to late June. (Dates vary from year to year.)

Location
Banff is 120 kilometers west of Calgary. Bus service to Banff is available from the Calgary airport.

History
"The Banff Centre for the Arts is a place for artists, and is dedicated to lifelong learning and professional career development in the arts, acting as site and catalyst for creative activity and experience. Located in the mountains of Canada's first national park, the Banff Centre for Continuing Education is a unique Canadian institution playing a special role in the advancement of cultural and professional life, internationally recognized for its leadership in arts and management, and for developing and hosting conferences on contemporary issues."

What They Offer
Playwrights may spend one to four weeks working on a final manuscript with the opportunity for consultation with and commentary from a dramaturge of his or her choice. The playwright may also work with a professional cast of actors to further explore and refine the text. This work, under the direction of Kim McCaw, is the final step in preparation for rehearsal and/or production. Typewriters are available upon request. The cost of the colony is $273 per week for tuition, $182 per week for your room, and $92 per week for the meal plan. (These are Canadian dollars.) Some full and partial fee abatement awards are available. In exceptional

cases, some individuals may be provided with a travel allowance. Contact the Centre to apply for travel assistance.

Facility Description

Banff was Canada's first National Park. At 1,383 meters and surrounded by mountains, the town of Banff (pop. 7000) is a major tourist destination. The Banff Centre has performance theatres, recital halls, art galleries, an extensive library, a well-equipped recreation and fitness complex, and a campus store. The Leighton Studios, part of the Centre's complex, are set in a mountainside pine grove slightly apart from the main buildings. There are eight studios specially designed as workspaces for composers, writers, and artists. A ninth, for potters, is in the Visual Arts building. Studios are accessible twenty-four hours a day. Each comfortably furnished studio has a private view, a kitchenette, and a washroom. Studios have large windows, a skylight, and a large open space that allows for work on the walls or floors. They are equipped with adjustable track lighting, studio sinks, large work tables, and movable equipment trolleys. Easels are available. Leighton's ceramics space (in Glyde Hall) provides potter's wheels, kilns (electric, gas, wood, soda, and raku), a slab roller, an extruder, a sandblaster, an outdoor working pad, a plaster room, a clay mixing room, and a glaze room. The music studios are equipped with pianos. The writing studios have ample desk space, and typewriters and drafting boards are available.

How to Apply

Send a SASE for application and brochure. Return completed application with a nonrefundable fee of $48 (Canadian) or $42 (U.S.), a script (packaged and labeled according to instructions), and, if you are requesting a reduction in cost, your written request for award and/or travel assistance with documentation of need.

Deadline

February 3, 1995. Date may vary slightly from year to year.

Approximate Cost of a Four-week Residency

$2,188 (Canadian), plus transportation, materials, and incidentals.

The Banff Centre   Banff, Alberta
WRITING STUDIO PROGRAM   CANADA

The Banff Centre for the Arts
Box 1020, Station 28
107 Tunnel Mountain Drive
Banff, Alberta T0L 0C0 Canada

Attention: Registrar
(403) 762-6180, (800) 565-9989 (U.S. and Canada toll free), (403) 762-6345 Fax

Type of Facility/Award

Residency.

Who Can Apply

Writers.

Provisos

This program is open to applications from all sectors of Canadian society. Successful applicants will have published a body of work (books, stories, poems, or belles-lettres in magazines or anthologies) and will be working on a book-length manuscript or manuscript-in-progress and will be interested in working with an editor during their residency.

Dates of Operation

Late October to late November. Dates vary from year to year.

Location

Banff is 120 kilometers west of Calgary. Bus service to Banff is available from the Calgary airport.

History

"The Banff Centre for the Arts is a place for artists, and is dedicated to lifelong learning and professional career development in the arts, acting as site and catalyst for creative activity and experience. Located in the mountains of Canada's first national park, the Banff Centre for Continuing Education is a unique Canadian institution playing a special role in the advancement of cultural and professional life, internationally recognized for its leadership in arts and management, and for developing and hosting conferences on contemporary issues."

What They Offer

Twenty people are selected to work independently on their projects and consult individually with the resource faculty at the Centre as required. "The program is designed to give support not readily available elsewhere to writers at a crucial stage of their careers." Fees for the studio session are $1,500 tuition, plus $1,085 for your room, and $470 for the meal plan. (These are Canadian dollars.) Limited financial aid is available (by application) for a reduction of up to eighty percent of the cost.

Facility Description

Banff was Canada's first National Park. At 1,383 meters and surrounded by mountains, the town of Banff (pop. 7000) is a major tourist destination. The Banff Centre has performance theatres, recital halls, art galleries, an extensive library, a well-equipped recreation and fitness complex, and a campus store. The Leighton Studios, part of the Centre's complex, are set in a mountainside pine grove slightly apart from the main buildings. There are eight studios specially designed as workspaces for composers, writers, and artists. A ninth, for potters, is in the Visual Arts building. Studios are accessible twenty-four hours a day. Each comfortably furnished studio has a private view, a kitchenette, and a washroom. Studios have large windows, a skylight, and a large open space that allows for work on the walls or floors. They are equipped with adjustable track lighting, studio sinks, large work tables, and movable equipment trolleys. Easels are available. Leighton's ceramics space (in Glyde Hall) provides potter's wheels, kilns (electric, gas, wood, soda, and raku), a slab roller, an extruder, a sandblaster, an outdoor working pad, a plaster room, a clay mixing room, and a glaze room. The music studios are equipped with pianos. The writing studios have ample desk space, and typewriters and drafting boards are available.

How to Apply

Send a SASE for an application and brochure. Return completed application with an application fee $48 (Canadian) or $42 (U.S.), a résumé (list publication credits on a separate sheet), a description of your proposed project, a statement about what you hope to accomplish during the program, names and addresses of two references, and a work sample. Appropriate work samples are: *Poetry:* two copies of a segment of a book-length manuscript or work in progress, supported by a portfolio of published or unpublished work (total of twenty-five to forty pages). *Prose:* two copies of a segment of a book length manuscript or work in progress, supported by a portfolio of published or unpublished work (total of fifty to seventy-five pages). Those requesting financial aid must supply appropriate documentation of need.

Deadline

April 30. Notification on or before June 30.

Approximate Cost of a Four-week Residency

$3,055 (Canadian), plus transportation, materials, and incidentals. Limited financial aid available.

BEMIS CENTER FOR CONTEMPORARY ARTS   NE

Bemis Center for Contemporary Arts
724 South Twelfth Street
Omaha, Nebraska 68102-3202

Attention: Spencer Hall, Residency Coordinator
(402) 341-7130 or (402) 341-9791 Fax

Type of Facility/Award

Residency.

Who Can Apply

Visual artists.

Provisos

Bemis Center does not discriminate on the basis of sex, race, religion, or national origin. They welcome artists from anywhere in the world but they expect applicants to have a command of the English language.

Dates of Operation

Open year-round.

Location

The Center is in a renovated factory building on the fringe of downtown Omaha, Nebraska.

History

Bemis Center for Contemporary Arts (originally titled Alternative Worksite) was established in 1981 by a group of artists in Omaha as a unique opportunity for ceramic artists. The major portion of the project took place at a functioning brick factory, the Omaha Brick Works. Between 1981 and 1984, more than 100 artists came to work at the site, the direct outgrowth being the Bemis Center for Contemporary Arts — a nonprofit organization dedicated to supporting exceptionally talented visual artists of all types. It is supported by the efforts of private and corporate donors and public funding.

What They Offer

Residency is from two to six months. Artists are provided a well-equipped studio space, living accommodations, and a monthly stipend ranging from $200 to $500 per month. Part of the residency may be spent on a farm or in studios in the small, historically-preserved town of Brownville. It is hoped that residency will be directed toward exploration and self-challenge rather than "producing" for a possible show. Residents are expected to give an informal slide presentation of their work sometime during their stay and to leave one piece of work done during the residency as a donation to the Bemis. Artist and director together select the piece to be donated. Ask about their summer programs at the Art Farm and the studios in Brownville.

Facility Description

Bemis Center is located in a large warehouse. Space has been divided to form several studio/apartments averaging 1,800 square feet with twelve- to sixteen-foot ceilings. Each unit has good natural light, heating, air conditioning, a kitchen, and bath. Sculptors and ceramic artists receive slightly smaller studio/apartments and share a 6,000-square-foot workspace on the ground floor. (Facility description may not be 100% accurate since the Center moved to another building one block from its old location, adding a new sculpture facility and general offices. The old location will now focus on works by Midwest artists.) All work-related equipment is provided, as well as 200-, 100-, and 20-cubic foot kilns, an overhead bridge crane, two forklifts, and welding equipment. There are a woodshop with tools, ample metal working equipment, the new sculpture facility, and a small photographic darkroom with film cameras and projectors, a videotape camera, and editing equipment. Access to printmaking equipment is also available. The Center has a gallery that annually carries eight exhibitions of contemporary art in all media. Work from some of the residencies may be included in the shows. The Center hosts receptions, performances, concerts, and lectures. The Center houses a fine collection of books, videos, and magazines in their Clare Haas Howard Art Library.

How to Apply

Send a SASE for an application and brochure. Return completed application with a $25 nonrefundable application fee, ten slides (labeled according to instructions) of work completed within the last two years (and an adequate SASE for their return), three references who are authorities in your field and are familiar with your work, and a résumé. You may include any reviews, catalogs, or other support materials for the selection committee's evaluation, but they will not be returned.

Deadline

March 1. Notification in May. (1995 dates.)

Approximate Cost of a Four-week Residency

$25, plus transportation, meals, materials, and incidentals — offset by stipend.

BLUE MOUNTAIN CENTER   NY

Blue Mountain Center
Blue Mountain Lake
New York, New York 12812-0109

Attention: Harriet Barlow, Director
(518) 352-7391

Type of Facility/Award

Residency.

Who Can Apply

Established creative and nonfiction writers and other artists and musicians.

Provisos

"The committee is particularly interested in fine work that evinces social and ecological concern and is aimed at general audiences." Established creative and nonfiction writers and other artists and musicians who do not require exceptional facilities are invited to apply.

Dates of Operation

Center is open from June 15 to October 15. (Dates approximate.)

Location

Located in the heart of the Adirondack Mountains, BMC is two hours from the Albany airport and a five-hour drive from New York City.

History

The Blue Mountain Center was established in 1981. They sponsor readings and discussions by guests who choose to share their work with the local community. For six weeks prior to and following the residency period (see below), BMC hosts seminars and work groups concerned with social, economic, and environmental issues.

The main house at Blue Mountain Center. (Photo courtesy Blue Mountain Center.)

What They Offer

Blue Mountain Center runs four separate sessions each summer. Up to fifteen artists at a time are invited to spend four weeks in residence each session. Writers are
housed in the lodge with the bedrooms serving as their studies. Visual artists and
composers have separate studios. Breakfast and dinner are served in the dining
room. Lunch is served picnic-style to avoid interruption of work. Residents must
provide their own transportation to Center. Guests are asked to contribute to a
studio construction fund, but such contributions are entirely voluntary.

Facility Description

Guests are housed in individual bedroom/studies in a turn-of-the-century Adirondack lodge surrounded by woods, lakes, and mountains. Facilities include a tennis
court, lakes, boats, trails, a recreation room, a linen and laundry room, and a pho-
tocopy machine. There is a pay phone for guests' use.

How to Apply

Send a SASE for information and guidelines. Then submit a brief biographical sketch including your professional achievements, a statement of your plan for work at the Center, the names of any previous BMC residents you know, some samples of your work (and an adequate SASE for their return), copies of reviews of previously published books or shows if available, the $20 nonrefundable application processing fee, and your preference for an early, late summer, or fall residency. Proper samples are: *Writers:* ten pages. *Artists:* up to ten slides. *Musicians/Composers:* Call Center for appropriate submittal instructions. Spouses must apply separately and will be evaluated independently.

Deadline

February 1. Decisions by March 31.

Approximate cost of a Four-week Residency

$20, plus transportation, some materials, and incidentals.

BLUE SHORES   WI

Blue Shores
Lake Forest Park Road
Sturgeon Bay, Wisconsin 54235

Attention: Greg Jones or Terry Schuhmann
(414) 743-5126

Note: the owners of and inspiration for this facility on Lake Michigan facility announced in August 1995 that they are closing their retreat and selling the property.

THE BRANDYWINE WORKSHOP   PA

The Brandywine Workshop
Firehouse Art Center
730–32 South Broad Street
Philadelphia, Pennsylvania 19146

Attention: Edwin Arocho, Assistant Gallery Director
(215) 546-3657

Type of Facility/Award

Residency.

Who Can Apply

Artists working in all media, including experimental forms.

Provisos

Applicants must reside in the United States and must have been out of school for at least one full year. No graduate or undergraduate students are eligible to apply.

Dates of Operation
Open year-round.

Location
Brandywine is located on the "Avenue of the Arts" in Philadelphia.

History
The Brandywine Workshop was founded in 1972 as a "nonprofit, culturally diverse institution dedicated to promoting interest and talent in printmaking and other fine arts."

What They Offer
Selected artists will receive paid travel, room, board, and a modest honorarium for a minimum of one week. (Brochure does not specify a maximum stay.) Usually fifteen short-term fellowships are awarded each year, depending on funding. Some partial fellowships for local artists are also available on a restricted basis. Artists produce limited edition (100 or less) prints during their stay. The artist keeps half and Brandywine keeps half of each print run. Artists are required to leave their mylars and separation sheets with the Center to document their creative processes.

Facility Description
Brandywine operates an offset lithography and screenprinting facility. Since expanding into the Firehouse Art Center, they now have galleries, classrooms, a museum shop, archives, and an expanded printmaking workshop.

How to Apply
Send a SASE for application and brochure. Return completed application with ten 35 mm slides of your current work (labeled according to instructions), an accompanying descriptive sheet, and a résumé.

Deadline
May 1. Notification within thirty days.

Approximate Cost of a Four-week Residency
No cost except some materials and incidentals.

THE ARCHIE BRAY FOUNDATION   MT

The Archie Bray Foundation for the Ceramic Arts
2915 Country Club Avenue
Helena, Montana 59601

Attention: Josh DeWeese, Resident Director
(406) 443-3502 Office, (406) 443-2969 Studios, (406) 442-2521 Clay Business

Type of Facility/Award

Artist-in-Residence Program.

Who Can Apply

Ceramists.

Provisos

None listed.

Dates of Operation

Open year-round.

Location

The Foundation is three miles from downtown Helena on a 26-acre site of the former Western Clay Manufacturing Company.

History

The Archie Bray Foundation was founded in 1951 as a nonprofit public educational foundation by Archie Bray, Branson Stevenson, and Pete Meloy. It is dedicated to the enrichment of the ceramic arts. The list of ceramic artists who have worked at the Bray is a Who's-Who of American ceramists.

What They Offer

Full-time residency for one year provides each artist with a studio at a rent of $150 per month. Some short-term residencies are available in the summer months. Glazing and kiln facilities are shared. Fuel and material costs are the artist's responsibility. Clay and other materials are purchased by the Foundation in large lots to keep costs to artists low. Artists may consign their work to the Foundation gallery for a one-third commission. Residents are expected to be self-motivated and willing to help with various jobs around the studio to maintain the Bray. No housing is provided, although residents usually find reasonable accommodations in Helena. Transportation is necessary to reach the studios just outside Helena. Resident artists teach throwing and handbuilding classes for the community.

Facility Description

In addition to the artists' studios and workshops, the facility maintains a gallery space to exhibit and offer for sale the work of the resident artists. The Foundation also operates a retail ceramic supply business with an extensive inventory of pre-mixed and dry clays, studio equipment, glaze materials, and ceramic literature.

How to Apply

Send a SASE for brochure. Then submit twenty slides of current work (and an SASE for their return), a résumé, a statement of intent (including desired length of residency), two letters of recommendation, and a $10 nonrefundable application fee.

Deadline

March 1.

Approximate Cost of a Four-week Residency

$150 per month, plus $10 application fee, transportation, housing, meals, materials, and incidentals.

Bucknell University
BUCKNELL SEMINAR FOR YOUNGER POETS   PA

Bucknell University
Bucknell Seminar for Younger Poets
Stadler Center for Poetry
Lewisburg, Pennsylvania 17837

Attention: John Wheatcroft, Director
(717) 524-1944 or (717) 524-1853

Type of Facility/Award

Fellowship.

Who Can Apply

Poets.

Provisos

Students from American colleges who have completed their sophomore, junior, or senior years may compete for the ten fellowships awarded annually.

Dates of Operation

Four weeks each summer in June and July. Dates vary from year to year.

Location

Lewisburg, Pennsylvania.

History

Young poets are provided with an extended opportunity to write and to be guided by established poets. Private time for writing is balanced with disciplined learning in an atmosphere of peer support and camaraderie.

What They Offer

Each fellow receives tuition, room, board, and space to write. Ten students are chosen annually. Staff poets conduct two workshops each week, offer readings of their own verse, and are available for tutorials. Interaction with Bucknell's Poet-in-

Residence is a valuable feature of this program. Fellows are also given the opportunity to participate in weekly readings. All academic, cultural, and recreational facilities of the University are open to Fellows.

Facility Description
Poets are housed in the Stadler Center for Poetry on the Bucknell campus.

How to Apply
Send a SASE for information. Applications should include an academic transcript, two supporting recommendations (one must be from a poetry writing instructor), a letter of self-presentation (a brief autobiography stressing commitment to poetry writing, experience, and any publications), and a ten- to twelve-page portfolio. Include an adequate SASE if you want your portfolio returned.

Deadline
March 1.

Approximate Cost of a Four-week Residency
Transportation and incidentals.

CARINA HOUSE   ME

Carina House: A Monhegan Residency
William A. Farnsworth Library and Art Museum
P.O. Box 466
Rockland, Maine 04841

Attention: Director
(207) 596-6457

Type of Facility/Award
Residency.

Who Can Apply
Painters, drawers, printmakers, sculptors, or photographers (others, see Provisos).

Provisos
For 1995, the program was for visual artists (painting, drawing, printmaking, sculpture, or photography) who are at least twenty-one years old and legal residents of the state of Maine. Students currently enrolled in a degree program are not eligible. The program is aimed at serious artists who have not yet won wide recognition for their work and whose financial resources would otherwise not allow them an extended stay on Monhegan. (May provide residencies for writers or other artists in other years — check with director.)

Dates of Operation
Session A: June 1 to July 5. Session B: July 28 to August 31. (1995 dates.)

Location

Monhegan Island, Maine.

History

Because of its unparalleled natural beauty, Monhegan Island has attracted artists for over a hundred years. "The Monhegan residency is designed to give back to Maine artists part of their heritage and tradition, including a tradition of creative experimentation and exploration." The residency is funded by the contributions of anonymous individual donors and the William A. Farnsworth Library and Art Museum.

What They Offer

Two artists will each be awarded a five-week long residency and a $500 stipend. The cottage is not big enough for more than one, so no family, overnight guests, or pets are allowed. Residents must provide their own transportation to the island.

Facility Description

The Carina House is a small, simply but adequately furnished artist's cottage.

How to Apply

Send a SASE for brochure. Submit a brief letter summarizing your professional background, experience, and expectations for the Monhegan residency along with a curriculum vitae and four references who are not family — two personal and two professional. Provide no more than twenty slides of your recent work (and a SASE adequate for their return).

Deadline

March 17, postmarked or hand-delivered. Notification on or before April 15. (1995 dates.)

Approximate Cost of Four-week Residency

Transportation, meals, materials, and incidentals — offset by stipend.

CARVING STUDIO & SCULPTURE CENTER   VT

The Carving Studio & Sculpture Center
Marble Street
P.O. Box 495
West Rutland, Vermont 05777

Attention: Lucy Biddle, Executive Director
(802) 438-2097 Phone and Fax

Type of Facility/Award

Residency.

Who Can Apply

Carvers and sculptors (primarily stone).

Provisos

None listed.

Dates of Operation

Open year-round.

Location

West Rutland, Vermont.

History

The Carving Studio sits on the edge of Vermont's first marble quarry. The studio was patterned after the Carrara studio in Italy. After suffering years of neglect, the old company store was turned into studios that offer various courses on carving (from granite to wood to soapstone) as well as workshops on casting bronze and working with power tools.

What They Offer

The Studio offers individual artists, who are looking for an opportunity to work on special projects, the time, space, and use of the equipment for short or long periods of time throughout the year. The idea is to encourage experimentation and exploration of new media, large- or small-scale work, and work that combines several media. The Carving Studio also offers a small stipend, plus room and board in exchange for studio responsibilities such as assisting the participants with stone-moving, kitchen detail, and studio maintenance. Those accepted into the Work-Study Program may participate in courses and/or work independently. Opportunities are limited. College credit is available for some of CSSC's courses.

Facility Description

The Carving Studio is made entirely of marble blocks. Another building is being renovated as residence space for artists within easy walking distance of The Studio.

How to Apply

Send a SASE for brochure. There is no formal application process outlined in the brochure. The Studio sounds like it's open to supporting clearly defined projects of potential merit, with studio space, a residency, or a work-study (work-exchange). Call or write for specific details.

Deadline

Rolling application process.

Approximate Cost of a Four-week Residency

Transportation, housing, meals, materials, and incidentals, which may be partially offset by a stipend and/or work-study exchange.

CENTER FOR EXPLORATORY AND PERCEPTUAL ART   NY

The Center for Exploratory and Perceptual Art (CEPA)
700 Main Street, Fourth Floor
Buffalo, New York 14202

Attention: Robert Hirsch
(716) 856-2717, (716) 856-2720 Fax, or E-mail: CEPA@AOL.COM

Type of Facility/Award
Residency.

Who Can Apply
Photographers.

Provisos
The Center did not clarify this in time, but it is my perception that applicants must be from one of the eight western New York counties or the territories of the Tuscarora and Seneca Nations. Write or call for clarification.

Dates of Operation
Open year-round.

Location
CEPA is located in the downtown theater district of Buffalo, New York.

History
"CEPA supports, encourages, and funds projects from both emerging and established visual artists, and is committed to supporting artists from groups traditionally underrepresented in cultural spaces. CEPA also functions as a research and education center for the exploration of new technologies in the photographic arts."

What They Offer
CEPA offers funding, housing, and support for visiting artists. Residents interact with the local community through public lectures, studio visits with student artists, and discussions at regional high schools. CEPA also commissions art for public transit vehicles and offers gallery exhibitions, satellite exhibitions, a guest lecture series, publications, education, technical support, and an internship program in photography, photo-related art, and film.

Facility Description
CEPA has an exhibition gallery, studios, classrooms, darkrooms, and a computer facility (which is currently being updated).

How to Apply
Send a SASE for application guidelines. Submit twenty slides (packaged and la-

beled according to instructions) with a descriptive sheet, a résumé, a one-page (typed) project description, and an adequate SASE for return of your slides. If you have questions, send them in writing and include a SASE for immediate reply.

Deadline

Rolling application process.

Approximate Cost of a Four-week Residency

Transportation, meals, materials, and incidentals — offset by stipend.

CENTER FOR THE ARTS AND RELIGION   DC

Center for the Arts and Religion
Wesley Theological Seminary
4500 Massachusetts Avenue, N.W.
Washington, D. C. 20016

Attention: Elly Sparks Brown, Administrative Director
(202) 885-8608 or (202) 885-8660 Faculty Office

Type of Facility/Award

Fellowship.

Who Can Apply

All artists.

Provisos

The Center will consider applications from artists of all faiths whose work evidences concern with issues of the religious community, artists who work at the boundary between the secular and the sacred, and artists who are willing to articulate the relationship between their work and their faith.

Dates of Operation

Academic year (September through May).

Location

Washington, D.C.

History

None provided.

What They Offer

Artists may stay at the Center for one academic year, one semester, or one (concentrated) six-week period. The Center provides the use of an art studio, a stipend (amount not specified), and/or room and board (depending upon the nature of the residency), free audit of one seminary class per semester, the opportunity to teach classes to members of the community for a stipend, the opportunity to participate in an on-campus exhibit of your work, and invitations to forums, lectures, concerts, etc. sponsored by the seminary and the Center for the Arts and Religion. Artists have use of the seminary library and ongoing affiliation with other artists, faculty, and staff in an inclusive and ecumenical context. There is access to some of the best museums, galleries, and theaters in the nation. In return, the Center expects residents to participate in the artistic community through support, instruction, and critique of one another's work. They are also expected to participate in community outreach (e.g., exhibits, lectures, etc., with entrepreneurial arrangements to be negotiated between the artists and the sponsoring institution) and to donate one piece of work to the Center/Wesley Theological Seminary that will become part of Wesley's permanent art collection.

Facility Description
None provided.

How to Apply
Send a SASE for information. If interested, submit a résumé (with professional credentials, a personal statement explaining why you are interested in working at the seminary and how your artistic process and product work in relationship to your spirituality), a portfolio with twenty slides of your recent work (labeled according to instructions), and a cover letter. A telephone interview (unless you can come in person) will be arranged after review of your submitted material.

Deadline
Rolling application process.

Approximate Cost of a Four-week Residency
Transportation, housing, meals, materials, and incidentals — offset by stipend. No specifics given — please inquire directly of the Center for details.

CENTRUM ARTISTS RESIDENCY PROGRAM   WA

Centrum Artists Residency Program
P.O. Box 1158
Port Townsend, Washington 98368

Attention: Carol Jane Bangs, Director
(360) 385-3102 or (360) 385-2470 Fax

Type of Facility/Award
Residency.

Who Can Apply
Writers, visual artists, printmakers, composers, and choreographers.

Provisos
None listed. Previous residents may reapply. Minority candidates are encouraged.

Dates of Operation

January through May, and September through December.

Location

Fort Worden State Park is near Port Townsend, Washington, on the northeastern tip of Washington's Olympic Peninsula. The nearest major airport is Seattle-Tacoma.

History

Centrum residencies were established 1978. Centrum is a nonprofit arts and education organization that also sponsors workshops, festivals, performances, and conferences. Two hundred writers, visual artists, architects, actors, dancers, and musicians have benefited from the program since its inception. The program was restructured from 1993 to 1994 and began accepting applications again in early 1995.

What They Offer

Between fifteen and twenty artists are selected each year for fully subsidized one-month residencies, which include housing, studio space (where applicable), a stipend of $300, and $100 allowance for materials for visual artists using the printmaking studio. Former residents are eligible for residencies of up to three months, but they must cover the cost of their own housing and studio rental (if applicable), and they do not receive a stipend or materials allowance. Linens and bedding are supplied. No residencies will be scheduled in June, July, or August.

Facilities

Artists stay in individual cottages on the grounds of historic Fort Worden State Park, a 440-acre former military fort on the Strait of Juan de Fuca. Cottages are on a grassy knoll overlooking the water. Each contains a living room, two or three bedrooms, a bathroom, and a kitchen equipped with basic cooking and eating utensils. Cottages are simply furnished and have no phone, no TV, and no radio. There is a laundromat on the grounds.

How to Apply

Send a SASE for application and brochure. Return completed application with a nonrefundable $10 application fee, a description of your proposed project, a current résumé/vita, and examples of your recent work as follows. *Writers:* a copy of your most recent book and/or photocopies of recent periodical publications. *Visual artists:* fifteen to twenty slides. *Composers:* an audiocassette sampling of your recent work (written transcription encouraged). *Choreographers:* a videocassette with at least one complete choreographic work. Samples of three other pieces may be included as well. Include a SASE adequate for the return of your materials.

Deadline

October 1 for new applicants. Former residents may apply at any time.

Approximate Cost of a Four-week Residency

$10, plus transportation, meals, materials, and incidentals — offset by stipend.

Chester Springs Studio
1668 Art School Road
P.O. Box 329
Chester Springs, Pennsylvania 19425

Attention: Residency Program
(610) 827-2722

Type of Facility/Award

Residency.

Who Can Apply

Visual artists.

Provisos

Visual artists who are residents of or are working in the United States are eligible to apply. Students enrolled in a degree program will not be considered. "The Studio is particularly interested in artists who continue to turn to the landscape as a source to develop ideas — whether they are expressed in a non-traditional or traditional form."

Dates of Operation

August 12 to September 2. (1995 dates.)

Location

Thirty miles west of Philadelphia in the historic village of Yellow Springs.

History

Chester Springs Studio is a nonprofit art center committed to the support of serious visual artists through teaching, exhibition, and residency opportunities.

What They Offer

Four grants are available for visual artists to work in the studios on projects in ceramics and other two- or three-dimensional media. Resident artists are provided with studio and living space, a materials and/or firing allowance of up to $300, and a stipend of $600 for the three weeks. The Studio also offers two residencies for ceramic projects requiring a wood-burning kiln or other outdoor firing facilities such as raku kilns for functional or sculptural work. There are a pit and other primitive firing areas. An assistant will be on hand to answer technical questions on wood-firing.

Facility Description

The Studio is housed in a mid-18th-century stone barn. The ceramic studio dimensions are 36' x 20'. There are two portable propane raku kilns, a sprung-arch downdraft wood kiln, a cross-draft two-chamber wood/salt kiln; and a Baily's Gas

Kiln (31 $^{1}/_{2}$" x 36 $^{1}/_{4}$" ID). For two- or three-dimensional projects, the studio is 36' x 36' x 20' H with a large northern skylight.

How to Apply

Send a SASE for an application and brochure. Return completed application with a description of work you plan to undertake, materials needed, and firings required. Also send a résumé listing education, awards, and exhibitions. Send slides (labeled according to instructions) of up to ten works and include some details. Do not send original or only copy slides. Include a SASP for notification of receipt of slides/ application. Also include a SASE adequate for the return of your slides.

Deadline

May 1 (postmark). Notification May 15.

Approximate Cost of a Four-week Residency

Transportation, housing, meals, materials, and incidentals offset by stipend and materials/firing allotment.

CHESTERFIELD FILM COMPANY   CA

The Chesterfield Film Company
8205 Santa Monica Boulevard, #1-200
Los Angeles, California 90046-5912

Attention: Writer's Film Project
(818) 777-0998

Type of Facility/Award

Fellowship.

Who Can Apply

Fiction, theater, and film writers.

Provisos

There are no age or academic requirements. Acceptance is based solely upon story-telling talent — regardless of the genre or form of the submission.

Dates of Operation

Open year-round.

Location

Los Angeles, California.

History

"For the past five years, the Writer's Film Project has been operated by the Chesterfield Film Company. The program was developed with generous support from Steven Spielberg's Amblin Entertainment and Universal Pictures. Each year, a mix of writers — fiction, theater, and film — has been chosen to participate." Some have been affiliated with university writing programs and some have not. Selected writers form a screenwriting workshop, using their storytelling skills to begin a career in film. Many program graduates have been signed by major literary agencies. Some have been hired by major studios for writing assignments and some have had their scripts acquired by various studios and production companies.

What They Offer

Up to five writers may be chosen to participate. Each will receive a $20,000 stipend to cover living expenses. The program requires participants to live in the Los Angeles area for the year. Fellows form a workshop that meets three to five times a week to consider story ideas, script outlines, and first and second drafts of each screenplay. Throughout the year, selected film professionals will meet with the writers to share their opinions and experience. Each writer is grouped with a professional screenwriter and a studio executive mentor. By the end of the fellowship year, each writer will have created two original, feature-length screenplays, which he/she can use as talent samples within the film industry. WFP writers are introduced to various literary agents and agencies. Chesterfield intends to produce the best screenplay from each program year's work. For each screenplay produced, Chesterfield will pay its author no less than the current minimums established by the Writers Guild of America (February 1995: $25,740 to $52,686, depending on film's budget).

Facility Description

This is a nonresidential fellowship. Fellows group meetings are held in a conference room at Amblin Entertainment. In the future, though, this location may change.

How to Apply

Send a SASE for application and brochure. Return two copies of the completed application with the $39.50 nonrefundable application fee, your writing samples, a SASE, and a SASP (to acknowledge receipt of materials). Applicants may submit writing samples in any one or more of the categories that follow. Indicate which samples are most representative of your work. *Fiction:* two or more short stories and/or one novel or novel-in-progress. *Plays:* one or two plays, including a one-paragraph synopsis of each play no more than three or four sentences in length attached to the front of the play. *Screenplays:* one or two screenplays, including a one-paragraph synopsis of each screenplay, no more than three to four sentences in length attached to the front of the script. Bind each screenplay with white paper and standard brads.

Deadline

June 1. Notification by December 15.

Approximate Cost of a 4-week Residency

$39.50, plus transportation, housing, meals, materials, and incidentals — offset by stipend.

THE CLAY STUDIO   PA

The Clay Studio
Evelyn Shapiro Foundation Fellowship
139 N. 2nd Street
Philadelphia, Pennsylvania 19106

Attention: Sybille Zeldin, Resident Artist
(215) 925-3453 or (215) 925-7774 Fax

Type of Facility/Award
Artist-in-Residence Program.

Who Can Apply
Open to ceramic and clay artists of all levels of interest and proficiency.

Provisos
None listed.

Dates of Operation
Residency runs from September 1 to August 31.

Location
Philadelphia, Pennsylvania.

History
The Clay Studio was founded in 1974 as a nonprofit educational arts organization. It is dedicated to the ceramic arts and to the work of new clay artists through its gallery, studio space, and lecture series.

What They Offer
The Evelyn Shapiro Foundation Fellowship provides the finalist one year of free studio space rental (200 square feet), a monthly subsistence stipend of $400, a materials and firing allowance, access to electric and gas firing kilns, access to glaze materials, and opportunities to teach in the Studio's school and to exhibit work in the Studio's gallery and shop. There is also a solo exhibition of the Fellow's work toward the end of the residency. The Clay Studio also has other programs: for a minimal fee and membership, the *Resident Artists Program* provides studio space for up to five years (by application/competition), and the *Associate Artists Program*, which is not juried, but offers work space (for a minimal fee) on a first come basis to applicants with some clay experience (not for novices). They also offer *Guest Artist Residencies* by invitation.

Facility Description
The Clay Studio houses a gallery, artists' studios, classroom space, and a retail shop.

How to Apply
Send a SASE for an application and brochure. Submit completed application with

a résumé, a statement of your reasons for participating in the Fellowship Program, and ten slides of recent work. Include an adequate SASE if you want your slides returned.

Deadline
May 15.

Approximate Cost of a Four-week Residency
Transportation, housing, meals, and incidentals — offset by stipend.

THE CLEAVELAND HOUSE B&B   MA

The Cleaveland House B & B
P.O. Box 3041
West Tisbury, Massachusetts 02575

Attention: Cynthia Riggs, Manager
(508) 693-9352

Type of Facility/Award
Retreat.

Who Can Apply
Caters specifically to poets and writers, but welcomes all guests.

Provisos
None listed.

Dates of Operation
Open year-round.

Location
Located at the center of Martha's Vineyard Island in Massachusetts, the house is three miles from the airport, six and a half miles from the Vineyard Haven ferry dock, and nine and a half miles from Oak Bluffs.

History
The Cleaveland House has been in the family of poet Dionis Coffin Riggs for more than 200 years. Therefore, the house has both the charm and the inconveniences of a house that's over two centuries old. However, indoor plumbing and electricity were added in various remodeling phases.

What They Offer
This is a bed and breakfast that caters to poets and writers. It is a gathering place for local intellectuals. On Wednesday afternoons, Mrs. Riggs holds a poetry workshop. Guests are invited to bring their poems to read and join in the critique session, or to simply listen. Room rates in 1995 were as follows: the upstairs guest rooms, which

share one bath, are the East Chamber Room (double bed, fireplace) at $75 per day or $420 per week and the South Bedroom (single bed) at $60 per day or $350 per week. Both rooms together as a suite cost $125 per day or $625 per week. There is one guest room downstairs with twin beds and a fireplace at $75 per day or $420 per week. Access to the downstairs shared bathroom is through the kitchen.

Facility Description

The classic, gray shingled house has large airy rooms (some with fireplaces), antique furniture, shared baths, small closets, and no televisions.

How to Apply

Send a SASE for brochure. Then call or write for reservations. First-come, first-served. No application process.

Deadline

None.

Approximate Cost of a Four-week Residency

$1,400 to $1,680, plus transportation, meals, and incidentals.

CONTEMPORARY ARTISTS CENTER   MA

Contemporary Artists Center
The Beaver Mill
189 Beaver Street
North Adams, Massachusetts 01247

Attention: Artists Residencies Program
(413) 663-9555

Type of Facility/Award

Artist-in-Residence.

Who Can Apply

Visual artists — all media.

Provisos

Artists should be serious, working artists. Artists from around the world are invited to apply. Grants are not available for CAC alumni — but they are eligible for special returning rates.

Dates of Operation

June 25 through August 13. (1995 dates.)

Location

The Contemporary Artists Center is on a twenty-seven-acre wooded site adjoining Natural Bridge State Park. North Adams is also the future home of the Massachusetts Museum of Contemporary Arts, which was conceived by Thomas Krens, who is now the Director of the Guggenheim Museum. A former mill town in the Berkshire Mountains, North Adams is about three hours from New York City, two and a half hours from Boston, and one hour from Albany. It is accessible by bus or train.

History

The Center was founded in 1990 by multimedia artist Eric Rudd and sculptor Martin Hatcher. "The Center provides freedom of space, materials, and processes to encourage experimentation and growth in each artist. There are no artistic separations of sculpture and painting or printmaking."

What They Offer

The summer residency program invites serious, working artists to spend one to seven weeks at the Center working without non-art interruptions. They offer one three-week grant and two one-week grants by separate application (a fee of $10 is charged to apply for grants). Grants fully cover tuition, room, and board. Additional limited financial aid is available to other artists through the regular application process. Twenty-five artists at a time are provided with room, board, some materials, and distraction-free time. Tuition is based on the amount of time you choose to stay: one week is $800, an additional second week is $500, third week is $400, fourth week is $350, fifth week is $300, sixth week is $250, and seventh week is $200. For all seven weeks, the total cost would be $2,800. Throughout the session, artists visit and give talks. Studios are open twenty-four hours a day. There are additional fees for artists signing up for the special eighth week silicone intaglio ($850 plus $100 lab fee) and experimental monoprinting sessions ($800 plus $50 lab fee). They also offer a work week. Contact the Center directly for more information.

CAC also offers independent studio residencies from September through November and from March through May 15. The basic rate is $300 per week for a private room, use of the kitchen (basic foodstuffs are supplied, but not prepared meals), and access to the large working studios. Discounts are available for returning artists. Write or call for specific details.

Facility Description

The Beaver Mill is a 130,000-square-foot brick building. The industrial loft, common-space studios have high ceilings, big windows, and ample room for projects of all types including large-scale and site-specific installations. They also have a wood shop, a basic black-and-white darkroom, and printmaking facilities. CAC has hydraulic presses, a monster press (image size 4' x 8'), and a vulcanizing (heated) press. They also have many other industrials tools and materials. Residents can use (or learn to use) the monumental monoprinting press, air brush equipment, or the industrial foam-spraying equipment.

How to Apply

Send a SASE for application and brochure. Return the completed application with a résumé (or fill in the section on the application form) and some slides of your recent work. If you are applying for a grant, you must return the grant application form, a $10 nonrefundable application fee, a résumé, the CAC application form, evidence of need, and up to ten slides of your recent work. Also enclose an adequate SASE for return of your slides.

Deadline

March 31 for grant applications. Notification by April 15. No deadline listed for regular applications, but space is limited.

Approximate Cost of a Four-week Residency

$2,050, plus transportation, some materials, and incidentals (without grant or financial aid). Limited financial aid is available. $10, plus transportation, some materials, and incidentals (with grant for one week or three weeks).

Council on Foreign Relations
EDWARD R. MURROW FELLOWSHIP   NY

Council on Foreign Relations
58 East 68th Street
New York, New York 10021

Attention: Elise Lewis, Director of Membership and Fellowship Affairs
(212) 734-0400 or (212) 861-2701 Fax

Type of Facility/Award

Fellowship.

Who Can Apply

Journalists.

Provisos

Each applicant must be a U. S. citizen who is serving as "a correspondent, editor or producer for radio, television, a newspaper or magazine widely available and esteemed in the United States, who is either now serving abroad, or having been based overseas recently, plans to return to a foreign post in the near future."

Dates of Operation

Nine months of the year, but specific dates were not provided.

Location

Council of Foreign Relations offices in New York City.

History

The fellowship, made possible by a grant from the CBS Foundation, was first awarded in 1949. "The purpose of the Edward R. Murrow Fellowship is to help the Fellow increase his/her competence in reporting and interpreting events abroad and to give him/her a period of nearly a year for sustained analysis and writing free from the daily pressures that characterize journalistic life. The Fellowship is expected to promote the quality of responsible and discerning journalism that characterized the work of Edward R. Murrow during his life."

What They Offer

The Council, which is a nonprofit and nonpartisan organization, has no affiliation with the U.S. government and takes no position on foreign policy. It provides to the Fellow, who is an "outstanding correspondent, editor, or producer, who has been living abroad and has been preoccupied with short deadlines, an opportunity to broaden his/her perspective through a coordinated program of reading, study, discussion, writing, and renewed contact with the American domestic scene." Fellow is provided office space at the Council's building in New York and a stipend based on the Fellow's previous salary.

Facility Description

Not provided.

How to Apply

Send a SASE for application guidelines. One may be nominated or may nominate oneself by sending or faxing to the Council a letter of nomination that includes the name and address of the candidate, a brief description of his or her background, and the reasons for nomination. Qualified candidates will be asked to complete an application with full biographical details, current and previous employment information, educational information, and the names and addresses of five references who are well acquainted with the applicant's work. Also include a statement of 2,500 words or less summarizing your experience as a foreign correspondent, how the fellowship would contribute to your professional development, a letter from your employer granting a leave of absence if you are selected, approximately five samples of your work from abroad, a résumé, and an 8" x 10" glossy photo.

Deadline

November 15 for letters of nomination. February 1 (postmarked) for applications.

Approximate Cost of a Four-week Residency

Transportation, housing, meals, materials, and incidentals — offset by fellowship.

CREATIVE GLASS CENTER OF AMERICA   NJ

Creative Glass Center of America
1501 Glasstown Road
Milville, New Jersey 08332

Attention: Denise Gonzalez-Dendrinos, Program Coordinator
(609) 825-6800, ext. 2733

Type of Facility/Award
Residency.

Who Can Apply
Glass artists.

Provisos
Glass artists must be over twenty-one years of age when fellowship commences. All applicants must have basic English language skills. Fellowship applicants should have basic hot glassworking skills.

Dates of Operation
January 2 to March 29, April 8 to July 5, and September 16 to December 13. (1996 dates.)

Location
Wheaton Village is located in rural southern New Jersey.

History
Established in 1983, The Creative Glass Center of America is a division of the Wheaton Cultural Alliance, Inc. CGCA provides creative artists with the time, space, and equipment to work out their creative concepts without the restrictions imposed by production costs and sales needs. This allows artists to establish a body of work, regardless of personal financial limitations.

What They Offer
Four Fellows at a time are given access to the glassworking facilities at Wheaton Village, all the glass they can use, free (shared) housing in the Center's four bedroom Cape Cod house just two blocks from the campus, and a $500 monthly stipend to defray expenses. Term of fellowship is three months. Fellows are responsible for their own cooking and cleaning. A studio technician is available for consultation and to familiarize artists with the equipment and its use. Fellows take turns assisting one another with glassblowing and casting support. Fellows generally work in teams of two. Teams rotate throughout the session. The hot shop closes during the last week of each fellowship session to allow time for finishing work and packing. Interaction and exploration of ideas with Wheaton Inc.'s research and development people are encouraged. Fellows must work in view of the museum visitors twelve hours per week, not including assisting time. Fellows are asked to donate

one of their works made during the residency for permanent inclusion in the CGCA collection in the Museum of American Glass at Wheaton Village.

Facility Description

The center sits on an eighty-eight-acre site that features the Museum of American Glass with over 7,500 objects (including over 100 works by past Fellows) and a 2,000-volume library of glass history and technology. The studio is located in a re-created 1888 glasshouse. The up-to-date, fully equipped 15,000-square-foot facility can accommodate most glass processes. Equipment includes: 500 lb. clear tank, 500 lb. color tank, four top loading annealers (24" H x 60" W x 36" D; 24" H x 48" W x 36" D; 18" H x 52" W x 30" D; and 15" H x 23" W x 13" D), one car kiln (casting, 26" H x 30" W x 40" D), two pick-up ovens (16" H x 24" W x 14" D and 6" H x 16" W x 16" D), one 15" ID glory hole (single 8" door), a two car garage, 23" ID glory hole (8" & 15" layered doors), two flat grinding wheels, a felt wheel (3 ¹/₂" W x 12" dia), a pumice wheel (2 ¹/₂" W x 16" dia), a belt sander (106" L, 4" W belts), two Reciprolaps, a sandblaster (36" H x 48" W x 36" D), a self-feeding Diamond saw with 24" dia. blade, another Diamond saw with a 12" dia. blade, a stone lathe with assorted wheels, hand held orbital diamond grinder, two benches, compressed air, two propane torches, hand-operated pressing machines, 19th century cast iron molds, plaster and clay room, and a woodworking shop for limited use.

How to Apply

Send a SASE for an application and brochure. Return eight copies of each of the following: the completed application, a current résumé, a brief statement explaining how you would use the Fellowship to benefit your artistic and career development, and two letters of recommendation (letters may be sent directly to CGCA who will be responsible for making multiple copies). Include ten slides of your work (labeled according to instructions) and an adequate SASE for their return. Include a paragraph about you and your work to be used for publicity purposes.

Note: Slides submitted by applicants chosen for the fellowships or as alternates become the property of the Creative Glass Center of America.

Deadline

August 1 (all sessions).

Approximate Cost of a Four-week Residency

Transportation, meals, some materials, and incidentals — offset by stipend.

CREEKWOOD WRITERS COLONY RESIDENCIES   AL

Creekwood Writers Colony Residencies
Alabama School of Fine Arts
Creative Writing Department
1800 Eighth Avenue North
Birmingham, Alabama 35203

Attention: James R. Nelson, Executive Director
(205) 252-9241

Notice: Creekwood Writers Colony is no longer in operation. No inquiries please.

CUMMINGTON COMMUNITY OF THE ARTS   MA

The Cummington Community of the Arts
R.R. 1, Box 145
Cummington, Massachusetts 01026

Notice: Cummington ceased operation in 1995. No inquiries please.

DENVER CENTER THEATRE COMPANY   CO

The Denver Center for the Performing Arts
Denver Center Theatre Company
1050 Thirteenth Street
Denver, Colorado 80204

Attention: Donovan Marley, Artistic Director
(303) 893-4000 ext. 2339 or (303) 825-2117 Fax

Type of Facility/Award
Opportunity for Playwrights.

Who Can Apply
Playwrights.

Provisos
They are looking for full-length plays that have not yet had a professional production. No one-act plays, no musicals, no plays for children, no translations, and no adaptations.

Dates of Operation
Open year-round.

Location
Denver, Colorado.

History

Denver Center for the Performing Arts is a nonprofit arts organization. They previously hosted the U.S. West Theatrefest (playwright's) competition. No other background information was provided.

What They Offer

The Denver Center Theatre Company holds readings and developmental workshops of new plays and full production of selected plays. The 1995/96 season lists twelve plays on the schedule from the end of September through mid-June.

Facility Description

Arts and theater center.

How to Apply

Send a SASE for information. Then send your clean, legible, securely bound script with a cover letter, a résumé of your experience as a writer, and a brief description of any readings, workshops, or amateur productions the script has received. Include an adequate SASE for return of the script (make sure your name, address, and telephone number are on the title page). Unsolicited manuscripts will only be accepted from residents of Arizona, Colorado, Idaho, Iowa, Minnesota, Montana, Nebraska, New Mexico, North Dakota, Oregon, South Dakota, Utah, Washington, and Wyoming. Residents of other states should send a letter of inquiry before sending a script.

Deadline

No deadline. Scripts accepted all year.

Approximate Cost of a Four-week Residency

Not applicable for this listing.

WALT DISNEY PICTURES & TELEVISION FELLOWSHIP   CA

Walt Disney Pictures & Television
500 Buena Vista Street
Burbank, California 91521

Attention: Brenda Vangsness, Program Administrator
(818) 560-6894

Type of Facility/Award

Fellowship.

Who Can Apply

Writers.

Provisos

The programs is meant to seek out and employ culturally and ethnically diverse new writers. Writers with WGA credits are eligible for this program and should apply through the Guild's Employment Access Department at (310) 205-2548.

Dates of Operation

One-year period beginning mid-October.

Location

Los Angeles, California.

History

Program was in its sixth year in 1995.

What They Offer

Ten to fifteen Fellows per year may be chosen. A $30,000 salary is provided for the year's work. Fellows from outside of the Los Angeles area will be provided airfare and one month's accommodations. Housing and work space are not included.

Facility Description

Major motion picture film studio/offices.

How to Apply

Send a SASE for an application and brochure. Return application with a completed writing sample, a one-page résumé, and a notarized standard letter of agreement which allows them to read your material (provided with application materials). Partner submissions are acceptable only if both writers submit applications together with one script. All scripts must contain a cover page with your name, address, and telephone number. Include a statement of interest in the program (fifty words or less). Appropriate samples for the features division include: a completed live-action motion picture screenplay (approximately 120 pages) or a full length two-to-three act play. Appropriate samples for the television division are a current full-length half-hour television script, e.g., *Ellen, Frasier, Mad About You, Roseanne* (all approximately forty-five pages), or a full length play (including one-acts over twenty-four pages). Include a SASP for submission acknowledgment. No fax applications.

Deadline

April 7 (postmarked). Applications are accepted between March 13 and April 7. Selections in late August. Notification dates are subject to change. (1995 dates.)

Approximate Cost of a Four-week Residency

Housing, meals, materials, and incidentals — offset by salary.

DJERASSI RESIDENT ARTISTS PROGRAM   CA

Djerassi Resident Artists Program
2325 Bear Gulch Road
Woodside, California 94062-4405

Attention: Admissions (year for which you are applying, i.e., 1997)
(415) 747-1250 or (415) 747-0105 Fax

Type of Facility/Award
Residency.

Who Can Apply
Choreographers, writers, composers, visual artists (painters, sculptors, installation artists, photographers), media artists (filmmakers, video artists, performance artists, experimental theater artists, and sound and radio artists).

Provisos
Emerging and established artists are welcome to apply. Applications from artists of varied cultural and ethnic backgrounds are encouraged. Collaborators and/or couples must apply separately. Applications must be returned in printed or typewritten English. Smoking is only allowed in designated outdoor areas. Alumni must wait three years before reapplying. The program does not discriminate with regard to race, sex, sexual preference, disabilities, religion, marital status, or national origin.

Dates of Operation
April through October.

Location
One-hour south of San Francisco in Woodside, California.

History
"The Djerassi Resident Artists Program was established in 1979 by Carl Djerassi in memory of his daughter Pamela, a painter and poet, as a retreat for artists. Since that time, it has provided 'The Gift of Time' for 800 residencies awarded competitively."

What They Offer
Sixty artists per year are provided with housing, all meals, and studio space for one month. Writers are housed in the Artists' House. Visual artists, composers, and choreographers are housed in the barn. No families. No pets. Choreographers may request to have up to two dancers in residence with them. (Additional dancers are welcome to work in the studio on weekdays and weekends by special arrangement.)

Facility Description
The Djerassi facility is located on 600 acres of rangeland, redwood forest, and hiking trails. Writers' rooms, located in the seven-bedroom Artists House, have large desks, workspaces, and outdoor decks. The Artists' House is where you'll find

the main kitchen, the dining area, a library, and a large deck. The unique twelve-sided barn has a darkroom, three visual art studios with sleeping lofts, a kitchen, and a common area. "The barn also houses the professional choreography studio and the composers' studio, equipped with a grand piano and a MIDI keyboard."

How to Apply

Send a SASE for an application and brochure. Return completed application with the $25 nonrefundable application fee and the following: a résumé, a project proposal (include a description of your working process), a list of special requirements (living, work space, or equipment needs), a list of your three most important professional achievements, the names and addresses of two references (professionals in your field who are familiar with you and your work), and a current work sample. *Dancers:* send a cued VHS video tape (labeled according to instructions) of two examples of choreography not more than ten minutes total with an accompanying descriptive sheet. *Writers:* send three sets of six to ten poems, short fiction, chapter(s) or section of a book (maximum of twenty-five pages) or a playscript (all labeled according to instructions). Unpublished material is welcome. Securely clip all pages together. *Composers:* send two full compositions on audio cassette, CD, or DAT. If submitting cassettes, send each composition on a separate tape. Include accompanying scores or a brief descriptive statement. *Visual artists:* send six color slides (packaged and labeled according to instructions) with descriptive sheet. *Media artists/new genre artists:* send a video cassette tape, slides, or text, whichever is most appropriate (labeled according to instructions), and an accompanying descriptive sheet. Enclose an adequate SASE for return of your sample(s). Samples will not be returned if you are accepted. Also return the notification postcard sent with your application packet.

Deadline

February 15. Notification no later than August 15. (1996 dates.)

Approximate Cost of a Four-week Residency

$25, plus transportation, materials, and incidentals.

DORLAND MOUNTAIN ARTS COLONY   CA

Dorland Mountain Arts Colony
Box 6
Temecula, California 92593

Attention: Admissions
(909) 676-5039

Type of Facility/Award

Residency.

Who Can Apply

All artists in music, literature, and the visual arts.

Provisos

Dorland has no electricity. If your work requires electrical apparatus (computers, tools, etc.), this is not the place for you. Spouses and collaborators may be in residence at the same time, but they must apply and will be considered separately.

Dates of Operation

Open year-round.

Location

Dorland is approximately 100 miles from Los Angeles, about sixty miles from San Diego, and about eight miles from the town of Temecula. The closest airport is in San Diego. A private van will take you from the airport to the Colony for a fee.

History

An internationally recognized haven for artists, writers, and composers, Dorland grew from the dream of Ellen Babcock Dorland, a world famous concert pianist, and her friend Barbara Horton, an environmentalist. "Between 1974 and 1988, Dorland was under the stewardship of The Nature Conservancy, an international land preservation group. The Conservancy designated Dorland as a nature preserve to protects its unique plants and wildlife. Dorland is also recognized as an Indian burial ground and considered sacred by neighboring Indian tribes. In July 1988, the Conservancy deeded the property back to the Dorland board of directors with the restriction that the land be protected from development in perpetuity." The lack of electricity at Dorland has become "a symbol of our separateness from the modern-day world."

What They Offer

Dorland offers residencies of two to eight weeks. The average stay is one month. Individual cottages house each artist. Kitchen utensils, linens, and housewares are provided. Residents are responsible for their meals. Weekly trips into town provide opportunities for shopping, banking, and laundry. A cottage fee of $5 per day is requested to cover the cost of firewood, wicks, and fuel. (Propane is used to fuel stoves and water heaters.) Residents communicate by placing notes in each other's mail boxes so as not to disturb one another's privacy. There is a pay phone for residents' use. Occasionally, residents organize potluck dinners or impromptu open studios. There is an eclectic library. Dorland is serious about privacy; no overnight guests are allowed without prior staff approval. Children may not stay overnight. Day visitors may be allowed with prior staff approval. No pets are allowed.

Facility Description

Cottages have a kitchen, a bathroom, and living and working areas. The cottages are heated by woodstoves. Kerosene or Coleman lamps are used to provide light. If you like to walk or hike, there are miles of natural trails on the grounds. There's also a spring-fed pond if you feel like cooling off.

How to Apply

Send a SASE for an application and brochure. Return the original application and three copies with a brief description of your proposed project and reasons for wanting a Dorland residency, three copies of your educational and professional experience, two references in your field, and a sample of recent work. *Composers:* send three copies of two tapes or scores (no records, please). *Poets:* send three copies of at least six poems. *Visual artists:* send three sets of six slides in plastic sleeves. *Writers:* send three copies of three works (short manuscripts or chapters). You may include other items to help the selection committee evaluate your work. If accepted, you have two years in which to schedule your residency, are on a first-come, first-served basis, so plan ahead. Within ten days after scheduling, you are required to send a $50 nonrefundable processing fee (to hold your dates).

Deadline
March 1; notification May 15. September 1; notification November 15.

Approximate Cost of a Four-week Residency
$190, plus transportation, meals, materials, and incidentals.

Note: This listing was taken from brochures and guidelines for the 1993/94 season. Call the facility about program changes. Requests for an update went unanswered.

DORSET COLONY HOUSE   VT

Dorset Colony House
P.O. Box 519
Dorset, Vermont 05251

Attention: Dr. John Nassivera, Director
(802) 867-2223

Type of Facility/Award
Residency.

Who Can Apply
Writers, playwrights, composers, directors, designers, collaborators, and visual artists.

Provisos
Facilities are only suitable for visual artists who work on a small scale. There are no special studios and the quality of natural light varies.

Dates of Operation
March 20 through May 20. September 15 through November 30.

Location
Dorset, a small village on the National Register of Historic Places, is near the Green Mountains of Southern Vermont, a four-and-a-half-hour drive from New York City.

History
The Colony House was built in the early 1800's as a three-story farmhouse. Victo-

rian features were added later in the century. The last remodeling was by the Sheldon family in the 1920's, when the house was completely renovated and more than doubled in size. From 1960 to 1978, it was rented to Dorset's professional theater company as summer housing for the acting company. In 1979, the house was purchased by Dr. and Mrs. John Nassivera, with the assistance of the Clarence Geiger Trust, in order to assure that it would continue as the home for the Dorset Theatre Festival. The house is now available for use by writers, particularly playwrights, as a workspace and retreat during the months of the year when the acting company is not in residence. The colony has hosted new writers, Pulitzer Prize winners, and Academy Award winners. Most residents have been playwrights and writers.

What They Offer

The Colony House can accommodate up to eight writers at a time, operating from March 20 through May 20 and from September 15 through November 30. Periods of residency are flexible — from one week to several months, depending upon the artist's requirements. First-time residencies are granted for up to one month. The Colony House can also accommodate groups when scheduling allows. Food services are not provided for individuals, although they are available for groups and special occasions. Residency fee is $90 per week, which is less than 50% of the actual cost of operation. There are no application fees or other charges. Residents are responsible for their own transportation and meals during the stay; the kitchen is open at all times and fully equipped with utensils, paper goods, coffee, etc.

Facility Description

The house is a large three-story structure with eight private rooms (some with fireplaces), three public areas (where conversation and fellowship are encouraged) including the kitchen, a wood-paneled library/sitting room with a fireplace, and a large dining room, also with a fireplace, that can accommodate up to twenty people. The kitchen is fully equipped and capable of serving large groups. The house was fully winterized in 1979 and is well suited for efficient year-round operation. The Colony House is set off on three acres of lawn surrounded by tall maple, oak, and pine trees that seclude it from the street and from the rest of the village. Dorset village is within walking distance, as are open fields and streams, a pond, mountain trails for hiking, cross-country ski trails, and the Dorset Marble Quarry, a favorite swimming area.

How to Apply

Send a SASE for a brochure. Then send a letter with your requested residency dates, a description of your intended project, and a résumé of publications, readings, and/ or productions. First time residencies are granted for periods of up to one month.

Deadline

Rolling application process. Advance time is kept to minimum.

Approximate Cost of a Four-week Residency

$360, plus transportation, meals, materials, and incidentals.

DUMBARTON OAKS DC

Dumbarton Oaks
1703 32nd Street, N.W.
Washington, D.C. 20007

Attention: Office of the Director
(202) 342-3200 or by cable: HARDOAKS, Washington, D.C.

Type of Facility/Award
Fellowship.

Who Can Apply
Anyone wishing to do extensive research in three areas of study: Byzantine Studies (including related aspects of late Roman, early Christian, Western medieval, Slavic, and Near Eastern studies), Pre-Columbian Studies (of Mexico, Central America, and Andean South America), and Studies in Landscape Architecture.

Provisos
All applicants must be able to communicate satisfactorily in English.

Junior Fellowships are for students who at the time of application have fulfilled all preliminary requirements for a Ph.D. (or appropriate final degree) and will be working on a dissertation or final project at Dumbarton Oaks under the direction of a faculty member at their own university. In exceptional cases, applications may be accepted from students before they have fulfilled preliminary requirements.

Fellowships are for scholars who hold a doctorate (or appropriate final degree) or have established themselves in their field and wish to pursue their own research. Applications are also accepted from graduate students who expect to have a Ph.D. prior to taking up residence at Dumbarton Oaks. (Successful applicants will revert to the status and stipend of Junior Fellows if the degree has not been conferred.)

Summer Fellowships are for scholars on any level of advancement.

Dates of Operation
Academic Year: September to May — varies yearly. Academic Semester: September to January or January to May. Summer Session: Six to nine weeks beginning mid-June and ending mid-August.

Location
Washington, D.C.

History
Dumbarton Oaks is administered by the Trustees for Harvard University

What They Offer
Junior Fellowships: The full academic year award is approximately $16,400 for an

unmarried Junior Fellow. Support includes a stipend of $12,000, housing (a housing allowance may be offered instead of housing if Dumbarton Oaks is unable to provide accommodations), a research expense allowance of $800 for the year; lunch on weekdays, and Dumbarton Oaks's contribution to health insurance. Travel expense reimbursement for the lowest available airfare, up to a maximum of $1,300 may be provided for Junior Fellows residing outside the United States and Canada if support cannot be obtained from other sources.

Fellowships: The full academic year maximum award for a married Fellow from abroad accompanied by family members is $34,700. Support includes a stipend of $21,000; housing (a housing allowance may be offered instead of housing if Dumbarton Oaks is unable to provide accommodations); $1,700 (if needed) to assist with the cost of bringing and maintaining dependents here; a research expense allowance of $800 for the year; lunch on weekdays; and Dumbarton Oaks's contribution to health insurance. Travel expense reimbursement for the lowest available airfare, up to a maximum of $1,300 may be provided for Fellows residing outside the United States and Canada if support cannot be obtained from other sources. (Other grants or sabbatical salaries may supplement awards with the knowledge and permission of both the grantors and Dumbarton Oaks.)

Summer Fellowships: Awards provide a maintenance allowance of $150 per week (for six to nine weeks), housing in a Dumbarton Oaks apartment or at the Fellows Building, lunch on weekdays, Dumbarton Oaks contribution to health insurance, and travel expense reimbursement (not to exceed the lowest available airfare, up to a maximum of $1,300) if other travel support cannot be obtained. No housing allowances or dependents' allowances for families are available in the summer.

Facility Description

None provided.

How to Apply

Send a SASE for an application and brochure. Return ten complete, collated sets of the application letter including title of project, type of fellowship desired, field of study, and precise period for which the award is requested. Include in your letter the names of three scholars (two for Summer Fellowships) who will send letters of recommendation directly to Dumbarton Oaks (one of the three letters for Junior Fellows must be from your faculty advisor) and a proposal (up to 1,000 words) describing the work to be done in residence. Indicate progress already made, the anticipated time for completion, and use to be made of the resources at Dumbarton Oaks. Include personal and professional data, i.e., your name, address, telephone number, family status (including names and ages of dependents who would accompany you to Dumbarton Oaks), your education and academic degrees (with dates conferred, awards, and honors), present and past positions, your publications, papers read, field research, and your proficiency in the requisite languages, which must include facility in written and spoken English. Junior Fellowship applicants must have their university registrar send an official transcript of their graduate record directly to Dumbarton Oaks.

Deadline

Application must be postmarked by November 1 and received by November 15. Awards are announced in February and must be accepted by March 15.

Approximate Cost of a Four-week Residency

Most meals (daily lunches provided), materials, and incidentals — offset by stipend.

EXPERIMENTAL TELEVISION CENTER   NY

Experimental Television Center
109 Lower Fairfield Road
Newark Valley, New York 13811

Attention: Hank Rudolph, Program Coordinator
(607) 687-4341 Voice and Fax

Type of Facility/Award

Artist-in-Residence Program.

Who Can Apply

Video artists and artists working in all genres.

Provisos

Artists must have prior experience in video production or with other electronic systems. Experience with image-processing tools and computer systems is helpful, but not required.

Dates of Operation

February through June. September through January.

Location

Owego, New York.

History

The Experimental Television Center was founded in 1971. "The Center's original programs involved artists, students and teachers as well as the interested community in activities which included access to portable video equipment and editing facilities, a weekly community cable series, an extensive series of workshops and an annual exhibition series, research and development of imaging tools and systems, a residency program and support services for artists. Today the Center offers a unique concentration on electronic image-making by providing production, research and support services and a grants program for artists and arts organizations."

What They Offer

The Experimental Television Center invites artists of all genres to come and explore concepts of digital and analog imaging and to experiment with expanding the formal boundaries of the many different approaches to video. Artists operate the equipment themselves (there is no crew), but instruction and technical assistance are available from the program director. Artists retain the rights to material produced during the residency, but the center requires a copy of the completed work for their library. The Center does not offer residencies during the months of July and August. Residencies usually run between three and five days beginning on Wednesdays. Two days are required for instruction. Artists are encouraged to arrive in Owego the day before the residency begins. Artists are welcome to stay at the Center during the residency. Studio fee is $15 per day with an additional $15 per day donation requested for communication among artists. The program director's services as a production assistant may be hired at the rate of $75 per day. At the conclusion of the residency, the artist will provide the Center with a description of the work performed. Artist is asked to send a copy of the finished tape to the Center and keep them informed of any exhibition or distribution.

The Center also offers funding as follows: *The Grants Program* (direct support to film and electronic media artists in New York state), *Finishing Funds* ($500 toward completion costs of electronic media works currently in progress), *Presentation Funds* (grants to nonprofit organizations in New York State to assist with the exhibition of works of film and electronic art), and *Exhibition Regrants* (support for the public presentation of film and video exhibition series). Call or write for specific details if you are interested in any of these funding programs.

Facility Description

The system consists of analog devices such as colorizers and keyers as well as digital devices such as a frame buffer, several Amiga computers, and a Toaster. Record decks are $^{3}/_{4}$" and are not editors. A list of other equipment is available upon request.

How to Apply

Send a SASE for a brochure and application guidelines. Submit a project description indicating how you'd use their imaging system. Include a résumé with information relating to past video works and their exhibition, a clear indication of your knowledge of equipment operation, your choice of a five-day period (with alternative dates), and, if you are a first time applicant, a $^{3}/_{4}$" or VHS of recently completed works (and an adequate SASE for return of the tape). If you must cancel your residency, the Center asks for at least four weeks' notice. Without such notice, you may have difficulty getting rescheduled for another residency.

Deadline

December 15 for February through June residencies. July 15 for September through January residencies.

Approximate Cost of a Four-week Residency

$30 per day, plus transportation, meals, materials, and incidentals.

THE EXPLORATORIUM   CA

The Exploratorium
3601 Lyon Street
San Francisco, California 94123

Attention: Melissa Alexander, Arts Program Assistant
(415) 561-0324 (Arts Program), (415) 563-7337, or (415) 561-0307 Fax

Type of Facility/Award
Artist-in-Residence Program.

Who Can Apply
Visual artists.

Provisos
Artists whose interests are relevant to the thematic concerns of the museum are invited to send informal proposals. (See *How to Apply*, below.) The museum's central theme is human perception. The Exploratorium is looking for interesting exhibits (using any form of artistic media) that will work, will last, and will stand up to the heavy use of children. As an interactive science museum, successful candidates will be those artists who like to experiment, who invite challenge, and who like the idea of working with an enlightened and exploratory scientific community.

Dates of Operation
Open year-round.

Location
The Exploratorium is located in San Francisco's Marina District, near the Presidio and the Golden Gate Bridge.

History
"The Exploratorium, San Francisco's museum of science, art, and human perception, was founded in 1969 by Dr. Frank Oppenheimer, a noted physicist and teacher. From the beginning, the museum has used the observations made by artists as means of developing a clearer understanding of nature among our visitors.

"Though the Exploratorium is best known as a science museum, the museum has used the perceptions of both artists and scientists to establish notions of how we see, know, and understand the world around us. Artists' works illustrate the reoccurrence of natural processes in a multiplicity of contexts, and they thus convey a sense of the unity between nature and culture which encompasses both art and science."

What They Offer
Four to six artists each year come to the Exploratorium and produce works of art. Each selected concept is negotiated separately, based on a formal proposal. The program functions more as a laboratory for artistic investigations than as a studio.

Artists get to use the shop and its mechanical and human resources to explore scientific instruction, construction, and the collaborative investigation of their (the artist's) vision, as well as to provide new exhibits for the museum's collection.

Facility Description

The Exploratorium, located in San Francisco's cavernous Palace of Fine Arts building, is a center of cultural investigation. The artists have use of a sophisticated electronics and machine shop and the technical problem-solving skills of a staff fascinated by aesthetics. The Palace of Fine Arts building itself is a work of art and a famous San Francisco landmark.

How to Apply

Send a SASE for application guidelines and a brochure. After reading about (or visiting) the Exploratorium, those who share common interests with the museum should write a letter to the program coordinators telling them what they'd like to do. Include background information, slides, and other supporting materials. If there is staff interest in the idea, the artist will be invited to the museum to discuss the idea further, present past work to the staff, and to become more familiar with the staff and the facility. If the proposed idea seems viable, the artist will be asked to submit a formal proposal. That proposal should include the concept, a budget, any special requirements (such as equipment, access to people with special skills or knowledge or other needs), a timeline, and supporting materials. The proposal will be reviewed by a staff committee and ratified by the Arts Program Advisory Committee made up of a group of community artists, previous artists in residence, and arts affiliates. A contract is then negotiated and the residency is structured to include scheduling, press strategies, timelines, context and thematic tie-ins, and possible support activities such as workshops, artist talks, etc. Time schedules are determined by the scope of the project. Criteria for selection are quality of concept, quality of past work, ability to communicate, willingness to collaborate and to share new ideas, relevance of project content to other current projects or investigations at the museum, and expressed staff interest in the project and artist.

Deadline

Rolling application process, although most artists are selected in December as the Exploratorium begins planning its next fiscal year (begins in June).

Approximate Cost of a Four-week Residency

Not applicable in this listing. Each successful candidate must negotiate his or her own contract with the museum.

The Fabric Workshop Museum
1315 Cherry Street, 5th Floor
Philadelphia, Pennsylvania 19107

Attention: Artist Advisory Committee
(215) 922-7303 or (215) 922-3791 Fax

Type of Facility/Award

Artist-in-Residence Program.

Who Can Apply

Visual artists.

Provisos

Well-known and emerging artists of various disciplines who desire to broaden their aesthetic by doing silkscreen printing on fabric are invited to apply.

Dates of Operation

Open year-round.

Location

Philadelphia, Pennsylvania.

History

"The Fabric Workshop and Museum is the only nonprofit organization in the United States devoted to experimental fabric design and printing by nationally recognized and emerging artists representing all disciplines. Founded in 1977, The Fabric Workshop has developed into a renowned institution with an Artist-in-Residence program, an extensive permanent museum collection of unique contemporary art, the Museum Sales Shop, and comprehensive educational programming including exhibitions, lectures, tours, and student apprenticeships."

What They Offer

Ten to twelve artists each year are selected for this program. Artists receive an honorarium (no amount stated in Workshop's literature), photographic documentation of finished projects, and pieces of their experimental works. All materials necessary, including screens, ink, fabric, and the labor needed to complete the project in the Workshop's laboratories are provided. Technical assistance is available from the Workshop's highly skilled staff.

Facility Description

Facility includes print studios, dye and pigment mixing rooms, an exhibition area, and a museum sales shop.

How to Apply

Send a SASE for brochure. If you are interested in this program, send ten to twenty slides, a résumé, and any other materials of interest. The Artist's Advisory Committee meets quarterly to review the work of the artists to be invited in the next year or two. Some are solicited, others approach them independently.

Deadline

Rolling application process.

Approximate Cost of a Four-week Residency

Transportation, housing, meals, and incidentals — offset by honorarium.

THE FARM — AN ART COLONY FOR WOMEN   NY

The Farm — An Art Colony for Women
R.D. 3, Old Overlook Road
Poughkeepsie, New York 12603

Attention: Kate Millett
(914) 473-9267

Winter Address:
Kate Millett
295 Bowery
New York, New York 10003
(212) 473-2846

Type of Facility/Award

Artist-in-Residence Program.

Who Can Apply

Writers and visual artists.

Provisos

Women writers and women visual artists of all kinds from the United States and elsewhere are invited to apply.

Dates of Operation

May through Christmas.

Location

Poughkeepsie, New York.

History

The Farm is a self-supporting and economically independent colony for women artists. The crops, Christmas and landscape trees, help support the colony's expenses — keeping buildings in repair and providing studio space.

What They Offer

In exchange for housing, residents contribute five hours of work each weekday morning. From one o'clock until eight o'clock each evening when dinner is served, residents are free to work on their art. Everyone is free to do as they please on weekends. Every person contributes $70 per week for food.

They also offer a one-week intensive Master Class in writing. Tuition is $500, which includes room and board. No work exchange is required for this program.

Facility Description

Tree farm in New York.

How to Apply

Send a SASE for information and application guidelines. Then submit examples of your work, a description of yourself, your interest in the farm, and preferred dates of residency.

Deadline

Rolling application process.

Approximate Cost of a Four-week Residency

Transportation, $70 week for meals, plus materials and incidentals.

THE FINE ARTS WORK CENTER IN PROVINCETOWN   MA

The Fine Arts Work Center in Provincetown
24 Pearl Street
Box 565
Provincetown, Massachusetts 02657

Attention: Tom Murdock
(508) 487-9960 or (508) 487-8873 Fax

Type of Facility/Award

Residency.

Who Can Apply

Writers and visual artists.

Provisos

Writers and visual artists in the crucial early stages of their careers are invited to apply. Writers may apply in fiction, poetry, and creative nonfiction, but not in playwriting. All work submitted must be in English. Writers who are applying in more than one genre must pay the nonrefundable processing fee for each submission. In the visual arts, painters, sculptors, installation artists, printmakers, and photographers are considered. The Center has no facilities for videographers or

---

filmmakers. No welding or casting equipment is available — artists must provide their own. Minority candidates are encouraged to apply.

Dates of Operation

October 1 through May 1.

Location

Provincetown, Massachusetts.

History

In 1968, the Fine Arts Work Center was founded by a group of artists, writers, and patrons of the arts. "They believed that the freedom to pursue independent work within a community of peers was the best catalyst for creative growth, and the Work Center has dedicated itself to this goal for twenty-five years."

What They Offer

The Fine Arts Work Center provides twenty (ten for artists and ten for writers) seven-month fellowships each year. Writing Fellows are provided with live-in studios and a monthly stipend of $375. Visual Arts Fellows are provided with work studios, separate living accommodations, a monthly stipend of $375, and a monthly materials allowance of $75. Fellows have no duties except to do their own work. Group activities, such as communal dinners, are organized both formally and informally, and provide the Fellows with the opportunity to meet Program Committee members, Trustees, and local artists and writers. No pets are allowed.

Facility Description

Fellows are provided with live-in apartments and separate working studios. Studios are approximately 400 square feet and have good northern light. Additional facilities include a basic woodshop, a print shop with an etching press, and a darkroom (without equipment). The Center has no welding or casting equipment. Writing Fellows are housed in small one- to three-room apartments. All units are furnished and have kitchens. The Stanley Kunitz Common Room, with a seating capacity of 150, is used for presentations by visiting artists and writers as well as for readings by Writing Fellows. Visual Arts Fellows mount individual shows in the Center's Hudson D. Walker Gallery. Visiting artists and writers engage in dialogues with the Fellows throughout the year. (The Stanley Kunitz Common Room is handicapped accessible, as are two living spaces and two working studios.)

How to Apply

Send a SASE for an application and brochure. *Writers:* return completed application with the $25 nonrefundable processing fee, a brief history of your professional work and accomplishments and your educational experience, a statement explaining what you hope to accomplish at the Work Center, a SASP to acknowledge receipt of your application, a SASE for notification of the committee's decision, and a sample of your work. Fiction samples should not exceed thirty-five double-spaced pages (including synopsis). You may send short stories or chapters from a novel. If you send chapters from a novel, include a synopsis. Poetry samples should not exceed twenty pages. Imaginative nonfiction samples should not exceed thirty-five double-spaced pages. Published work is acceptable only in manuscript form. Notify the committee of any prior book contracts as well as those received during the application review period. Fellowships are primarily for those who have not received big advances or contracts from major publishers.

Visual Artists: return completed application with the $25 nonrefundable processing fee, a brief history of your professional work and accomplishments, your educational experience, a SASP to acknowledge receipt of your application, a SASE for notification of the committee's decision, and a sample of your work. First Stage: send no more than ten 35 mm slides (packaged and labeled according to instructions) with accompanying descriptive sheet. Two slides are projected at one time. Also include an adequate SASE for return of your slides. Do not send announcements, catalogs, reviews, or letters of recommendation; they will not be reviewed or returned. Second Stage: approximately thirty applicants will be invited to submit original work. You will be notified in mid-March if you are a finalist. Original work must be received by the deadline date in April. (Finalists will be notified of date.) Work should include four to six drawings or works on paper, and three paintings or three pieces of sculpture or equivalent documentation. Include a SASP in a separate envelope at the time the artwork is sent for acknowledgment of receipt of work. Containers of work must be durable, simple, and easily returnable to sender. Applicant must include detailed, accurate instructions on repackaging. Work delivered by hand must be picked up by May 15. Return shipments will be C.O.D.

Deadline
February 1 (received). Notification on or before May 1.

Approximate Cost of a Four-week Residency
$25, plus transportation, meals, materials, and incidentals — offset by stipend.

Note: Information in this listing was from brochures and application guidelines for the 1993/94 season. Please call the facility to inquire about any program changes. Requests for updated information went unanswered.

Franciscan Canticle, Inc.
CANTICLE ARTS CENTER   CA

Franciscan Canticle, Inc.
Canticle Arts Center
675 N. Palm Canyon Drive
Palm Springs, California 92262

Attention: Vincent B. Gonzales, Director of Development
(619) 416-1338 or (619) 416-1344 Fax

Type of Facility/Award
Retreat.

Who Can Apply
Artists of all disciplines.

Provisos
Canticle is open to artists from anywhere in the world.

Dates of Operation
Open year-round.

Location
Palm Springs, California.

History
Canticle is the result of the dreams of four Los Angeles artists. In 1983, the Canticle Arts Center was formed to encourage men and women artists to use their gifts through their own artistic expressions. The term "Canticle" describes a spontaneous song of praise for creation. In July of 1989, the Center moved to a spacious and inspirational location in the Mojave Desert. As of this writing, the Center has moved to the Palm Springs location, which is described as "even more spectacular than our retreat center in Victorville, California."

What They Offer
The Center offers short- and long-term residencies based on the submitted application. Canticle provides you with a private studio or workspace, living accommodations, and three meals a day for $1,250 per month. If you're willing to share studio space, the cost (including living accommodations and meals) is $1,000 per month.

Facility Description
No description of the new, Palm Springs, facility was provided.

How to Apply
Send a SASE for an application and brochure. Return completed application, which requests the names of three references and asks for both personal and professional background information. Include a résumé and photo. Twenty-five percent of the cost

of the retreat must be paid one month prior to arrival; the balance is due on arrival.

Deadline

Rolling application process.

Approximate Cost of a Four-week Residency

$1,250, plus transportation, materials, and incidentals (for private studio). $1,000, plus transportation, materials, and incidentals (for shared studio).

FRANKLIN FURNACE   NY

Franklin Furnace
112 Franklin Street
New York, New York 10013

Attention: Performance Proposals or Emerging Performance Artists Series
(212) 925-4671

Type of Facility/Award

Fellowship/Grant.

Who Can Apply

Performance artists.

Provisos

Emerging performance artists or performance artists developing new works are invited to apply. Artists from all fifty states and other countries will be considered. Funded performances must take place somewhere in the state of New York.

Dates of Operation

Open year-round.

Location

New York City.

History

Artist Martha Wilson founded Franklin Furnace in 1976. Its mission at that time was to collect, catalog, conserve, and exhibit contemporary, artist-produced books and multiples. In 1993, their collection was acquired by The Museum of Modern Art in New York. This merger made it possible for Franklin Furnace to shift their focus to the expansion of its performance art and exhibition programs, as well as its innovative education programs in public schools. "Franklin Furnace has been at the forefront of the contemporary art world's fight for freedom of expression."

What They Offer

They have two programs: *The Fund for Performance Art* and *The Emerging Performance Artists Series*. The Fund for Performance Art awards $2,000 to $5,000 to artists to allow them to produce an important work anywhere in the state of New

---

York. The Emerging Performance Artists Series offers an honorarium for a one-night performance. They provide the venue, most of the technical equipment, technical assistance, and publicity for the event.

Facility Description

No description of facilities is given, except that their original basement performance space was closed by the Fire Department in 1990 after an anonymous caller claimed they were an "illegal social club." Now they mount their performances "in exile" in places such as the Judson Memorial Church, The Great Hall at Cooper Union, and in Woolman Hall and the New School for Social Research.

How to Apply

Send a SASE for an application and brochure. Return application with a (minimum) fifty-word summary of your proposed work. Include a VHS videotape cued for five minutes. You may also include an audio cassette, slides, or photos. Include a budget, information on any other funding sources, an adequate SASE for return of your materials, and if you wish, include a résumé, reviews of previous work, and any other support materials you feel would be helpful to the selection committee.

Deadline

April 1 (postmarked) for Fund for Performance Art Awards. April 1 (postmarked) for Emerging Artists program.

Approximate Cost of a Four-week Residency

Not applicable in this listing. See *What They Offer* above.

FUND FOR NEW AMERICAN PLAYS   DC

The Fund for New American Plays
The John F. Kennedy Center for the Performing Arts
2700 F Street, N.W.
Washington, D.C. 20566

Attention: Sophy Burnham, Manager or Iris Bond
(202) 416-8024 (General), (202) 416-8020 (Iris Bond), or (202) 416-8026 Fax

Type of Facility/Award

Playwright's Offering.

Who Can Apply

Theater groups and affiliated playwrights.

Provisos

Nonprofit professional American theaters are invited to apply. Fund was established to encourage playwrights to write new plays and to stimulate the development of plays and plays with music. The Fund does not provide funds for musicals or translations of foreign plays.

Dates of Operation
Full calendar year for production.

Location
Various locations throughout the U.S.

History
The Fund has awarded more than two million dollars to nonprofit theaters through-out the country to enable them to produce forty-nine new plays by fifty playwrights. 1995 was the Fund's ninth year. Three of the plays have won Pulitzer Prizes and others have been nominated for various awards, including Tonys and Outer Circle Critics Awards. Some have been produced in New York and other U.S. cities.

What They Offer
The Fund provides grants to underwrite specific or extraordinary expenses relating to creative support (expenses exceeding the theater's budget, and expenses allowing the playwright's choice of director or designer), actor support (costs of guest artists exceeding the theater's budget and productions that have larger casts than the the-ater can support), and production support (living and travel expenses of playwrights during the rehearsal and performance in order to guarantee a minimum four-week rehearsal period and give the author the opportunity to remain at the theater for rewriting during the play's run). Funding for sets or costumes may be considered under special circumstances. No funding is offered for publicity, marketing, payroll taxes, box office, or other non-artistic aspects of production. Playwright receives an award of $10,000. A separate grant for $2,500, The Roger L. Stevens Incentive Award, is given from time to time to playwrights of exceptional promise.

Facility Description
Varies according to theater.

How to Apply
Send a SASE for information and guidelines. Submit one proposal, five copies of the play, a production budget, proof of nonprofit status, a copy of the exclusive arrangement between the playwright and the theater, a history of the play's read-ings, workshops or other developmental work, disclosure of any encumbrances to the script, biographies of the playwright and any artist for whom financial support is being requested, disclosure of any co-production agreements with other theaters or producers in regard to the script, and a short paragraph about the theater. Also include a short bio, two black and white headshots of the playwright, a short para-graph about the artistic director, and a synopsis of the play suitable for press releases.

Deadline
March 15. Announcements — Fall.

Approximate Cost of a Four-week Residency
Not applicable in this listing. See *What They Offer* above.

GELL WRITERS CENTER OF THE FINGER LAKES   NY

Gell Writers Center of the Finger Lakes
Naples, New York

Administration:
Writers & Books
740 University Avenue
Rochester, New York 14607

Attention: Joseph Flaherty, Executive Director of Writers & Books
(716) 473-2590 or (716) 729-0982 Fax

Type of Facility/Award

Retreat. They also have a residency program, but residencies at this time (1995) are by invitation only. They may open up to "by application" residencies in 1997 if the pilot program is successful and receives funding.

Who Can Apply

Writers (including, but not limited to, poets, playwrights, novelists, magazine editors, and journalists).

Provisos

The retreat is ideal for working writers who wish to write in the serenity and beauty of the Finger Lakes area.

Dates of Operation

Open year-round.

Location

The Gell House is in Naples, New York, at the foot of the Bristol Hills. Located at the end of Canandaigua Lake, the area is one of the world's great grape-growing regions. The Finger Lakes region is easily accessible by major highways, by rail, or via Rochester International Airport, forty-five minutes to the north.

History

"Writers & Books is a Literary Arts Center providing Western New York with a variety of programs supporting the creation and appreciation of contemporary literature. These programs include readings by regional and national writers, an extensive workshop series, and community outreach programs. Writers & Books is supported in part with grants from The New York State Council on the Arts and The National Endowment for the Arts, as well as by corporations, memberships, and contributions."

What They Offer

Retreats at the Gell House are available through Writers & Books. Members are charged $25 per night per person and non-members are charged $35 per night per person. Please note: The house is equipped with two private bedrooms, each containing separate writing areas. If you choose to be alone in the house, you must pay for both bedrooms.

Writers & Books currently offers eight paid fellowships each year, providing room, board, and a stipend as part of a three-year pilot program. In return, Fellows are asked to take part in programs, including readings and workshops in a variety of community settings in the area. This is a "by invitation" pilot program, for which applications are available at Writers & Books. Inquire if you are a regional resident interested in this program.

Facility Description

The comfortable and charming Gell House is a completely furnished hillside home with a beautifully landscaped yard surrounded by twenty-three acres of woodlands and trails. The house has two bedrooms, two baths, a living room, a dining area, a fully-equipped kitchen, and indoor and outdoor porch areas. There is a wonderful territorial view from several large windows in the house and it is not uncommon to see deer near the spring-fed brook that falls along a terraced waterway. The setting is ideal for quiet study and reflection. "Planning is now underway to add a new building at the center, The Gleason Lodge, which will house up to eighteen writers for residencies, workshops, and seminars."

There are also many cultural and recreational attractions nearby, including The Bristol Valley Playhouse, Cumming Nature Center, Mees Observatory, the Finger Lakes Hiking Trail, High Tor Wildlife Management Area, and The Finger Lakes Performing Arts Center. In winter, the area is great for downhill skiers and cross-country skiers — at other times, you can hike, bike, swim, sail, or simply enjoy the rolling landscape. Also nearby are many fine restaurants, vineyards, and wineries.

How to Apply

Call or write for reservations, which are on a first-come, first-served basis. If you write, indicate your preference of dates and desired length of stay.

Deadline

None.

Approximate Cost of a Four-week Residency

$700 for members, plus transportation, meals, materials, and incidentals. $980 for non-members, plus transportation, meals, materials, and incidentals. (If you are a resident of the region, contact Writers & Books about the fellowship program.)

The Glassell School of Art
5101 Montrose Boulevard
Houston, Texas 77006

Attention: The Core Program
(713) 639-7500

Type of Facility/Award

Fellowship.

Who Can Apply

Visual artists.

Provisos

Visual artists who are just finishing their undergraduate or graduate Fine Arts training are invited to apply. Certificates of Achievement may be earned in painting,
drawing, printmaking, sculpture, ceramics, photography, and jewelry.

Dates of Operation

September through May.

Location

Montrose/Museum District of the city of Houston, Texas.

History

The Glassell School of Art (formerly The Museum School) was founded in 1927 as
part of the Houston Museum of Fine Arts. Established in 1982, The Core Program
provides talented young artists with a stimulating work environment between formal school training and professional life. The focus is on intensive studio experience and self-motivated investigation of the visual arts.

What They Offer

Up to ten Fellows, who will work in close proximity to each other in order to
promote dialogue and the exchange of ideas, may be selected each year. Each Fellow receives approximately 450 square feet of studio space (with twenty-four-hour
access), a tuition waiver, and a $5,000 stipend, which is paid out in monthly incre-
ments over the nine months of the program. Additionally, Fellows may attend
special seminars and participate in an annual group exhibition. They may have
their work critiqued by visiting artists and critics. In exchange, Fellows give five
hours each week in service to the school or museum. The school does not provide
housing, but affordable housing is usually available within walking distance. Most
Fellows find it necessary to take part-time employment. Eighty percent of the Core
Fellows apply for a second and final year in the program. Their slides are juried with
the finalists for the following year.

Facility Description

The school is in spacious, modern building next to the Lillie and Hugh Roy Cullen Sculpture Garden and across the street from The Museum of Fine Arts and The Contemporary Art Museum. There are a 4,600-square-foot indoor/outdoor sculpture shop, a 3,000-square-foot indoor/outdoor ceramics shop, a fully-equipped printmaking shop for lithography and intaglio, a state-of-the-art light metals and jewelry shop, a gang style darkroom, studios (for drawing, painting and design), a lecture hall, and a main gallery with a 33-foot atrium and mezzanine exhibition space.

How to Apply

Send a SASE for brochure. Submit twelve slides of recent work, a résumé, a statement of intention, three letters of recommendation, and a SASE adequate for return of your slides.

Deadline

April 1 for the following September to May program. Notification May 1.

Approximate Cost of a Four-week Residency

Transportation, housing, meals, materials, and incidentals — offset by stipend.

GLENESSENCE   CA

Glenessence
Arts Associates International, Inc.
1447 W. Ward
Ridgecrest, California 93555

Attention: Allison Swift, Owner
(619) 446-5895 or (619) 446-6782 Fax

Type of Facility/Award

Retreat.

Who Can Apply

All writers — male or female, all genres, all ages, all stages.

Provisos

Non-competitive application process. All writers (nonsmokers) may apply.

Dates of Operation

February through June. September through November.

Location

Glenessence is located in California's high desert town of Ridgecrest, which is east of Bakersfield and north of Barstow. The closest airport is Inyokern. Transportation from Inyokern airport, a short commuter flight offered by American Eagle (American) airlines, can be arranged by owner.

History

Glenessence is a private estate in the upper Mojave Desert. Previously operated as a bed and breakfast for business travelers, it was recently converted to a writers' colony.

What They Offer

Writers may rent an individual room with a private bath for $565 per month. Each person buys his/her own groceries, stores them in the kitchen, and cooks to suit their own individual taste. No foundation subsidizes the operation of Glenessence. Rental income offsets utility and maintenance costs. The owner is the dean of the local college and can provide access to the college's computer lab, library, and bookstore. The best months for a visit are February through June and September through November. July and August are too hot. December and January are too cold. (Call if you need to book space during those months.) A car is not necessary.

Limited financial assistance is available in the form of fellowships for those who are unable to pay the regular monthly rate. If you are interested in a fellowship, mention your financial need when applying. For fellowships, writing samples and a letter of recommendation are necessary before reservations can be confirmed. Notification of status takes one month. Call for details.

Facility Description

Glenessence is a luxury villa with a distinctive architectural design incorporating a heavy beam structure with foot-thick earthen walls and handcrafted cedar trim. The grounds include a tiled courtyard, and a pool and spa with splashing fountains.

In the courtyard at Glenessence. (Photo courtesy of Glenessence.)

There are five designer rooms, each with private bath, available for guests: the San Miguel room has a Mexican motif, the Santa Fe room has an American southwest motif, the Serengeti has an East African motif, the County Mayo has an Irish motif, and the Independence has a Colonial motif. Guests are allowed shared use of the library, living room, dining room, fitness center, writing rooms, kitchen, laundry, swimming pool and spa (in season), and the sunny courtyard. Glenessence is peaceful and elegant,.

In 1995, Glenessence added private phone lines and cable TV to some rooms. They also implemented a physical fitness program for those who wish to participate. They've added the following exercise equipment poolside: an exercise bike, a weight lifting bench (with a variety of weights), a workout bench for sit-ups and crunches, and a Nordic Track.

How to Apply

Send a SASE for brochure or call for reservations. A $100 deposit is required to hold dates. You may request specific rooms, but rooms are reserved and assigned on a first-come, first-served basis. There is no formal application process. No writing samples are required.

Deadline

None. Based upon availability. Call for reservations.

Approximate Cost of a Four-week Residency

$565, plus transportation, meals, materials, and incidentals. Limited financial aid is available.

Goshen College
THE GOSHEN COLLEGE PEACE PLAY CONTEST   IN

The Goshen College Peace Play Contest
Goshen College
Goshen, Indiana 46526

Attention: Lauren Friesen, Professor of Drama

Type of Facility/Award

Opportunity for Playwrights.

Who Can Apply

Playwrights.

Provisos

The one-act play contest is open to everyone, but the College is especially interested in scripts from college students and from historical peace churches. As the title of the contest suggests, plays with contemporary peace concerns are encouraged. Preference is given to plays that "present non-violent alternatives, the tragedy of violence, or seek understanding and reconciliation across the boundaries that divide the human community."

Dates of Operation
October (even-numbered years only).

Location
Goshen, Indiana.

History
Goshen College is a Mennonite college. The contest is held every other year on even-numbered years. All winning plays have been produced by the college. Some have gone on to tour various off-campus settings.

What They Offer
The winning entry will receive a cash award of $500 and full production of the play.

Facility Description
Goshen College's theatre is called The Umble Center. No details were provided.

How to Apply
Send a SASE for application guidelines. Submit your one-act play (with an adequate SASE for its return) to the address above before deadline.

Deadline
December 31 (odd-numbered years). Notification around June 1.

Approximate Cost of a Four-week Residency
Not applicable in this category.

THE GUEST HOUSE AT NEW LIGHT STUDIOS   WI

The Guest House at New Light Studios
Box 343, Turtle Town Hall Road
Beloit, Wisconsin 53511

Attention: Rolf Lund, Proprietor
(608) 362-8055 or (608) 362-1417

Type of Facility/Award
Retreat.

Who Can Apply
Artists, writers, musicians, or anyone seeking solitude in a peaceful, rural setting.

Provisos
Best suited for those seeking a quiet, nurturing atmosphere.

Dates of Operation
Open year-round.

Location
Beloit is located two hours north of Chicago, an hour and a half southwest of Milwaukee, and forty-five minutes south of Madison, Wisconsin. Beloit is accessible by bus from Chicago's O'Hare Airport; transportation from the bus stop at Beloit College is available if prearranged.

History
The three hosts are working artists: a musician, a writer, and a sculptor. They established the Guest House as a retreat center for artists seeking solitude.

What They Offer
Inspiration and rejuvenation are their primary offerings. The Guest House is a self-sufficient cottage with two bedrooms, a kitchen, a bathroom with shower, and a living room. It has cooking appliances, cooking utensils, a refrigerator, a furnace, and a wood stove. Guests must supply their own food. Rates are $40 for one bedroom per night and $50 for two bedrooms per night. There are private guest rooms down the road at the studio of another artist. Rooms have chalkboards, desks, and space for drawing or painting. In the past, the hosts have accepted paintings and readings as partial payment of guests' bills. Work exchange (practical things like painting the barn, gardening, etc.) is also an option if prearranged. If you go, plan on paying for your stay. If you can work out other arrangements, great. If you wish to schedule an exhibit or reading, solo or in collaboration with others, the hosts of the Guest House will be glad to help with arrangements and accommodations.

Facility Description
The Guest House is a two-bedroom cottage on a Wisconsin farmette. Guests may enjoy a swim in the pool, a game of basketball or ping-pong, or a hike or drive through the countryside. Additionally, there are creeks nearby for canoeing, and the prairie provides an excellent place for cross-country skiing in the winter.

How to Apply
Send a SASE for brochure. There is no application process. Call or write for reservations. The Guest House is booked on a first-come, first-served basis.

Deadline
None.

Approximate Cost of a Four-week Residency
$1,120 (one bedroom) or $1,400 (two bedrooms), plus transportation, meals, materials, and incidentals. (1995 rates.)

Gull Haven Lodge
94770 Highway 101 North
Florence, Oregon 97439

Attention: Larry, Host and Manager
(503) 547-3583

Type of Facility/Award
Retreat.

Who Can Apply
Anyone.

Provisos
None listed.

Dates of Operation
Open year-round.

Location
Gull Haven Lodge is eight miles south of Yachats and eighteen miles north of Florence on the Oregon coast. The Lodge is situated on a bluff overlooking the Pacific Ocean and borders the Siuslaw National Forest.

History
None provided.

What They Offer
Gull Haven has a variety of accommodations available at different rates. Here are some. *South Up:* an apartment with a panoramic view through floor-to-ceiling windows, a living-dining area with queen bed, a full-sized kitchen, a private bedroom with full bed, and three window-seat bunks in the living room that sleep extra people (accommodates six). *North Up:* a four-room apartment with two private bedrooms (one with a queen bed and one with a full), a complete kitchen (with microwave), a cedar-lined living room with wood-burning stove, a full bed off the dining area, and two window-seat bunks (accommodates six). *The Gathering Place:* a three-room cabin with a private deck and picnic area. It has sleeping space for four in the living room (a sofa-bed and two window seat bunks), a fireplace, a full bed in the private bedroom, and a large kitchen. *Northwest Down:* A romantic suite for two with a kitchenette/dining area combination and a private bedroom with queen bed. *Rose Room:* one room with a queen bed, a twin bed, and a small dining area located in front of three large windows for a view of the beach. *The Shag's Nest:* a one-room cabin with a private deck at the edge of the sea cliff with spectacular views on three sides. It has a fireplace, a queen bed, and a small kitchenette for light cooking. There is a bathroom located on lower level of the Lodge. Gull Haven also

offers two sleeping rooms for the budget-minded. Guests of these rooms share a bathroom (with shower) and a small kitchen with a refrigerator, a hot plate, and a sink. *The Lavender Room* is cedar-lined with large windows, a queen bed and a small dining set. *The Garden Room* is also cedar-lined and has a double bed, a small dining set, and views to the west and south through large windows. Pets are permitted for an additional $8 per pet per day.

Facility Description

A quiet hideaway perched atop a bluff overlooking the ocean, Gull Haven offers a variety of cedar-paneled rooms with paintings, prints, or photographs by Oregon artists. All units have breathtaking, unobstructed views of the sea and sky. Most units have living rooms, equipped kitchens, and modern tiled bathrooms. Some have small libraries of books and magazines. Each unit is uniquely different. Gull Haven is not a motel, it's a retreat.

How to Apply

Call for reservations. A fifty percent deposit is required prior to arrival. Thirty days notice is required for cancellation of reservations made more than two months in advance. Forty-eight hour notice is required for all other reservations. There is a two night minimum on weekends; and a three night minimum on holiday weekends. Call for current rates. Gull Haven offers a discount from regular rates to those who mention this listing.

Deadline

First-come, first-served.

Approximate Cost of a Four-week Residency

Room rental (varies by room, but ranges from $35 per night to $85 per night for two people), plus transportation, meals, materials, and incidentals.

HAMBIDGE CENTER   GA

The Hambidge Center for Creative Arts and Sciences
P.O. Box 339
Rabun Gap, Georgia 30568

Attention: Judith Barber, Executive Director
(706) 746-5718 or (706) 746-9933 Fax

Type of Award

Residency.

Who Can Apply

Writers and visual artists of all types.

Provisos

Applicants must be twenty-one years of age or older. Self-sufficient, emerging artists as well as mature, professionals seeking to engage in creative work or research are invited to apply. Residents of Fulton County, Georgia, may be eligible for a fellowship through the Fulton County Arts Council (inquire directly).

Dates of Operation
March through mid-December.

Location
The Hambidge Center is three miles from Dillard, 120 miles from Atlanta, and ninety miles from Asheville, North Carolina.

History
The Center was founded in 1934 by Mary Crovatt Hambidge. Hambidge serves approximately a hundred fellows each year. Since 1974, over a thousand artists have lived and worked at the Center.

What They Offer
The Hambidge Center for Creative Arts and Sciences offers stays of two weeks to two months. Residencies begin on a Monday and end on a Friday. The Center provides housing, either in individual dwellings/studios, or in the Rock House. From May through October, weeknight dinners are prepared and served at the Rock House, but Fellows must provide their own breakfasts, lunches, and weekend meals. Bed and bath linens are provided. A car is unnecessary, but helpful. Each resident is asked to pay $125 per week toward the costs. Financial aid may be available for those in dire need. Inquire when applying. The Center also offers workshops, speaker's forums, and gallery exhibitions that are open to the public.

Please note: No meals are provided for residencies taking place during the months of November, December, March, and April.

Facility Description
The Hambidge Center is listed on the National Register of Historic Places. Located in the Blue Ridge Mountains, it includes 600 acres of unspoiled, wooded land in a mountain valley with several creeks and waterfalls. Numerous nature trails alive with wild flowers cross the property. The Center offers guided nature walks through-out the year. There are seven isolated and private individual cottage/studios for residents' use, each with its own fully-equipped kitchen and bath. The Rock House (a large stone house with five bedrooms and two and a half baths) is where residents are served their evening meal. Residents using the pottery studio may be housed in the Rock House. Rock House residents share use of the bathrooms and the main kitchen. The Center also has a gallery (and a small shop) that hosts five or six shows each season.

How to Apply
Send a SASE for an application and brochure. Return the completed application with a $20 processing fee and a résumé of your education and/or training — note

any awards, honors, grants, exhibitions, or performances to help the committee to understand your commitment to your field. Append publicity materials such as copies of reviews, notices, etc. that your work has received, a list of your five most significant professional achievements, three letters of recommendation from people in your field who are familiar with your work, and some samples of your work. *Visual artists:* send at least ten slides of your recent work. *Choreographers, dancers, film, and video artists:* send video tapes of your recent work. *Poets and writers:* send three copies of a manuscript or a published work. If you send a published book, one copy will suffice. Attach a separate page telling the selection committee why a stay at the Center would be helpful to your career. Include an adequate SASE if you want your samples returned.

Deadline

January 31 (received). Late applications may be considered if there are cancellations. Notification in April.

Approximate Cost of a Four-week Residency

$520, plus transportation, some meals, materials, and incidentals (May–October). $520, plus transportation, meals, materials, *and* incidentals (November, December, March, and April).

Harvard University
NIEMAN FOUNDATION   MA

Harvard University
Walter Lippmann House
One Francis Avenue
Cambridge, Massachusetts 02138

Attention: Program Officer, Nieman Fellowships for Journalists
(617) 495-2237 or (617) 495-8976 Fax

Type of Facility/Award
Fellowship.

Who Can Apply
Journalists.

Provisos

U. S. and international journalists of all ages are invited to apply. There are no educational prerequisites for applicants. The Foundation is looking for working mid-career journalists of particular accomplishment and promise. *International journalists* must be fluent in spoken and written English. *U.S. journalists* must be citizens of the United States. *International and U.S. Journalists* must be full-time staff or freelance journalists working for the news or editorial department of newspapers, news services, radio, television, or magazines of general public interest; must have had at least three years of professional work in the media (most successful applicants have had five to ten years experience); and must obtain the employer's consent for a leave of absence for the academic year.

Dates of Operation

Academic year (September to June).

Location

Harvard University, Cambridge, Massachusetts.

History

The Nieman Foundation's objective is "to promote and elevate the standards of journalism in the United States and educate persons deemed specially qualified for journalism." The money was bequeathed by Agnes Wahl Nieman in memory of her husband, Lucius Nieman, founder and publisher of the *Milwaukee Journal*.

What They Offer

Approximately twelve U.S. and twelve foreign journalists are selected each year.

U. S. journalists receive a stipend of $25,000 for the academic year. Support for international journalists varies. Each journalist is allowed to choose a study plan of their own design. Fellows do not receive course credit or a degree for work done. Tuition, classroom, and library fees are covered by the fellowship. Most Fellows choose between two and four audited courses (one each semester is required.) If Fellows have children, they get a modest monthly allowance for childcare. Weekly "informal beer and cheese" meetings with selected faculty members, noted newspeople, and politicians are part of the tradition. Funding for international journalists is not provided by the Nieman Foundation. Those applicants must seek funding through other sources, although the Nieman Foundation has access to a few restricted grants. Selected Fellows must agree: to return to their employer at the end of the sabbatical year; to refrain from professional work during the fellowship term; to complete all the work in their academic courses (one in fall, one in spring semester); and to remain in the Cambridge area during the term of their fellowship while classes are in session.

Facility Description

Fellows are housed in the Walter Lippmann House, which was built in 1836 by Ebenezer Francis. The house has been "a school for 'young ladies,' a private residence, and the manse of a local church. In January 1978, the building was renovated and restored to become the Walter Lippman House of the Nieman Foundation and home for Nieman Fellows."

How to Apply

Send a SASE for an application form and brochure. Return completed application form (which asks for education, employment, professional, and award information) along with a (not more than 1,000 word) statement describing your journalistic experience, career plans and aims; a (not more than 500 words) statement discussing your proposed field of study at Harvard; and some samples of your recent (no older than one-year) professional work according to guidelines received with your application.

Deadline

January 31 (postmarked) for U.S. journalists. Interviews in Spring. Announcements in May. March 1 (received) for international journalists.

Approximate Cost of a Four-week Residency

Transportation, housing, meals, materials, and incidentals offset by stipend. (Grants to international journalists vary and may include transportation.)

Harvard University
HARVARD SCHOOL OF PUBLIC HEALTH   MA

Center for Health Communication
Harvard School of Public Health
677 Huntington Avenue
Boston, Massachusetts 02115

Attention: Jay A. Winsten, Ph.D., Associate Dean and Center Director
(617) 432-1038 or (617) 432-4490

Also contact: Terri Mendoza
(617) 432-4488 or (617) 731-8184 Fax

Type of Facility/Award

Fellowship.

Who Can Apply

Experienced print or broadcast journalists and accomplished freelance writers.

Provisos

Project must be book-length coverage of a health-related subject(s).

Dates of Operation

Academic year.

Location

Boston, Massachusetts.

History

"The Harvard Center for Health Communication was established in January of 1986 to provide *reliable health* information to journalists; to investigate and evaluate the *role of* mass communication in public health; to provide *educational and research opportunities* for journalists; and to develop a graduate-level curriculum in mass communication and public health for health professionals." The Harvard

Journalism Fellowship for Advanced Studies in Public Health was established in 1987 with a $375,000 grant from the Alfred P. Sloan Foundation.

What They Offer

Three journalists each year are chosen to spend a full academic year in residence exploring the problems in public health through a combination of self-directed study and structured seminars. Each fellow receives a stipend of $22,000 and up to $2,000 in a housing/relocation allowance. (These are the 1993/94 figures. The program was suspended for 1994/95, but will hopefully be reinstated for 1995/96 academic year as a book writing fellowship. Call the Center if interested.) Fellows have access to resources throughout Harvard University. They may choose to audit certain courses and attend selected lectures and seminars, or to seek out professors individually. Faculty advisors help guide Fellows in their courses of study. Periodically, there are small informal lunch time seminars with Harvard faculty and other Boston-area health experts to help Fellows with research beyond their individual fields. The Center also sponsors some formal evening seminars to explore critical problems in public health policy, analysis, and reporting. Applicants should be free of reporting assignments during the fellowship term.

Facility Description

University campus. No on-campus housing is provided.

How to Apply

Send a SASE for information and guidelines. Submit a letter of application (with name, address, and phone number on first page) containing the following: how you hope to benefit as a journalist or writer from the fellowship, a description of the public health problem(s) you propose to explore, and a broad outline of your project (book proposal). Include a letter of endorsement from a senior editor at your news organization, providing assurance you will be able to return to regular employment at that organization at the end of the fellowship year and assuring that you will not have any regular news assignments while at Harvard. Freelance writers should include a letter of recommendation from a former editor or other associate who can attest to applicant's professional skills and commitment. All candidates should include a curriculum vitae or résumé and five samples of previous work.

Deadline

March 1. Notification on or before May 1. (1993/94 dates. These dates may change with the program's 95/96 restructuring.)

Approximate Cost of a Four-week Residency

Transportation, housing, meals, materials, and incidentals offset by stipend and relocation allowance.

HARVESTWORKS, INC.   NY

Harvestworks, Inc.
The Audio Arts Organization
596 Broadway (602)
New York, New York 10012

Attention: John McGeehan
(212) 431-1130, (212) 431-8473, or E-mail: jfxm@echonyc.com

Type of Facility/Award

Artist-in-Residence Program.

Who Can Apply

Media artists (audio, film, dance, video, radio, music, theater, and performance
artists) and composers.

Provisos

No students, groups, or ensembles. Two years must pass before previous Harvestworks
AIR's can reapply. Emerging artists and artists of color are encouraged to apply
regardless of technical skills.

Dates of Operation

Open year-round.

Location

New York City.

History

Harvestworks is a nonprofit audio arts organization that has received funding support from a number of arts organizations. They receive hardware and software support from various multimedia hardware and software companies.

What They Offer

There are two types of residencies: *The Project Residencies* give media artists and composers twenty to forty hours of studio production time to create a new audio work for
public presentation. Twenty residencies per year are awarded (two alternates are selected in the event of a cancellation). Residencies are at Studio PASS. They include
access to a professional audio studio, a full-time engineer, tape, and other materials.
Priority is given to the creative use of the PASS facility and the innovative use of
sound. Selection criteria include: professional experience of the artist, a solid public
performance or broadcast commitment for the proposed work, and feasibility that
the project can be completed in the time provided using PASS resources.

The Programming Residencies give composers up to forty hours of studio time to
receive instruction in and to experiment with computer music MIDI systems. The
residencies include a professional software instructor and access to the Studio PASS
Macintosh computers, music software, and MIDI equipment. Priority will be given

to composers of acoustic and electronic music who would like to explore, and incorporate into their work, the capabilities of computer music MIDI systems. Projects intended for public performance are not required for this grant, however, specific areas of interest or works in progress will enhance the learning process. The artist's professional experience is part of the selection criteria.

Facility Description

Studio PASS is equipped with a live recording room, audio to video synchronization, Macintosh computer-controlled music sequencing capabilities, and ProTools, a Macintosh IIx computer-based digital recording and editing program by Digidesign. This is a well-equipped, state-of-the-art facility with a digital audio workstation, a multimedia workstation, tape recorders, outboard equipment, microphones, monitor speakers, synthesizers, video and synthesizers, other MIDI equipment, and software. They also offer (for use and for sale) hardware and software from the STEIM research center in the Netherlands.

How to Apply

Send a SASE for an application and brochure. Return six copies of the completed application with a detailed project description, plus one copy of a two-page résumé summarizing your experience in the field. (Do not send reviews, reference letters, program notes, or record albums.) Include a work sample. Cue a ten-minute audio or video segment for panel's consideration, or send a up to eight slides. Label all samples with your name. Formats include ¼" reel-to-reel audio tape, cassette, DAT, Beta, VHS, ¾" videotape, or slides in a clear plastic slide sheet. Do not send masters or originals. Include an adequate SASE if you want your materials returned, or you may pick up your samples in person at Harvestworks after December 31.

Deadline

November 1. Notification before January 1. (1994 dates.)

Approximate Cost of a Four-week Residency

Transportation, housing, meals, materials, and incidentals.

The Hastings Center
JOURNALIST-IN-RESIDENCE   NY

The Hastings Center
255 Elm Road
Briarcliff Manor, New York 10510

Attention: Strachan Donnelley, Ph.D., Director of Education
(914) 762-8500 or (914) 762-2124 Fax

Type of Facility/Award

Artist-in-Residence.

Who Can Apply
Professional journalists.

Provisos
Research project must be on some specific issue in biomedical ethics.

Dates of Operation
Open year-round.

Location
Briarcliff Manor, New York.

History
The Hastings Center is the oldest independent, nonpartisan, interdisciplinary research institute of its kind. They have a staff of twenty-eight, the collective talents of over a hundred elected fellows, an excellent bioethics library, and 12,000 associates around the world. Research is the central activity at the Center.

What They Offer
Journalists may spend from one week to one month at the Center pursuing an independent research project on some specific issue in biomedical ethics, or doing general work in applied ethics and in reflecting on how best to present ethical issues and dilemmas in medicine, the life sciences, and the professions to the general public. Visiting journalists are expected to become involved in the everyday life of the Center, participating in luncheon discussions and project meetings. The Center can arrange for fairly inexpensive local housing, but does not offer a stipend.

Facility Description
Office building. No housing is provided.

How to Apply
Send a SASE for an application and brochure. Return completed application form indicating area of interest, dates you're applying for, and source of funds while in residence. Include a three-page description of your project; your curriculum vitae; a sample of your recent work; and the names and addresses of two current references.

Deadline
Rolling application process.

Approximate Cost of a Four-week Residency
Transportation, housing, meals, materials, and incidentals.

Hawk, I'm Your Sister
P.O. Box 9109
Santa Fe, New Mexico 87504-9109

Attention: Beverly Antaeus
(505) 984-2268

Type of Facility/Award

Retreat/Respite.

Who Can Apply

Women, sometimes men, sometimes children.

Provisos

All participants are expected to be in good general health. Some trips are more strenuous than others. Some trips are restricted to women only — others are coed — others allow children.

Dates of Operation

Various.

Locations

The calendar of events for 1995 listed trips to Heron Lake, New Mexico; the Missouri River, Montana; Big Bend National Park; the Bahamas; Russia; Baja, California (Mexico); and Peru.

History

Hawk, I'm Your Sister is truly unique. They organize and lead canoe expeditions all over the world. Some are for women only, others include men, some allow children. Many have a theme (such as their *Writing Retreat*). The nonprofit group was founded by river guide (since 1975) Beverly Antaeus. She decided to specialize in canoe trips for women because of "the great satisfaction of sharing the growth, enthusiasm, and cohesive spirit of women exploring the wilderness as people of competence and power." *Sister Hawk* raises money for *The Wildlife Center*, which specializes in raptor (birds of prey) rehabilitation and the care and restoration of other wild animals until they can be released back into their native environment. The trips are fully staffed with an interesting array of people who do everything from cook to dive. Some have various first aid, CPR, and lifesaving certifications. Writing affiliates of note (such as Deena Metzger, Sharon Olds, Michael Ortiz Hill, and Milly Sangama) often join on the expeditions and share their experience and knowledge with other participants.

What They Offer

Unlike the other programs for writers listed in this book, this program speaks to the other side of writing — the side that requires thought, experience, and time with the elements, which is why I decided to include it. Therefore, unlike the other programs, this is a "respite" for which you must pay, as you would for any other vacation.

Hawk, I'm Your Sister provides all major equipment: canoes, paddles, life jackets, tents, food, cooking and eating utensils, and toilet tissue. You provide your own sleeping bag and personal gear. (They will send you a recommended list of useful gear and clothing.) Trips range from 7 to 17 days.

Facility Description
Various.

How to Apply
Send 55¢ in stamps for their calendar/brochure.

Deadline
Different for each trip.

Approximate Cost of a Four-week Residency
Prices vary according to length of trip and location. 1995 prices ranged from $1,095 for one-week trips in the U.S. to $2,500 for their trips to Russia and Peru. You pay the cost of transportation to designated airport(s).

HEADLANDS CENTER FOR THE ARTS   CA

Headlands Center for the Arts
944 Fort Barry
Sausalito, California 94965

Attention: Holly Blake, Director
(415) 331-2787, (415) 331-2887 for directions, or (415) 331-3857 Fax

Type of Facility/Award
Residency.

Who Can Apply
Visual, media, literary, and performing artists.

Provisos
Visual, media, literary, and performing artists residing in the California, Ohio, and North Carolina are invited to apply. (Residence restrictions may change as funding sources change — check with the Center.) North Carolina and California artists pursuing undergraduate or graduate degrees may not apply while enrolled in a degree-granting program. (See "How to Apply" below for specific artists' eligibility.) Bay Area artists may apply for the Affiliate Artists program (that listing follows this one) wherein they can rent studio space at Rodeo Beach for up to three years.

Dates of Operation

Open year-round.

Location

The Marin Headlands is located just north of the Golden Gate Bridge and west of the town of Sausalito. The Art Center is situated in eleven historic army buildings amidst 12,000 acres of coastal open space.

History

On the northern edge of San Francisco Bay, the Marin Headlands, once the home of the coastal Miwok tribe, is now a National Recreation Area. The Headlands Art Center is housed in historic Fort Barry, which was built in 1907 and occupied by the Army until 1972 when the Anti-Ballistic Missile Treaty was signed. The National Park Service entered into an arrangement with the Headlands Art Center (and other nonprofit groups) to let them occupy the buildings in exchange for their renovation. The Headlands Art Center was incorporated in 1982 to investigate the relationship between human and natural systems through the arts. The Artist-in-Residence Program began in 1987. More than twenty-five artists each year come from all over the world to live and work on-site.

What They Offer

Offerings vary by state of residence since each program is sponsored by that state's arts commission. Generally, three artists from Ohio and three artists from North Carolina are awarded three month residencies each year. In addition to shared living space (a 4-bedroom house shared with other resident artists), each artist is provided with either studio space or work space ranging from 200 to 2,000 square feet, a stipend of $500 per month, round trip airfare, use of the center's car for local trips, and dinner five nights each week. The same is provided for Bay Area residents, except for the airfare. In addition, Bay Area residents may qualify for an eleven month live-out residency program wherein they receive a stipend of $2,500, dinner two nights a week, and studio or work space ranging from 200 to 2,000 square feet. All AIR's attend dinner/discussions and take part in Open Houses (there were three in 1995). Traditionally, AIR's direct one evening's discussion about work that is of interest to him or her. Please be sure to call the center for updated offerings. All information is subject to change.

Facility Description

All of the Center's eleven historic buildings have been partially renovated and are scheduled for major improvements over the coming years.

How to Apply

Send a SASE for brochure. Then (all applicants) submit a résumé; a letter (no more than two-pages) indicating your interest in working with Headlands Center for the Arts: discuss how this residency will affect your work and what you can contribute to the community of the Headlands. *California residents only:* please state the category and the residency period (1, 2, 3, or 11 months) for which you are applying and indicate dates in August you are available to be interviewed. In addition to the items listed above, each state requires various support materials to be submitted, as well as a SASE adequate for their return. Support materials required for each state are listed below:

California & Ohio artists: Visual artists (painters, printmakers, photographers, sculptors, conceptual artists) submit no more than fifteen 35 mm slides (labeled according to instructions), or up to ten minutes of ¹/₂" video and/or audio tape. *Choreographers, dancers, performance and cross-disciplinary artists* submit slides, photographs, scripts, video documentation, and other materials that adequately describe your work. Review the information in other categories to determine what material you should submit. *Writers* (poets, fiction writers, nonfiction writers, and playwrights) submit one copy of no more than twenty pages of poems; thirty pages of prose; or three one-act plays. *Musicians, composers, radio and audio artists* submit up to thirty minutes of audio (cassette or CD) or ¹/₂" video tape of recent work. Please cue ten minutes of material for primary review. *Film or video artists* submit up to thirty minutes of 8 mm or 16 mm film; or ¹/₂" video tape. Please cue ten minutes for primary review.

California residents only: Arts professionals (critics, art administrators) submit sufficient material to evidence the breadth of your work and interests.

North Carolina artists: Visual artists (painters, printmakers, photographers, sculptors, craft artists, conceptual artists, or interdisciplinary artists) submit no more than fifteen 35 mm slides (labeled according to instructions), or up to ten minutes

Headlands Installation HCA Open House. (Photo courtesy Headlands Archives.)

of $^1/_2$" video and/or audio tape. *Writers* (poets, fiction and nonfiction writers) submit one manuscript copy of no more than twenty pages of poems or thirty of prose.

Deadline
June 3. (1994 date.)

Approximate Cost of a Four-week Residency
Some meals, materials, and incidentals — offset by stipend.

HEADLANDS CENTER FOR THE ARTS   CA

Headlands Center for the Arts
Affiliate Program
944 Fort Barry
Sausalito, California 94965

Attention: Holly Blake, Director
(415) 331-2787 or (415) 331-3857

Type of Facility/Award
Artist-in-Residence Program.

Who Can Apply
Visual artists, arts professionals, and a limited number of scholars in the humanities, sciences, and social sciences.

Provisos
Applicants must be residents of the San Francisco Bay Area.

Dates of Operation
Open year-round.

Location
The Marin Headlands is located just north of the Golden Gate Bridge and west of the town of Sausalito. The Art Center is situated in eleven historic army buildings amidst 12,000 acres of coastal open space.

History
On the northern edge of San Francisco Bay, the Marin Headlands, once the home of the coastal Miwok tribe, is now a National Recreation Area. The Headlands Art Center is housed in historic Fort Barry, which was built in 1907 and occupied by the Army until 1972 when the Anti-Ballistic Missile Treaty was signed. The National Park Service entered into an arrangement with the Headlands Art Center (and other nonprofit groups) to let them occupy the buildings in exchange for their renovation. The Headlands Art Center was incorporated in 1982 to investigate the relationship between human and natural systems through the arts. The Artist-in-Residence Program began in 1987. More than twenty-five artists each year come form all over the world to live and work on site.

What They Offer

The Affiliate Program provides studio or work space rentals on Rodeo Beach at Fort Cronkhite for up to three years. Affiliates may participate in two Open Houses each year and may attend the center's public programs such as readings, talks, and performances free of charge. There are scheduled monthly dinners for the Artists-

Headlands Center for the Arts. (Photo by Ed Beyeler.)

in-Residence and the Affiliates. Studio sizes range from approximately 110 square feet to 600 square feet. Open space rents for $.50 per square foot, and there are a few enclosed rooms available at $.65 per square foot. There are a limited number of studio spaces available for work exchange (call for information). A damage deposit of $100 is required of all artists. Studios are open twenty four hours a day, but may not be used as sleeping quarters. No smoking is allowed in the buildings. Artists are expected to show consideration for others with regard to noise and dust.

Facility Description

The former World War II army barracks buildings in Fort Cronkhite (buildings 1057, 1058, and 1062) serve the Affiliates. They are thinly built, two-story structures with lots of windows and have been used as artists' studios since 1987. There is no heat except for that provided by electric heaters. Each affiliate is charged a flat rate quarterly for electricity (110 volt, 30 amps). All studio buildings have cold running water. Building 1058 has a toilet.

How to Apply

Send a SASE for brochure. Then submit a résumé, contact information for three references, and a letter (no more than two-pages) indicating your interest in working with Headlands Center for the Arts. In addition to the items listed above, submit support materials (and a SASE adequate for their return) as listed below:

Visual Artists (painters, printmakers, photographers, sculptors, conceptual artists) submit no more than fifteen 35 mm slides (labeled according to instructions), or up to ten minutes of $1/2$" video and/or audio tape. *Performance and cross-disciplinary artists* submit slides, photographs, scripts, video documentation and other materials that adequately describe your work. Review the information in other categories to determine what material you should submit. *Writers* (poets, fiction writers, non-fiction writers, and playwrights) submit one copy of no more than twenty pages of poems; thirty pages of prose; or three one-act plays. *Composers and choreographers* submit up to thirty minutes of audio (cassette or CD) or $1/2$" video tape of recent work. Please cue ten minutes of material for primary review. *Film or video* artists submit up to thirty minutes of 8 mm or 16 mm film; or $1/2$" video tape. Please cue ten minutes for primary review. *Arts professionals* (critics, art administrators) or *Scholars*, submit sufficient material to evidence the breadth of your work and interests.

Deadline

October 21 (postmarked). (1994 date — may vary from year to year.)

Approximate Cost of a Four-week Residency

Transportation, studio rental (varies by number of square feet), housing, meals, materials, and incidentals.

Hedgebrook
2197 East Millman Road
Langley, Washington 98260

Attention: Writer's Residency Program
(360) 321-4786

Type of Facility/Award
Residency.

Who Can Apply
Writers.

Provisos
Women writers of all levels of experience, all ages, from all nations, of all racial, ethnic, and cultural groups who work in a variety of genres are invited to apply. Handicapped accessible.

Dates of Operation
January 9 to May 31. June 21 to December 8. (Dates vary from year to year.)

Location
Hedgebrook is located on Whidbey Island, a twenty minute ferry ride from the town of Mukilteo, which is about an hour's drive north of the Seattle-Tacoma International Airport.

A cottage at Hedgebrook. (Photo courtesy of Hedgebrook.)

History

Cottages at Hedgebrook was established as a not-for-profit organization in 1988 by founder Nancy Skinner Nordhoff to provide a natural place to work for women writers, published or not, of all ages, and from all cultural backgrounds.

What They Offer

Hedgebrook offers residencies of one-week to three-months to six writers at a time. Breakfast materials are supplied, lunch is brought to your cottage, and dinner is served at the farmhouse. Many meals are made from the bounty of the farm's award-winning vegetable garden. All necessities (and many non-necessities) are provided. All the writer needs to bring is her writing equipment, clothes, a bath towel, and flashlight. Typewriters and computers may be rented from a nearby shop. Limited travel scholarships and application fee waivers (based on need) may be available.

Facilities

Hedgebrook is situated on a woodsy thirty-acre farm on Whidbey Island in Puget Sound. The grounds include natural trails, a waterfall, ponds, a fire pit, and areas for horseshoes, volleyball, and croquet. Each writer has her own private, hand-crafted cottage with a writing space, a reading chair, bookshelves, a window seat, a small kitchen, a toilet, and a sleeping loft with stained glass windows. Cottages are fully furnished, including appliances, utensils, cleaning supplies, bed linens, a radio, a dictionary, and a thesaurus. All cottages have electricity and one is wheelchair accessible. Each has a wood stove for heat. (Wood is provided.) A bathhouse (with laundry facilities) serves all six cottages. The main farmhouse has a small library, a dining room, a living room, a telephone for resident's use, and the colony offices. Another telephone, located in the pumphouse near the cottages, is also available for writers' use. There are no phones or televisions in the cottages. No overnight guests are allowed. No pets. The utmost care is taken to give writers uninterrupted time to concentrate on their work.

How to Apply

Send a SASE for an application and brochure. Return completed application with a $15 nonrefundable application fee and five copies each of a description of the project you would work on at Hedgebrook, a statement about why a stay at Hedgebrook would be important to your work, and a sample of your writing (up to ten pages). No names on submissions other than application form.

Deadline

April 1 for Summer/Fall Session: June 21 to December 8. September 30 for Winter/Spring Session: January 9 to May 31. (1995 dates. May vary from year to year.)

Approximate Cost of a Four-week Residency

$0, plus transportation. Limited travel scholarships and application fee waivers are available.

Henry Street Settlement
Abrons Art Center
466 Grand Street
New York, New York 10002-4804

Attention: Visual Arts Program
(212) 598-0400 or (212) 505-8329 Fax

Type of Facility/Award

Artist-in-Residence Program.

Who Can Apply

Visual artists.

Provisos

None listed.

Dates of Operation

Open year-round.

Location

Lower East Side section of Manhattan.

History

None provided.

What They Offer

Five artists each year are selected to work in the center's collective studio. The studio is available on weekdays from 9 a.m. to 8 p.m., most Saturdays, and some Sundays. It is closed on national holidays. Residency term is for one year beginning in September. Artists are asked to make use of the studio at least twenty hours each week. Space is limited, so the center cannot accommodate large sculptures or printing equipment. In exchange, artists contribute three hours per week of "in-kind" services, such as teaching art workshops, leading gallery tours, installing exhibitions, or other special projects. Anyone accepted into the AIR program who is of Latino, African-American, Asian, or Native American background, under the age of thirty-five, with financial need, and a demonstrated commitment to the visual arts may also be eligible for the $5,000 *Van Lier Fellowship*. Application forms for this fellowship are included with the forms for the Artist-in-Residence Program.

Facility Description

This is an open-space art studio collective in the Abrons Art Center. It is suggested that artists thinking of applying to the program visit the Center beforehand.

How to Apply

Send a SASE for application and guidelines. Return the completed application with a résumé, ten slides of your work accompanied by a slide script (form included), a SASE for return of your slides, and a short statement about your work (optional). The four-page application asks for detailed information about your work, work habits, past experience, and income. It also asks for two letters of reference and two telephone references. The *Van Lier Fellowship* application asks you to briefly describe how this award will make a difference in your life over the next year.

Deadline
May 30.

Approximate Cost of a Four-week Residency
Transportation, housing, meals, materials, and incidentals. Studio space provided.

Howard University
HOWARD UNIVERSITY PRESS   DC
Howard University Press
1240 Randolph Street, N.E.
Washington, D.C. 20017

Attention: William S. Mayo
(202) 806-4940

Notice: The Howard University Press Book Publishing Institute's program is currently being evaluated with the idea of strengthening the curriculum. "Revitalized program will begin in 1996." If interested, send a SASE in early 1996 for new guidelines.

INSTITUTE FOR CONTEMPORARY ART   NY
Institute for Contemporary Art
P.S.1 Museum and the Clocktower Gallery
46-01 21st Street
Long Island City, New York 11101-5324

Attention: Alanna Heiss, President and Executive Director
(718) 784-2084, (212) 233-1440, or (718) 482-9454 Fax

Type of Facility/Award
Artist-in-Residence Program.

Who Can Apply
Visual artists.

Provisos
To be eligible for consideration, the applicant must be a professional artist. No high school, college, or graduate students will be considered. Applicants must be citizens or legal, permanent residents of the U.S.A., or citizens of Northern Ireland. Other

foreign artists may be able to apply through the International Studio Program — call or write for details.

Dates of Operation
Program is for one year — Fall to Fall.

Location
Studios are located at the Clocktower Gallery in lower Manhattan.

History
None given.

What They Offer
The Institute provides rent-free, non-living studio space in the Clocktower Gallery for a period of one-year. The Institute offers each artist individual studio space in which he or she can work within a professional, international art community. Participating artists at The Clocktower have access from 6 a.m. to 12 midnight weekdays, and from 12 p.m. to 8 p.m. on weekends. The Institute supplies light, security, and heat. Recently, they added a Northern Ireland studio. International residents may be eligible for a stipend. Amount of the stipend varies by country. There is no stipend for Americans. While there is no formal work-exchange program, some artists work within the Institute's school program. Work of residents is sometimes shown in the Annual New York Exhibition of Studio Artists.

Facility Description
Studios range in size from 375 to 530 square feet. There are no darkroom, printing, or welding facilities. Each artist must supply his or her own materials and equipment. Under no circumstances can studio workspaces be used as living quarters. Studio space in the Clocktower Gallery will only be available until 1997.

How to Apply
Selection of the artists is made by a panel comprised of individuals active in the field (artists, critics, curators, dealers) and one member of the staff of P.S.1. Studios are allocated by the selection panel and the executive staff of The Institute. International applicants must submit a video of their work on a U.S. format (VHS).

To receive details and guidelines for applying to the program, send a SASE to the address above in mid-January. No application forms are available before that date.

Deadline
April 15 (postmarked). Applications are available beginning January 15 each year.

Approximate Cost of a Four-week Residency
Transportation, housing, meals, materials, and incidentals. Free studio space.

Intersection for the Arts
446 Valencia Street
San Francisco, California 94103

Attention: Paul Codiga/Kate Moses
(415) 626-2787 or (415) 626-1636 Fax

Type of Facility/Award
Cash Awards.

Who Can Apply
Writers.

Provisos
Awards are meant to encourage young, unpublished writers to continue to write. Applicants must be between twenty and thirty-five years of age on January 31 of application year. Applicants for the *Joseph Henry Jackson Award* must be residents of northern California or the state of Nevada for three consecutive years prior to January 31 (of the year of application). Applicants for the *James Duval Phelan Award* must have been born in the state of California, but need not be current residents. Previous winners are ineligible to receive the same award again. Proof of birth, age, and residence may be required and must be furnished within ten days if requested.

Dates of Operation
Not applicable in this listing.

Location
Not applicable in this listing.

History
"The awards are made annually under the terms of the Joseph Henry Jackson Fund and the James D. Phelan Trust, housed at The San Francisco Foundation. A special fund, established by the author Mary Tanenbaum in memory of Joseph Henry Jackson, makes a third $1,000 award available to encourage nonfiction writing."

What They Offer
Cash awards in the amount of $2,000 each for the *Joseph Henry Jackson Award* and the *James Duval Phelan Award*, and $1,000 for the *Mary Tanenbaum Award*. Award winning manuscripts become the property of The San Francisco Foundation and become part of the Foundation's permanent archives. Authors retain full rights for the publication and distribution of their works.

Facility Description
Not applicable in this listing.

How to Apply

Send a SASE for an application and brochure. Return completed (official) application signed by you (you may use one application and one work sample to apply for all three awards) with a brief description of the work submitted. For the Phelan Award, the unpublished work-in-progress submitted may be fiction, nonfictional prose, poetry, or drama. For the Jackson Award, the unpublished work-in-progress may be fiction (novel or short stories), nonfictional prose, or poetry. Nonfiction writers who apply for either the Jackson or Phelan award, but are not selected as winners, are considered for the $1,000 Mary Tanenbaum Award for Nonfictional Prose. No separate application for this award is required. No candidate may win more than one award. Manuscripts must be no longer than 100 pages, 8 ½" x 11", typed, and double-spaced. Each manuscript must have a title page with the title of the work, author's name, and address. No handwritten or illegible manuscripts.

Deadline

February 6. Notification on or about June 15. (1995 dates.)

Approximate Cost of a Four-week Residency

Not applicable in this listing.

ISLE ROYALE NATIONAL PARK   MI

Isle Royale National Park
800 East Lakeshore Drive
Houghton, Michigan 49931

Attention: Artist-in-Residence Program
(906) 482-0984

Type of Facility/Award

Artist-in-Residence Program.

Who Can Apply

Writers, composers, and all visual and performing professional artists.

Provisos

Writers, composers, and all visual and performing professional artists whose work can be influenced by the north woods wilderness are invited to apply. The directors will consider all forms of art except those that manipulate or disturb the park's environment. The facility is not wheelchair accessible.

Dates of Operation

Mid-June to mid-September.

Location

Isle Royale is an island wilderness in Lake Superior. It is forty-five miles long and eight and a half miles wide. The park is fifteen miles from Grand Portage, Minnesota, seventy-three miles from Houghton, Michigan, and fifty-six miles from Copper Harbor, Michigan. There are no roads on the island — transportation is by boat or foot.

History

"Isle Royale's cultural history includes prehistoric Native American copper mining, lighthouses, fisheries, and maritime culture. Some of these resources are accessible from Rock Harbor via 165 miles of maintained trails or by various boat services. With Isle Royale's vast and varied cultural and natural resources, it presents itself as the ideal place for creative endeavors. The solitude and serenity of the island inspire creativity."

What They Offer

Residencies are for a minimum of two weeks; the brochure does not state a maximum. Artists are housed in a rustic cabin (former summer residence of the Dassler family) in Tobin Harbor, two miles by boat or trail from the park's major development at Rock Harbor. The cabin sleeps two. A guest house at the site can serve as a workroom and/or storage space. The accommodations are simple — a pit toilet and no electricity or running water. Basic cooking equipment, bedding, and fuel are provided, but the artist needs to bring personal gear, food, and art supplies. Food for the entire stay needs to be purchased before the trip. A canoe is provided for transportation. It is recommended the artist be self-sufficient, in good health, and well prepared. Expect cool temperatures, solitude, and simplicity. Selection is based on artistic integrity, ability to reside in a wilderness environment, a willingness to donate a finished piece of work inspired on the island, and the artist's ability to relate and interpret the park through their work.

Facility Description

The island is quite picturesque with its wave-washed shores, its boreal forests of spruce and fir, miles of ridge and valley topography, fascinating mammals (e.g., wolves and moose), and colorful birds. Hundreds of interesting plants and wildflowers grow in the forests. Ninety-nine percent of the island is wilderness, which is designated an International Biosphere Reserve.

How to Apply

Send a SASE for brochure. Return the entry form with a one-to-two page résumé, a summary of your creative works, a statement explaining what you hope to achieve from a wilderness residency, preferred dates, and support materials. These may include 35 mm slides (in standard mounts and labeled according to instructions) of your recent work, an audio cassette, a video cassette, or a manuscript excerpt, short story, or article. Include a SASE adequate for the return of your support materials.

Deadline

February 15 (postmarked).

Approximate Cost of a Four-week Residency

Transportation, meals, materials, and incidentals.

JACOB'S PILLOW   MA

Jacob's Pillow
Box 287
Lee, Massachusetts 01238-0287

Attention: Residency Group
(413) 637-1322

Type of Facility/Award
Residency.

Who Can Apply
Dance artists.

Provisos
None listed.

Dates of Operation
Various times during the year depending upon residency program.

Location
Lee, Massachusetts.

History
Jacob's Pillow is a theater company for dance artists.

What They Offer
Jacob's Pillow presents a twelve-week performance season (June through August) in the Studio/Theatre and a ten-week performance season in the Ted Shawn Theatre. Audience size ranges from 150 to 750. There are four types of residency programs.

In-Season Residencies: Residencies in this program are from two to three weeks during June through August. Artists are provided with studio space, housing, meals, and a modest fee. In exchange, artists are expected to open up their processes to the community through workshops, off-site outreach programs, or several informal presentations each week (open rehearsals, showings of nearly completed work) as part of the Pillow's *Inside/Out* series. These are free-to-the-public, outdoor presentations scheduled an hour and a half before Ted Shawn Theatre performances. At the end of the performance, the audience may ask questions or offer feedback. These activities should require from eight to ten hours per week of the artists' time.

In-School Residencies: These residencies range from one to four weeks and are usually scheduled for the spring or the fall. They require a commitment to education of grades kindergarten through twelve. Artists are provided with room and board, transportation, and a small fee. Studio space is provided at Jacob's Pillow when the artist is not in the schools. While in the schools, the artist may teach classes, lead workshops, lecture, or give demonstrations or informal performances for the benefit of the children. These activities take up three full school days per week.

Creation Residencies: Usually scheduled for spring or fall, Creation Residencies provide room and board and studio space, but no transportation or other fees. Artists are expected to give appropriate credit to the Pillow in any printed material referring to the work made while in residence. Use of theatrical lighting and technical support staff may occasionally be available at cost to these residents. In exchange, a portion of the artist's rehearsal process must be made open to the community.

Performance Residencies: These residencies are for performers in the Ted Shawn Theatre and Studio/Theatre who "usually stay off-campus, but occasionally are placed in residence for some period of time leading up to their performances. For these residencies, the artist is given room and board, studio and theatre space, and a fee. In exchange, artists may be required to participate (on a limited basis) in the Inside/Out series, teach classes or give workshops, hold open rehearsals, or participate in community outreach activities.

Note: This information was for the 1994 performance season. Make sure you request up-to-date information before applying.

Facility Description
None provided.

How to Apply
Send a SASE for application guidelines. Then send a letter of interest with support materials to the residency group.

Deadline
Rolling application process. Note months of residency terms.

Approximate Cost of a Four-week Residency
Materials and incidentals — offset by fee — for In-Season and In-School Residencies. Transportation, materials and incidentals for Creation Residencies. Transportation, materials and incidentals — offset by fee — for Performance Residencies.

KALA INSTITUTE   CA

Kala Institute
1060 Heinz Avenue
Berkeley, California 94710

Attention: Patrick McMenamin, Program Director
(510) 549-2977 or (510) 549-2984 Fax

Type of Facility/Award
Artist-in-Residence.

Who Can Apply
Visual artists.

Provisos

None listed. Artists from all countries are invited to apply.

Dates of Operation

Open year-round.

Location

Kala is in a light industrial area in the Oakland, Emeryville, Berkeley corridor.

History

Now in its twentieth year, Kala was founded by artists for artists, to provide them with access to technical equipment and assistance twenty-four hours a day, 365 days a year. Kala subsidizes eighty percent of the cost of maintaining a world-class intaglio and lithography studio. Proceeds from gallery sales go to support Kala's other nonprofit programs, including lectures, demonstrations, and performances.

What They Offer

The Artist-in-Residence Program provides inexpensive studio space to selected artists for a fee. Some fellowships are available, depending on funding. Call Kala for specific details. New AIR's (signing a one- to three-month contract) with no prior Kala experience are charged $313 per month with a reduction of $40 available in exchange for ten hours (per month) of work in the office or workshop. Previous Kala Artists-in-Residence are eligible for various levels of discounts depending on the length of their affiliation with the Institute and whether or not their contract is prepaid. (For example, a 12-month prepaid contract by an AIR with previous Kala experience and work exchange would cost the artist $198 per month for studio space. They also have senior rates, limited-use rates, single-day-use rates, media-lab-use rates, and various other rate categories. Listed are for 1995. They will be increased four percent on the first day of each new calendar year. Kala averages fifty to eighty AIRs per year. Half of these artists are from outside the U.S.

Facility Description

Kala's gallery, graphic arts workshop, art archive, consignment sales department, office, and media lab occupy 8,000 square feet. The workshop studio equipment includes: two American French Tool etching presses — 48" x 78" and 40" x 70"; three Griffin etching presses — 54" x 32 $1/2$", 44" x 21 $1/2$", and 32" x 18"; KB etching press — 26" x 47"; Takach-Garfield motorized litho press — 56" x 32"; Bumpodo litho press — 45" x 34"; Vandercook letterpress — (SP-20) cylinder proof press; Nu Arc Plate Maker (Arc-lamp); aquatint box; and darkroom. In addition to its intaglio and lithography equipment, Kala provides facilities for silk-screen, letterpress, and an electronic media laboratory for digital imaging, video editing, and multimedia productions. Media lab equipment includes: one Quadra 950 computer with 24 mb of RAM and a 1.5 external gigabyte drive; two Quadra 700's, each with 24 mb of RAM; a 44 mb Syquest drive; a flat bed opaque/transparency, 24-bit scanner; a Photo-CD compatible CD-ROM drive; a video translator and mixer. Computer software includes: Aldus Photoshop, Illustrator, Painter, MacroMind Director, Premier, HyperCard, and QuickTime.

How to Apply

Send a SASE for information and guidelines. Then, if you live nearby, make an appointment with the Director for a review of your portfolio. If you are applying by mail, send a résumé and some slides of your work. Include a SASE.

Deadline

Rolling application process.

Approximate Cost of a Four-week Residency

$313, plus transportation, housing, meals, materials, and incidentals. Limited fellowships available. $40 per month reduction on studio fees in exchange for ten hours' work in the workshop or office.

KALANI HONUA   HI

Kalani Honua
Institute for Cultural Studies
R.R. 2, Box 4500
Pahoa, Hawaii 96778-9724

Attention: Richard Koob, Artistic Director
(808) 965-7828 or (800) 800-6886 for reservations only

Type of Facility/Award

Retreat. Artist-in-Residence Program.

Who Can Apply

Visual, media, performing, folk, literary, and humanities artists.

Provisos

The main consideration is the professionalism of the artist and his or her ability to complete the proposed project.

Dates of Operation

Open year-round.

Location

Kalani Honua is situated near Kalapana on the big island of Hawaii, forty-five minutes from the city of Hilo, and one hour from Hawaii Volcanoes National Park. From Honolulu, book inter-island service on Hawaiian Air or Aloha Airlines to Hilo. Rent a car in advance or have the Center's van pick you up at the airport. Transfer fee is $25 per person. Advance reservations are required.

History

The Center was established in 1980 as an intercultural retreat and conference center, and as a retreat for professional artists by dance artists Richard Koob and Earnest Morgan. Kalani Honua means "the harmony of heaven and earth" in Hawaiian. The 1995 calendar of events includes several week-long workshops in topics like Energy, Self-discovery, Firewalking, a Hula Festival, Biokinetics, Men's and Women's Spirit Revivals, Bellydancing, Tai-Chi, a Men's Conference, a National Sacred Dance Conference, a Hawaiian Intercultural Dance Festival, and several Youth Summer Programs. Other workshops are available on an ongoing basis: Contemporary Dance, Yoga, Olelo Hawaii, Art of Self Defense, Hula, Qigong, Life Drawing, Fitness Training, Massage, Watsu, and Acupuncture.

What They Offer

Artists are welcome year-round at regular rates. Stipends for reductions in lodging fees are available by application. More stipends are available in the periods of May to July and September to December than at other times. Stipends (maximum allotment $1,275 per month) provide fifty percent of the lodging costs. Stipends may not be applied to dorm lodging or camping, or toward a reduction in food or transportation costs. Fees are $65 per night for a single with private bath/$75 per night for a double with private bath; $52 per night for a single with shared bath/$62 per night for a double with shared bath. Multiple occupancy rooms are $28 per night per person; camping is $15 per night per person; and private cottage units (single and double beds, bath, and living room with an ocean view) are $85 per night (single or double) and $15 for each additional person. An additional fee may be required if a private studio or work space is needed. A ten percent lodging discount is available on stays of seven nights or longer. Group rates are available. Children under three are free; children three to twelve are $10 per night. Breakfast, lunch, and dinner are served buffet style and consist of mostly vegetarian cuisine. Priced individually, all three meals together run about $25 per day. Children three to twelve are half price. There are kitchen facilities in each of the lodges for your convenience. A residency at Kalani Honua provides the artist with the impetus to complete works in progress, strike out in new directions, or simply exchange ideas with other resident artists from many disciplines, ethnic backgrounds, and cultures.

Facility Description

Site is located on twenty acres of secluded forest and dramatic coastline within Hawaii's largest conservation area. "Unlike virtual 'destinations,' Kalani Honua treats you to real healthful cuisine, thermal springs, a dolphin beach, spectacular Volcano National Park, and traditional culture." Four two-story wooden lodges and four private cottages provide simple but comfortable accommodations. Each lodge offers private rooms, has a 500- to 1000-square-foot multipurpose studio space with an ocean view on the upper level, common kitchen facilities, and shared or private bath options. Visual artists and dancers use the studio spaces as needed. Writers generally work in their rooms, outdoors, or in the reading lounge or café. Every effort is made to protect the artist's privacy during working hours. Studio visits without prior arrangement are discouraged. Telephone messages are delivered only in an emergency.

Activities available on-site include: pool, spa, volleyball, tennis, track, ping-pong, basketball, fitness room, and a massage/meditation lanai. Nearby you'll find snorkeling, warm springs and steam bathing, and sea cliff meditation.

How to Apply

Send a SASE for an application and brochure. If you are not requesting a fee reduction, there is no application process. Just call the 800-number for reservations. If you are requesting a fee reduction, return the completed application (preferably at least one month in advance of your intended residency) with a $10 nonrefundable processing fee, a description of your proposed project, a list of your professional achievements, a current résumé, two black and white glossy or Velox-type photos of you or your work for publicity and documentation purposes, two references (authorities in your field who have been informed about your application and are familiar with your work), and samples of your recent work (with an SASE for their return). *Visual artists:* send ten 35 mm color slides (packaged and labeled according to instructions) and an accompanying descriptive sheet. *Performing artists:* send one copy of performance reviews, news articles, or other documentation and one copy of a video (VHS format only) of work in rehearsal or performance. *Writers:* send one copy of some writing samples with your name on each (ten poems or two short stories or two chapters of a novel or one act of a play, and a synopsis). *Photographers:* send ten photographs.

For retreat reservations only, call toll-free: (800) 800-6886. For information, call the main number listed above. A deposit (one night's lodging cost) is required at the time of reservation confirmation. If you cancel your reservation no less than two weeks prior to arrival, your deposit, less $20, will be refunded. No refunds will be given if reservation is canceled less than two weeks prior to arrival date.

Deadline

Rolling application process. Applications are reviewed monthly. Space is awarded on a space-available basis. (To date, over eighty percent of the applications for fee reductions have been approved.)

Approximate Cost of a Four-week Residency

Variable, depending upon choice of accommodations and whether or not you purchase or cook your own food. Lodging varies from $450 for camping, to $840 for a dorm room, to $1,560 for single with shared bath — fifty percent fee reduction possible, to $1,950 for a single with private bath — fifty percent fee reduction possible, to $2,550 for a private cottage — fifty percent fee reduction possible. Meals can be purchased individually — three meals average $25 per day — or meals may be prepared in the shared kitchen facilities of the lodges.

Kansas Newman College
THE MILTON CENTER'S
POST GRADUATE FELLOWSHIPS   KS

The Milton Center
Kansas Newman College
3100 McCormick Avenue
Wichita, Kansas 67213-2097

Attention: Virginia Stem Owens, Director
(316) 942-4291, (800) 736-7585 toll free, or (316) 942-4483 Fax

Type of Facility/Award
Fellowship.

Who Can Apply
Writers.

Provisos
Writers who are Christians are invited to apply.

Dates of Operation
Academic year (September to June).

Location
Wichita, Kansas.

History
The Milton Center was founded in 1986 to "support work by writers who seek to animate the Christian imagination, foster intellectual imagination, and explore the human condition with honesty and compassion." 1994/95 was the first academic year of the award. The fellowship was designed to give Christian writers an opportunity to complete their first book-length manuscript of fiction or poetry.

What They Offer
The Center provides living expenses (housing is not prearranged) and a stipend of $6,000, disbursed over the nine months. Two fellowships each year are awarded. In exchange, Fellows will work no more than ten hours each week at the Center, helping with the newsletter, planning conferences, etc. Peer review of manuscripts in progress is available. The Fellow is also invited to become part of the worshipping community at Kansas Newman College while in residence.

Facility Description
College campus. Fellow arranges for his or her own living accommodations.

How to Apply
Send a SASE for an application and brochure. Return completed application with

a $15 nonrefundable application fee, a résumé, three letters of reference, a two or three page book proposal, two sample chapters or ten poems, and a one-page statement explaining what you aim to accomplish at the Milton Center. None of these items will be returned to you.

Deadline
January 31. (1996 date.)

Approximate Cost of a Four-week Residency
$15, plus transportation, meals, materials, and incidentals — offset by stipend.

THE JOHN MICHAEL KOHLER ARTS CENTER   WI

The John Michael Kohler Arts Center
608 New York Avenue
P.O. Box 489
Sheboygan, Wisconsin 53082-0489

Attention: Lynne Shumow, Arts/Industry Coordinator
(414) 458-6144 or (414) 458-4473 Fax

Type of Facility/Award
Artist-in-Residence Program.

Who Can Apply
Visual artists (all disciplines).

Provisos
Applying artists need not be trained ceramists or metal sculptors. However, they must be able to quickly understand industrial technologies. Artists may work in the Pottery or the Foundry/Enamel Shop or both, depending upon space availability.

Dates of Operation
Open year-round.

Location
The John Michael Kohler Arts Center is fifty miles north of Milwaukee and 150 miles north of Chicago in Sheboygan, Wisconsin, which is just five miles from the Kohler Company in the Village of Kohler.

History
"Arts/Industry is undoubtedly the most unusual ongoing collaboration between art and industry in the United States. Conceived and administered by the John Michael Kohler Arts Center of Sheboygan, Wisconsin, the program makes industrial technologies and facilities available to artists through long-term residencies, short-term workshops, tours, and other programming so that they may further their artistic explorations. Major funding is provided by Kohler Company and the National

Endowment for the Arts." The program serves four artists concurrently, benefiting approximately fifteen artists each year. Since its inception in 1974, the program has served hundreds of artists.

What They Offer

Residents are provided with studio space in the factory, which is accessible twenty-four hours a day, seven days a week. The Center provides shared housing for the four resident artists in a furnished, four-bedroom house near the site. Round-trip transportation from each artist's home to Sheboygan (within the continental United States) is reimbursable. The Center encourages artists to bring their own cars. Residents also receive a stipend of $120 per week. In addition, artists receive free materials, use of equipment, technical assistance, and photographic services. Residency terms are from two to six months. Upon arrival, artists receive an extensive orientation on the use of professional industrial equipment. This enables the artists to explore forms and concepts not possible in their own studios and to develop new ways of thinking and working. The Arts/Industry Program provides artists with materials and equipment normally used in factory production, free of charge. Tools and materials not normally used at the factory must be provided by the artists, who are asked to pay minimal amounts for the use of brass in excess of 100 pounds and for "A-1" company products. Artists do their own work with technical advice from the Art Center's technicians and Kohler Company's industrial craftspeople and engineers. Much of the work produced during a residency is documented on 35 mm slides. Artists receive a copy of the slide documentation.

All work produced by an artist during a residency belongs to the artist. However, artists are asked to donate one work each to the John Michael Kohler Arts Center and the Kohler Company. Additionally, artists are asked to give one day per month to educational activities such as slide lectures, video interviews, tours of their work space, or other activities.

"Internships are available for undergraduate and graduate art students. Interns generally aid the artists-in-residence and, in addition, may work with John Michael Kohler Arts Center staff on the documentation, maintenance, and exhibition of the Arts/Industry collection or on other aspects of the Art Center's program and operation. Interns usually have some access to the industrial technologies for their own art."

Facility Description

The Pottery: Kohler Company's Pottery is the largest pottery in the world under one roof. "Artists use a strong, off-white vitreous china clay which is once-fired in oxidation to 2400° F (cone 10). A kiln fired to 2100° F (cone 5) is also available. The clay is superb for slip casting and carving but is less effective for throwing and hand building. It is in slip form and is piped under pressure to the artist's studio space. Artists use plaster to make their own molds for slip-casting their work. Discarded production molds and ware also can be utilized. Cast pieces can be assembled in various ways before or after firing. Even the plaster is sometimes used to create sculpture. Artists are encouraged to experiment with the range of glaze possibilities.

Color variations may be made by adding ceramic stains (no oxides) to a variety of clear and white glaze bases. Kohler Company has an extensive Research and Development Laboratory where artists are able to develop glazes."

The Iron Foundry: "The Kohler Company Iron Foundry, the largest in Wisconsin, allows artists to cast or free-pour iron shapes. Artists may create their own patterns and molds, use production discards, or incorporate scrap metal into their work. An array of materials is available for making patterns, including wood, plaster, clay, metal, urethane, Styrofoam, and found objects. Artists may use pep-set, green sand, or natural sand for making molds and cores. Enamel-base iron is used for casting. Welding and cutting facilities may also be used at certain times. Artists working in the Iron Foundry may have periodic access to the Brass Die Cast area where they may cast forms in brass using pep-set or green-sand molds. At times, they may also add sprayed metal surfaces to the iron. Carpentry shops are available for fabricating supports, patterns, and armatures."

The Enamel Shop: "The Enamel Shop allows artists to use enamel powders directly on red-hot cast iron in single or multiple applications. The Enamel Shop contains thirty-six large enameling ovens; the use of one oven is usually reserved for artists. The Enamels Laboratory allows artists to experiment with and test the brilliant vitreous enamels available. Past artists-in-residence have developed liquid and paste enamels for use on somewhat cooler iron and with a variety of stencils."

How to Apply

Send a SASE for an application and brochure. Return completed application with an up-to-date résumé, twenty slides of your recent work (packaged and labeled according to instructions; slides will not be returned), a cover letter describing the work you propose to undertake during a residency, why the industrial facility is appropriate for your work, the extent of your experience in materials and processes you wish to use, a brief statement about your work — e.g. aesthetics, working methods, and catalogs, reviews, and/or other publications about your art. Also choose three alternative residency periods in order of preference and include the names, addresses, and telephone numbers of six references (describe their relationships to you, i.e., employer, gallery owner, etc.) who know you and your work well and who may be contacted at a later date. Drawings of the works you wish to undertake may be helpful in the selection process, but are not mandatory with your submittal.

Deadline

August 1 (received) for residencies beginning the following year.

Approximate Cost of a Four-week Residency

Meals and incidentals — offset by stipend.

LADAN RESERVE   CO

Ladan Reserve
Box 881239
Steamboat Plaza, Colorado 80488

Attention: Jeffrey Hayden, Director
(303) 723-4916

Notice: Ladan Reserve's program will begin in 1997. Contact in late 1996 to be added to their mailing list (include a SASE). No program details were provided.

LAKESIDE ART AND CULTURE INTERNATIONAL   MI

Lakeside Art and Culture International
9129 Golf
Lakeside, Michigan 49116

Attention: Laurie R. Wilson
(616) 469-5840, (616) 469-3033, or (616) 469-1101 Fax

Notice: At present, this is a very small program supporting only one invited artist at a time. They are trying to establish a new program for the future that will be based in Benton Harbor. Send a SASE in 1996 or 1997 to check offerings.

LEDIG HOUSE
INTERNATIONAL WRITERS COLONY   NY

Ledig House International Writers Colony
43 Letter S Road
Ghent, New York 12075

Attention: Executive Director
(518) 392-7656, (518) 392-4766, or (518) 392-2848 Fax

Type of Facility/Award
Residency.

Who Can Apply
Writers.

Provisos
Professional writers from around the world are invited to apply, although proficiency in English is required. The colony welcomes fiction, poetry, translation, playwrights, screenwriters, and nonfiction writers. Nominations (for future residents) are welcome, too.

Dates of Operation
April 1 to June 26. August 14 to October 31. (1995 dates.)

Location

The Colony is about two and a half hours from New York City.

History

The Ledig House was named in honor of the great German publisher, H. M. Ledig-Rowohlt. The Writers Colony was founded in 1992. "Ledig House is sponsored by a group of international publishers, literary agents, charitable foundations, and friends. Our associations include the greater literary community, theatre, and film. Professionals from these fields are invited to meet with resident writers during each session. It is our hope to create opportunities for exchange between writers that geographical distance or political boundaries might otherwise deter."

What They Offer

Residency terms are from two weeks to two months. The Colony provides each writer with a combined bedroom/work space and all meals. Breakfast and lunch supplies are provided for self-service, and dinner is prepared. Transportation to the Colony is not provided; however, limited funds (based on need and/or economic disparity) for accepted international applicants may be available. At the end of your residency, Ledig House asks you to write a brief note about the value of the residency to your work.

Facility Description

The Ledig House is located atop a 130-acre compound overlooking the Catskill Mountains. The house, built in 1830, is a renovated farmhouse. Bedrooms are on the upstairs level, and common rooms, for dining and conversation, are located on the main level.

How to Apply

Send a SASE for application guidelines. Submit a letter of recommendation from one or more of the following: published writers, critics, editors, publishers, translators, or members of the Board of Directors or Board of Advisors of Ledig House. Also send a biographical sketch including a history of your published or performed works, one nonreturnable copy of your latest published work, and a one-page description of your proposed residency project.

Deadline

Rolling application process. Notification ninety days prior to session.

Approximate Cost of a Four-week Residency

Transportation and incidentals.

Light Work
316 Waverly Avenue
Syracuse, New York 13244

Attention: Jeffrey Hoone, Director, or Gary Hesse, Assistant Director
(315) 443-1300

Type of Facility/Award
Residency.

Who Can Apply
All artists working in photography.

Provisos
None listed.

Dates of Operation
Open year-round.

Location
Syracuse, New York.

History
None provided.

What They Offer
Twelve to fifteen artists each year are invited to spend a month in Syracuse, sharing
an apartment with other invited guests of Light Work. They receive a $1,200 sti-
pend, use of a private darkroom, and have twenty-four hour access to the photo
and computer lab facilities. "Participants are expected to use their month to pursue
their own project, i.e., photographing, printing, book or portfolio preparation, etc.
They are not obligated to teach though we hope that the artists are friendly and
accessible to local artists." In return, Light Work asks each artist to leave them with
a few examples of the work made during their residency, some of which will be
featured in their quarterly journal *Contact Sheet*.

Facility Description
Light Work's lab can accommodate almost any black and white process from film
processing to mural printing. They have a Hope RA-4 20" color processor in their
color lab, and a Macintosh Quadra 950 and a Quadra 660AV equipped with flat-
bed and film scanners, Photoshop, Painter, and Quark Xpress software in their
digital computer lab.

How to Apply
There are no application forms or deadlines. Send a letter of intent, describing

generally the project or type of work you wish to accomplish while in residence, along with twenty slides of your work, your résumé, and a short statement about your work. Include an adequate SASE if you want your materials returned.

Deadline
Rolling application process. Light Work will try to respond to all applications within two or three months.

Approximate Cost of a Four-week Residency
Transportation, meals, some materials, and incidentals offset by stipend.

LILA WALLACE-READER'S DIGEST FUND AWARDS   NY

The Lila Wallace-Reader's Digest Fund
Two Park Avenue, 23rd Floor
New York, New York 10016

Attention: Program Director
(212) 251-9800 or (212) 679-6990 Fax

Notice: I have included information on this program because the Fund supplies various types of grants, fellowships, and funding for all aspects of the arts. It is a valuable resource for all artists. If you are interested in their programs, please write and ask for information. Specify your field of interest and they will send the appropriate booklet, detailing all the offerings available in that category.

Type of Facility/Award
Fellowships/Grants/Funding.

Who Can Apply
Artists and organizations involved in theater, dance, multidisciplinary arts, visual arts, literary arts, folk arts, arts education, adult literacy, urban parks, and other forms of art.

Provisos
Will be specified in program literature.

Dates of Operation
Ongoing.

Location
Various.

History
"The mission of the Lila Wallace-Reader's Digest Fund is to invest in programs that enhance the cultural life of communities and encourage people to make the arts and culture an active part of their everyday lives."

What They Offer

Various types of awards, grants, and fellowships. Send for their brochure.

Facility Description

Various.

How to Apply

Send a SASE with a letter requesting the brochure for your particular artistic discipline. (Writers ask for Writer's Awards, etc.)

Deadline

Deadline information will be detailed in specific brochures.

Approximate Cost of a Four-week Residency

Not applicable in this listing.

The Loft
THE LOFT-McKNIGHT AWARDS   MN

The Loft
Pratt Community Center
66 Malcolm Avenue Southeast
Minneapolis, Minnesota 55414

Attention: Loft-McKnight Awards
(612) 379-8999

Type of Facility/Award

Cash award.

Who Can Apply

Writers of creative prose and poetry.

Provisos

Applicants must have been legal residents of Minnesota for twelve months prior to application. Past winners of the Loft-McKnight Awards may not reapply in the same genre. Past winners of the Loft-McKnight Award of Distinction may not reapply. Applicants may only apply for one award — the Loft-McKnight Award or the Loft-McKnight Award of Distinction. Those applying for the Award of Distinction must have published at least one book or three stories in at least two different magazines.

Dates of Operation

Not applicable in this listing.

Location

Not applicable in this listing.

History

"The Loft-McKnight Awards and the Loft-McKnight Awards of Distinction were created to provide Minnesota writers of demonstrated ability with an opportunity to work for a concentrated period of time on their writing."

What They Offer

Eight Loft-McKnight Awards are presented annually. They provide winners with an award of $7,500 paid in monthly installments over a one-year period. Two Loft-McKnight Awards of Distinction are presented annually. Winners are provided with an award of $10,500 paid in monthly installments over a one-year period.

Facility Description

Not applicable in this listing.

How to Apply

Send a SASE for application guidelines. Follow the detailed instructions provided.

Deadline

Mid-November. (Date may vary from year to year.)

Approximate Cost of a Four-week Residency

Not applicable in this listing.

THE LORD LEEBRICK THEATRE COMPANY   OR

The Lord Leebrick Theatre Company
540 Charnelton Street
Eugene, Oregon 97401

Attention: Northwest Playwrights Series
(503) 465-1506

Type of Facility/Award

Opportunity for Playwrights.

Who Can Apply

Playwrights.

Provisos

Only authors currently or previously residing in Oregon, Washington, Idaho, Montana, Alaska, and northern California are eligible to submit plays. Plays having previous professional production will not be considered.

Dates of Operation

Three-week festival begins in mid-August.

Location

Eugene, Oregon.

History

None provided.

What They Offer

Selected polished scripts will receive full workshop production to be presented in alternating repertory over the three-week period of the festival (held in mid-August). Other selected scripts may receive staged readings performed once a week during the festival. All selected playwrights will be invited to attend the production process.

Facility Description

Theater.

How to Apply

Send a SASE for application guidelines. Submit a full-length or one-act play with a SASE adequate for its return. Plays having previous professional production will not be considered.

Deadline

May 1. (1995 date.)

Approximate Cost of a Four-week Residency

Transportation, housing, meals, and incidentals.

Lynchburg College in Virginia
RICHARD H. THORNTON ENDOWMENT   VA

Lynchburg College in Virginia
Richard H. Thornton Endowment
English Department
1501 Lakeside Drive
Lynchburg, Virginia 24501-3199

Attention: Thomas C. Allen, Chair
(804) 522-8267

Type of Facility/Award

Fellowship.

Who Can Apply

Writers.

Provisos

Fiction writers, playwrights, or poets who have published at least one book are eligible. Applicants are expected to have qualifications for success in teaching.

Dates of Operation

Academic semesters (Fall or Spring).

Location

Lynchburg, Virginia.

History

None provided.

What They Offer

Residents are provided with housing and meals at the college and an $8,000 stipend. Term of the residency is eight weeks. The resident must also teach a weekly seminar to advanced-level undergraduate writers, give one public reading on campus, and visit classes as a guest speaker.

Facility Description

Lynchburg College campus.

How to Apply

Send a SASE for application guidelines. Submit a résumé and a cover letter outlining your qualifications.

Deadline

March 1 for Fall term. September 1 for Spring term.

Approximate Cost of a Four-week Residency

Transportation, materials, and incidentals — offset by stipend.

THE MacDOWELL COLONY NH

The MacDowell Colony
100 High Street
Peterborough, New Hampshire 03458

Attention: Admissions Coordinator
(603) 924-3886, (212) 966-4860, or (603) 924-9142 Fax

Type of Facility/Award

Residency.

Who Can Apply

Writers, composers, visual artists, photographers, printmakers, architects, filmmakers, video artists, dramatists, and interdisciplinary artists.

Provisos

Applicants should be established in their field, although emerging artists with promising talent are encouraged to apply. The facility is wheelchair accessible. "The Colony encourages artists from all backgrounds to apply. It does not discriminate against anyone on the basis of age, race, handicap, sex, religion, marital status, or national origin in its admission policies or in access to its programs and activities. No one with the AIDS virus, ARC, or HIV shall be denied admission as long he or she is otherwise qualified." Collaborators must apply separately, but may submit a joint project description. Couples must apply and will be considered separately.

Dates of Operation
Open year-round.

Location
Peterborough, New Hampshire.

History
Composer Edward MacDowell bought the Peterborough's farm in 1896 and found he tripled his creative activity after moving there. Mrs. MacDowell later founded the Colony, attracting early applicants such as Edwin Arlington Robinson and later residents James Baldwin, Stephen Vincent Benet, Leonard Bernstein, Willa Cather, Aaron Copland, Frances Fitzgerald, Max Frankel, Arthur Kopit, Sara Teasdale, Studs Terkel, Virgil Thompson, and Thornton Wilder. Many colonists have been Guggenheim, Prix de Rome, or Pulitzer Prize winners, as well as Fulbright and MacArthur Fellows.

What They Offer
MacDowell offers stays of no more than eight weeks. Residents receive room, board, and individual studio space. A few studios also serve as the artists' living quarters. Breakfast and dinner are served in the Colony Hall; lunches are brought to the studios. The Colony hosts thirty-one artists in the summer and twenty-two in the other seasons. The average stay is six weeks. Previous residents must wait a year before reapplying. There are no accommodations for families or spouses. No pets are allowed. There are no medical facilities at the Colony and service in Peterborough is limited. Some financial travel assistance is available.

Facility Description
"The Colony has 450 acres of woodlands and fields, and forty-two supporting buildings." Studios are simply furnished and private. "Almost no studio is within sight of another." All main buildings have barrier-free access as do some studios.

How to Apply
Send a SASE for an application and brochure. Return completed application with the $20 nonrefundable processing fee, a description of your proposed project, a list of any special studio requirements, a list of your five most important professional achievements (vita, performances, recordings, exhibitions, filmography, videography, or published works), the names and addresses of two references, a list of any professional training, and a recent (within the last four years) sample of your work. If you want your sample returned, you must enclosed an adequate SASE. Appropriate samples vary by discipline. *Architecture/landscape architecture:* If you plan to do written work, submit five sets of a published article or a ten-page sample of your writing (as closely related to the type of work you proposed as possible). If you plan

to do design work, submit five sets of images (slides, photographs, photocopies) or drawings of your finished projects with a descriptive sheet. *Music composition:* Send two clearly reproduced scores with a separate cassette tape of each work. Label cassettes according to instructions. One piece should be in large form (a string quartet, a sonata, or an orchestral piece). *Film/video arts:* Send two films (16 mm or Super 8) or videos (³/₄" or ¹/₂" VHS video tapes), slides, or other documentation of your work. Film or video scriptwriters, send three copies of a script. *Interdisciplinary arts:* Send two videos (¹/₂" VHS video tape), slides, or other documentation of your work. *Visual arts:* Send five color slides packaged and labeled according to instructions. *Literature and drama:* Work samples should be in the same genre in which you intend to work at the Colony. If you submit a work-in-progress, you must also submit a finished work. If you are submitting a book, send one book and five sets of photocopies of up to twelve pages of a chapter. *Playwrights:* Send three copies of a complete script. *Poets:* Send six sets of a book or six to ten poems. *Fiction:* Send six sets of a book or an excerpt from a novel (if still in manuscript form). *Nonfiction:* Send six sets of a book or two or three essays. Call the Admissions Coordinator to discuss an appropriate work sample if your project does not fall clearly into one of the above categories.

Deadline

January 15 (received) for stays in May, June, July, and August. April 15 (received) for stays in September, October, November, and December. September 15 (received) for stays in January, February, March, and April. Notification within eight weeks after deadline.

Approximate Cost of a Four-week Residency

$20, plus daily contribution (based on ability to pay), transportation, materials, incidentals.

Note: The information in this listing was taken from brochures and application guidelines for the 1993/94 season. Please call the colony to inquire about any program changes. My requests for updated information went unanswered.

MAINE RETREAT   ME

Maine Retreat
c/o Nightshade Press
P.O. Box 76
Ward Hill
Troy, Maine 04987-0076

Attention: Roy Zarucchi and Carolyn Page, Owners
(800) 497-9258, (207) 948-3427, or (207) 948-5088 Fax

Type of Facility/Award

Retreat.

Who Can Apply

Writers, artists, and musicians.

Provisos

Only nonsmoking writers, artists, musicians are invited to apply. Retreat can only accommodate one artist at a time. Also, if you have allergies, this is not the place for you. (Owners have three cats, five geese, and two dozen chickens.)

Dates of Operation

April through October.

Location

The cabin is located on a fourteen-acre organic farm (woods and meadows) in the hills, twenty-five miles from the ocean and from Bangor, Maine. Guests have unrestricted access to over a thousand acres of wilderness.

History

The farm is owned by Roy Zarucchi and Carolyn Page, editors of Nightshade Press and the *Potato Eyes Literary Journal*.

What They Offer

Roy and Carolyn offer housing in an insulated, screened cabin in the woods. They provide all meals and incidental administrative support necessary for a writer, artist, or musician to work in peace. Cost is $150 for one week, $280 for two weeks, $390 for three weeks, and $500 for four weeks. (Minimum of one-half of total payment must be received prior to arrival.) Owners are willing to discuss a fee reduction in exchange for farm work. Owners will pick you up at the airport in Bangor if necessary. Bring your own car if you want to tour the area. This is a very quiet place.

Facility Description

The owners built a cabin in the maple grove of their property. It has electricity, but no indoor plumbing. There is an outhouse. The cabin can be used as a place for writing or thinking, or as an office or studio. You can also use the cabin as a living space and sleep there, but some people choose to sleep in the farmhouse. There is an upstairs bedroom available there with a private bath.

How to Apply

Send a SASE for information. Then send a sample of your writing, art work, or music for their review.

Deadline

Rolling application process.

Approximate Cost of a Four-week Residency

$500, plus transportation, materials, and incidentals.

MAITLAND ART CENTER   FL

The Maitland Art Center
231 Packwood Avenue
Maitland, Florida 32751-5596

Attention: Julie M. Mimms, Assistant to the Director
(305) 645-2181

Notice: Maitland's residency program was discontinued in 1984 for lack of funding. The program may be reinstated at a later date (perhaps in 2000 to 2002). If you inquire, please be sure to include a SASE.

George Mason University
INSTITUTE FOR HUMANE STUDIES   VA

Institute for Humane Studies
George Mason University
4084 University Drive, Suite 101
Fairfax, Virginia 22030-6812

Attention: Program Coordinator
(703) 934-6920, (703) 352-7535 Fax, or E-mail: IHS@mason1.gmu.edu

Type of Facility/Award
Fellowship.

Who Can Apply
Graduate students and undergraduate students.

Provisos
Graduate students and undergraduate students with junior or senior level standing in the next academic year are invited to apply. "The Humane Studies Fellowships are intended to support the studies of excellent students who are seeking degrees at any accredited school in the social sciences, the humanities, or in related fields of professional study; who intend to pursue an intellectual career; and who have demonstrated an interest in the ideal of a society of free and responsible individuals."

Dates of Operation
Academic semesters.

Location
Fairfax, Virginia.

History
"IHS is an independent center promoting the advanced study of liberty across a broad range of academic and professional disciplines. IHS is firmly grounded in the principles of the classical liberal tradition, which include the recognition of inalien-

able individual rights and the dignity and worth of each individual; protection of those rights through the institutions of private property, contract, and the rule of law, and through freely evolved intermediary institutions; and the ideal of voluntarism in all human relations, including the unhampered market mechanism in economic affairs and the goals of free trade, free migration, and peace." In 1993/94, they awarded over $500,000 in scholarships to seventy-three students from universities around the world.

What They Offer
Cash award of up to $18,500. (1995.)

Facility Description
University campus. No living accommodations provided.

How to Apply
Send a SASE for an application and brochure (not available at the time I requested information.) Follow instructions in guidelines.

Deadline
December 31.

Approximate Cost of a Four-week Residency
Transportation, housing, meals, materials, and incidentals — offset by fellowship.

George Mason University
INSTITUTE FOR HUMANE STUDIES   VA

Institute for Humane Studies
George Mason University
4084 University Drive, Suite 101
Fairfax, Virginia 22030-6812

Contact: Nonresidential Fellowships for Professionals
(703) 934-6920, (703) 352-7535 Fax, or E-mail: IHS@mason1.gmu.edu

Type of Facility/Award
Nonresidential fellowship.

Who Can Apply
College juniors, seniors, graduate students, or recent graduates.

Provisos
Applicants must be a college juniors or seniors, graduate students, or a recent graduates. They must have a clearly demonstrated interested in the "classical liberal" tradition of individual rights and market economies. They must intend to pursue a career in journalism, film, writing (fiction or nonfiction), publishing, or market-oriented public policy, and they must have arranged or applied for an internship,

training program, or other short-term opportunity related to their intended career. Nonresidential fellowships cannot be awarded for tuition or living expenses associated with pursuing a degree.

Dates of Operation

Operates year-round.

Location

This is a nonresidential fellowship.

History

"IHS Nonresidential Fellowships are awarded to appropriate candidates to help them take advantage of strategic short-term opportunities that can enhance their abilities and credentials to pursue careers that involve the communication of ideas."

What They Offer

Each fellowship consists of a stipend of up to $2,500 for a twelve-week period, housing, and travel assistance of up to $2,500, if required.

Facility Description

This is a nonresidential fellowship.

How to Apply

Submit a proposal of 500 to 1,000 words explaining what specific opportunity or opportunities you have arranged or applied for, how that opportunity would enhance your career prospects, and what financial assistance you would be need in order to accept the opportunity. Include a cover letter explaining your interest in classical liberal principles and how that interest fits in with your career plans. Submit a current résumé that includes your educational background (including major field and any academic honors received), your current educational status, your work experience (including summer positions and internships), and citations of any publications. Submit a writing sample or other samples of your work appropriate to your intended career. Also, provide the names, addresses, and telephone numbers of two academic or professional references.

Deadline

March 15 for summer positions. At least ten weeks in advance for other positions.

Approximate Cost of a Four-week Residency

Meals, materials, and incidentals — offset by fellowship.

MATTRESS FACTORY   PA

Mattress Factory
500 Sampsonia Way
Pittsburgh, Pennsylvania 15212-4444

Attention: Mattress Factory — Submissions
(412) 231-3169 or (412) 322-2231 Fax

Type of Facility/Award
Residency.

Who Can Apply
Visual artists.

Provisos
None listed.

Dates of Operation
Open year-round.

Location
Pittsburgh, Pennsylvania.

History
"The Mattress Factory is an alternative museum that commissions, presents, and collects site-specific installations in an environment whose resources are totally dedicated to that process."

What They Offer
Information provided by the Mattress Factory was light on detail, but if you are invited to work in residence, the Mattress Factory provides free housing, free studio space, free materials, transportation, and some meals.

Facility Description
The Mattress Factory provides work spaces and extensive resources "for artists and art forms that do not adapt easily to studio situations, but share a common need for a research and development environment."

How to Apply
Send a SASE for their information letter. If interested, send either 35 mm slides or VHS video tapes (include an adequate SASE if you want these materials returned) that best represent your work. Résumés are optional.

Deadline
Rolling application process.

Approximate Cost of a Four-week Residency
No cost except some meals and incidentals.

MEDICINE WHEEL ARTISTS RETREAT   MA

Medicine Wheel Artists Retreat
54 Nod Road
P.O. Box 1088
Groton, Massachusetts 01450

Attention: Director
(508) 448-3717

Type of Facility/Award
Retreat.

Who Can Apply
Artists of all disciplines.

Provisos
All applicants must be at least eighteen years old. Acceptance is based on talent, vision, and a readiness for the retreat experience.

Dates of Operation
Varies, but mostly in summer.

Location
Camp Massapoag is an hour from Boston. The Groton School is in Groton.

History
"Since its founding in 1989, Medicine Wheel has operated four artist retreats in Massachusetts, produced five animation festivals, and supported artists through workshops, seminars, and a quarterly resource newsletter. Medicine Wheel Artists believe that a focused and supportive setting is essential for artists to develop and complete new works of art. To that end, the Medicine Wheel Artists Retreat provides support and a retreat opportunity and recommends that working artists of all disciplines participate in such a residence experience at least once a year."

What They Offer
At the time of this writing, the Retreat has been leasing space from various local organizations. *Camp Massapoag*, owned by the YMCA, is only an hour away from Boston. Eight artists per week can retreat to the Camp from late August until late September. The Camp is ideal for painters, writers and others with their own equipment. Cost is $175 for a single per week, or $125 for a double per week. From mid-June until mid-July, the retreat is housed at *The Groton School*, an independent boarding school. The School has comfortable private rooms and can house sixteen artists at a time. The Groton School is good for acting companies, musical ensembles, dance troupes, and other groups. Cost is $295 for a single per week, or $225 for a double per week. At either retreat, artists are provided with three meals a day (one selection per meal is vegetarian). Artists may stay at either site for a

minimum of one week and a maximum of six weeks. A monthly payment plan is available, as are some full and partial scholarships.

Facility Description

Camp Massapoag is situated on a hundred-acre parcel of woodlands on a beautiful freshwater lake. Artists are housed in rustic cabins. Overlooking the Massapoag Pond and an abundance of wildlife is a beautiful lodge with a stone fireplace.

The Groton School sits on a lovely Georgian campus in a rural setting. It has large painting studios, a printing press, a kiln, darkrooms, piano and dance studios, an animation light table and stand, a 16 mm Bolex camera, and a library. If you're so inclined, you can go canoeing nearby on the Nashua River.

How to Apply

Send a SASE for an application and brochure. Return application with a description of your proposed project (include necessary equipment and facilities), a résumé (vita, biography, or short description of yourself), four to ten samples of your work (with an adequate SASE for their return), and a list of these samples. Be creative with your samples. Provide what you feels best represents you and your work.

Deadline

April 24. Applications accepted on a rolling basis until all positions are filled.

Approximate Cost of a Four-week Residency

$500 to $700, plus transportation, materials, and incidentals — Camp Massapoag. $900 to $1,180, plus transportation, materials, and incidentals — Groton School.

MILL MOUNTAIN THEATRE   VA

Mill Mountain Theatre
New Play Competition
Center in the Square
One Market Square, S.E.
Roanoke, Virginia 24011-1437

Attention: Jo Weinstein, Literary Manager
(703) 342-5730

Type of Facility/Award

Opportunity for Playwrights.

Who Can Apply

Playwrights.

Provisos

Open to all playwrights living in the United States. Only unpublished, unproduced scripts in English are eligible. No television or film scripts. Cast is limited to ten characters. No translations or adaptations.

Dates of Operation
Annual competition.

Location
Roanoke, Virginia

History
"Established in 1986, the Mill Mountain Theatre New Play Competition presents the best of new and innovative theatre by emerging American playwrights. The appropriate staging of our winning plays is the generating force behind The Norfolk Southern Festival of New Works. These presentations are consistently of high quality, and formulated to serve the needs of the author and the play."

What They Offer
Winner of the competition will receive a $1,000 cash award plus a staged reading, with the possibility of full production. Scripts may be for full-length or one-act plays of any subject matter and character variation. Each author is limited to one submission. No withdrawals, rewrites, or revisions will be accepted after submission except for those plays chosen as finalists that have undergone substantial structural revision. Finalists will be required to sign a statement of authenticity declaring: the play is an original work; it can be publicized as a world premiere; and it is not under consideration for publication or production. By submitting to this contest, the playwright agrees to the submission guidelines and to the production of their script. Plays having received developmental workshops may be submitted. After the staged reading, the author maintains all rights to the winning play. Winners are announced in the *Dramatists Guild Quarterly* and *American Theatre Magazine*. Mill Mountain reserves the right to withhold the prize and not declare a winner if no play of merit is found.

Facility Description
None provided.

How to Apply
Send a SASE for their flyer. Then submit your firmly bound, letter-quality manuscript with author's name, address, and phone number on the title page. Include an adequate SASE if you want your script returned. Also include a biography and history of the play, a cast of characters with brief descriptions, and a brief synopsis of the scenes. Include a SASP if you want notification that your materials arrived.

Deadline
January 1 (postmarked). Submissions are only accepted between October 1 and January 1. Notification on or around August 1.

Approximate Cost of a Four-week Residency
Not applicable in this category.

THE MILLAY COLONY FOR THE ARTS   NY

The Millay Colony for the Arts
Steepletop
East Hill Road
P.O. Box 3
Austerlitz, New York 12017-0003

Attention: Ann-Ellen Lesser, Executive Director or Gail Giles, Assistant Director
(518) 392-3103

Type of Award
Residency.

Who Can Apply
Writers, composers, and visual artists.

Provisos
None listed.

Dates of Operation
Open year-round.

Location
Austerlitz, New York, is approximately two and a half hours by car from New York
City — two hours from Boston.

History
"In 1925, Edna St. Vincent Millay and her husband bought a berry farm on a hill
in Austerlitz, New York, and named it Steepletop for the flower of the Steeplebush
which grows wild here." The house is a National Historic Landmark providing
quiet and beauty — the perfect place for artists to work. When the poet died in
1950, the estate was inherited by her sister, Norma Millay, who incorporated The
Millay Colony for the Arts as a nonprofit organization in 1973.

What They Offer
Residencies are for one month (usually from the first to the twenty-eighth). Colony
provides housing, studio space (if applicable), and all meals at no cost to residents.
Weeknight dinners are prepared. Breakfast and lunch food is available. Residents
prepare their own weekend meals. There is no application fee and no fee for a
Colony residency. However, the Colony does depend on gifts for its existence and
welcomes contributions. Residents must provide their own transportation to the
Colony. It is affiliated with the Pollack-Krassner Foundation which provides grants
to artists to cover the cost of a residency (i.e., shipping of materials, loss of income,
cost of maintaining your residence while at the colony). Ask for the Pollack-Krassner
brochure when you request an application if you need this type of assistance.

Facility Description

The Millay Colony for the Arts is located on a 600-acre estate in Austerlitz, New York. The Ellis studio is a year-round work and living space that can accommodate one visual artist, composer, or writer at a time. It has been described as ideal painter's studio, with 400 square feet of floor space and twelve-foot ceilings. There is a large northern skylight for natural light and the ceiling has movable clamp-on spotlights. A studio easel and a large movable wall are part of the facility. A porch off the studio overlooks a stream and woods in one direction and offers a long view of field and woods in another. There is an upright Steinway piano for composers. Steepletop Barn has four studios. Each artist working in the barn has a separate bedroom and studio. Studio dimensions are 14' x 20'. Two visual artists' studios are equipped with full-spectrum fluorescent lights as well as moveable clamp-on spotlights.

How to Apply

Send a SASE for an application and brochure. Return the completed application with a résumé, a description of your past work, a description of the work you intend to pursue at the colony, one professional letter of reference, and some examples of your work. Include an adequate SASE for return of your materials, as well as any documents you consider to be helpful to the admissions committee in making its decision. Include a SASP if you want acknowledgment of receipt of your application. Appropriate work samples follow. *Writers:* send several stories, one play, a manuscript of poems, or a published book. *Poets:* send ten to fifteen poems. *Short story writers:* send two or three stories. *Novelists and nonfiction writers:* send one or two chapters. *Screenwriters and playwrights:* send a short script or a portion of a script. *Visual artists:* send between six and ten slides labeled according to instructions and with an accompanying descriptive sheet. *Composers:* send one tape and standard-size scores. Colony will not process scores larger than 14" x 17".

Deadline

February 1 (received) for June through September residencies. May 1 (received) for October through January residencies. September 1 (received) for February through May residencies. Notification within two months of application.

Approximate Cost of a Four-week Residency

Transportation, materials, and incidentals. (Contributions welcomed.)

Montana Artists Refuge
Box 8
Basin, Montana 59631

Attention: M. J. Williams, Residency Coordinator
(406) 225-3525

Type of Facility/Award

Artist-in-Residence Program.

Who Can Apply

Musicians, graphic artists, painters, potters, writers, and dancers.

Provisos

The Refuge has no facilities for foundry work.

Dates of Operation

Open year-round.

Location

The Refuge is located in downtown Basin, Montana, where the Basin and Cataract Creeks flow into the Boulder River. It is twelve miles (as the crow flies) from Thunderbolt Mountain and the Continental Divide. Solitude can be found just ten minutes out of town in any direction.

History

The town, population 250, was established in 1862. It has two bars, a café, a tiny grocery, a production pottery, a post office, and a one-room school.

What They Offer

Visiting artists may stay of three months to one year. Rents range from $250 to $400 per month depending on facilities. From time to time, the Refuge provides financial assistance to artists in residence to defray rent. The upstairs of the Hewett Building rents for $400 per month. The downstairs apartment, with high ceilings suitable for some studio work, full kitchen, and a sleeping loft rents for $295. The pottery studio, which is a storefront used for display and sales, is 20' x 30'. It is suitable for three or four people to share (as a workspace). It has several wheels, an electric kiln, a glazing area, and work tables. There is a raku kiln out back. The pottery rents for $150 per month. Rent can be shared by the number of people using the space. Firing fees, clay, and glazing materials are separate. The Dyott Building has a studio apartment with a small kitchen area, a full bath, and a large room for sleeping and working. It is suitable for a weaver, writer, musician, or a potter working in the next door pottery. Rent is $250 per month. The Refuge is negotiating with members of the community for additional working and living spaces for artists.

Facility Description

Facilities include a large, two-story, brick building that was, in previous incarnations, the Hewett State Bank and a Masonic Hall. The lower floor houses the pottery studio and a large apartment with a high ceiling. The second floor is a spacious, two-room apartment with an adjoining 20' x 30' space suitable for performance, dance, weaving, painting, or other art projects. A dry goods store next door offers three modest living spaces, one of which is suitable for small studio projects. Behind the buildings, there is a large fenced yard with some trees and a little garden.

How to Apply

Send a SASE for a brochure and application guidelines. Then submit a résumé and a statement of intent, including desired length of residency, what you expect when you come here, what you want to accomplish during your stay, and the materials you will be using — to help decide which space is most suitable. Also send support materials according to your discipline: ten slides for visual artists and tapes or manuscripts for performance artists and writers. If seeking financial aid, indicate the amount needed and why you think you would be a worthy recipient.

Deadline

Rolling application process.

Approximate Cost of a Four-week Residency

Transportation, reduced-rent housing/studio space, meals, materials, and incidentals.

MORAVIAN POTTERY & TILE WORKS   PA

The Moravian Pottery & Tile Works
130 Swamp Road
Doylestown, Pennsylvania 18901

Attention: Apprentice Program
(215) 345-6722

Type of Facility/Award

Artist-in-Residence Program.

Who Can Apply

Ceramists.

Provisos

None listed.

Dates of Operation

Summer Session — June 5 to August 25. Fall Session — August 28 to November 28. (1995 dates.)

Location

Doylestown, Pennsylvania.

History

The Moravian Pottery & Tile Works, a National Historic Landmark, is maintained as a "living history museum" by the Bucks County Recreation and Park Department. The pottery's founder, Henry Mercer, was a major proponent of the Arts and Crafts movement in America. Handmade tiles are still produced there in a manner similar to that developed by Mercer. Since 1975, Moravian Pottery & Tile Works has offered apprentice workshops that teach, through practical experience in a production setting, Mercer's tile-making methods and relate them to the needs and interests of ceramists working today.

What They Offer

The Pottery sponsors two twelve-week workshop sessions each year — one in summer, one in fall. They offer three apprenticeships each session. Apprentices learn various forming and reproduction techniques, including tile and mosaic making, mold work, glaze application, saggar firing for controlled smoking of clay, and cement installation. Apprentices are provided with limited studio space in the Pottery, free materials, use of tools, technical advice, and biweekly pay based on the work produced under the Pottery's direction. Studios are accessible from 5 a.m. till midnight seven days a week. Apprentices work at the Pottery twenty-four hours each week for an hourly wage. "The clay provided is an impure local terra cotta, which when glazed is fired to cone 05 (1944° F). A variety of lead glazes and slips are provided for apprentice use. Smoked surfaces may be obtained through firing the clay in saggars. Plaster is provided for mold work; however, apprentices may not use molds which are the property of the pottery. Cement is available for the setting of tiles and mosaics."

Facility Description

The north wing of the Pottery, which is a reinforced concrete structure in a Spanish mission style, houses the primary studio space.

How to Apply

Send a SASE for brochure. Then submit a résumé, ten clearly labeled slides of recent work (they will retain these slides if you are selected), an artist's statement, two letters of recommendation, and a cover letter detailing the sort of interchange you desire from the experience and why the Moravian Pottery & Tile Works is appropriate to your needs.

Deadline

March 6 for Summer Session. June 5 for Fall Session. (1995 dates.)

Approximate Cost of a Four-week Residency

Transportation, housing, meals, and incidentals — offset by wage.

MY RETREAT   NY

My Retreat
Writers Colony and Bed & Breakfast
P.O. Box 1077, Lincoln Road
South Fallsburg, New York 12779

Attention: Cora T. Schwartz, Innkeeper
(800) 225-0256, (914) 436-7455, or (914) 434-2140 Fax

Type of Facility/Award
Retreat.

Who Can Apply
Poets, writers, and artists of life.

Provisos
Guests must be nonsmoking adults.

Dates of Operation
Main House — year-round. Cottages — May 1 through October 14.

Location
The Retreat is located ninety miles northwest of New York City in the foothills of the
Catskill Mountains. It is an eight-minute walk from the town of South Fallsburg (a
summer Mecca for the Hasidic community and well-known ashram) on a quiet, dead-
end road. The area is serviced by the ShortLine Bus Company at Port Authority in
New York City. The closest airport is Stewart International in Newburgh.

History
The colony opened June 1, 1993. Owner Cora Schwartz always dreamed of a private
place to write. She purchased two cottages across the road from her house and renovated and furnished them to accomplish this dream. "My Retreat was founded in the
spirit of Olga Kobylianskaia, a forerunner of the women's liberation movement and
a member of the Writers' Union of the U.S.S.R. Olga's dominant theme was
'aristocratism of the spirit' and the necessity for woman's liberation from the bondage
of primitive traditional laws. In her book, *Tsariva*, Olga portrays a woman of universal ideas who strives for greater enlightenment and desires to become a useful, independent member of society. In 1942, the Hitlerites decided to try Olga by court-
martial. Only death from illness saved her from violence. May Olga's talent for the
lyrical, her gift of observation, sensitivity and artistic taste live on at My Retreat."

What They Offer
Rooms are $85 per person per weekend (two nights) and $185 per person per week
(seven nights). Each room has a desk and a lovely view of the woods. A private suite
is available for $50 added to the above rates. Monthly rates are negotiable. Long-

term residencies are also available. Light breakfast foods are provided. Guests are responsible for the remainder of their meals, but kitchen facilities are available for cooking. In the summer, My Retreat offers workshops in fiction, poetry, publishing, photography, and other subjects of interest to writers and artists. During the rest of the year, workshops or lectures are offered monthly. No pets allowed.

Facility Description

The colony consists of a main house and two cottages. The two cottages have six furnished bedrooms, three kitchens, and four bathrooms. There are six screened and open porches. One of the cottages has a cool, basement library. There is a separate suite with a private entrance, bedroom, kitchen, and bath.

How to Apply

Send a SASE for brochure.

Deadline

My Retreat is booked on first-come, first-served reservation basis. A fifty-percent deposit is required seven days before arrival. The deposit will be refunded, less a $10 fee, if cancellation is received five days prior to arrival date.

Approximate Cost of a Four-week Residency

$740 (negotiable), plus transportation, lunches & dinners, materials, and incidentals.

NANTUCKET ISLAND SCHOOL OF DESIGN & THE ARTS   MA

Nantucket Island School of Design and The Arts
23 Wauwinet Road
P.O. Box 958
Nantucket, Massachusetts 02554

Attention: Fresh A.I.R. Program
(508) 228-9248 or (508) 228-2451

Type of Facility/Award

Residency.

Who Can Apply

Photographers, painters, sculptors, ceramists, textile artists, multimedia artists, writers, musicians, performance artists, and others.

Provisos

None listed.

Dates of Operation

Open year-round.

Location

Nantucket Island is thirty miles out to sea off the coast of Cape Cod. The Harbor Cottages are just five minutes from the center of town across from the Nantucket Harbor. The Sea View Farm Barn Studios are eight miles away in Wauwinet. The island is accessible by boat or by plane.

History

"The Nantucket Island School of Design and The Arts (NISDA), a year-round cultural and Arts Education Resource Center (AERC), is dedicated to exploring the interdependence of the arts, sciences, humanities, and environment, and to enhancing education through community and the quality of life through the arts." NISDA also hosts a lecture series and a summer program.

What They Offer

There are eight cottages of three different sizes at NISDA's Bar Harbor Cottages Artist Colony. They have small studio cottages; medium cottages with small, separate bedroom and living areas; and large cottages with larger living areas and storage lofts. All of the freshly renovated and winterized cottages have private kitchens and bathrooms. All sleep at least two people. NISDA doesn't mind if you bring a spouse, a friend, a partner, or a collaborator to share the cost of the cottage. NISDA will also attempt to pair applicants who may be interested in sharing. Artists with families are welcome. You may work in your room, outside, or at the Sea View Farm Barn Studios, which are eight miles from the cottages. Studios are accessible twenty-four hours a day.

From October to June, per person rates (which include your cottage and optional use of a Sea View Farm Barn studio) are: Small cottages (shared) are $140 per week or $560 per month. Medium cottages (shared) are $175 per week or $700 per month. Large cottages (shared) are $210 per week or $840 per month. If you want the cottage to yourself, rates are: Small, $245 per week or $980 per month; medium, $280 per week or $1,120 per month; and large, $315 per week or $1,220 per month. A ten-percent discount is available after the first month. Rates for July, August, and September are substantially higher. This fee does not include cottage utilities. A utility deposit of $125 per month is required, along with the total residency fee, upon acceptance. Each cottage (and school studio) has its own meter; billing will be adjusted according to your use. Residents must provide their own meals, materials, and incidentals. If for some reason you must cancel your residency, you will receive a refund, less a $25 handling fee, only if NISDA was able to fill your space. Otherwise, they will issue you a credit to be used within one year. NISDA has a work exchange program for fee-reduced residencies. You can save up to twenty percent of the cost of your cottage (not utilities) by teaching, caretaking, working in the office, or otherwise helping with school maintenance.

Facility Description

Nantucket Island is seven miles wide and fourteen miles long, sporting eighty miles of sandy beaches, heath-covered moors, and small pine forests. Some of the town's homes date back to the 1600's when Nantucket was the center of America's whaling industry. The Sea View Farm Barn Studios have a large open 2D or 3D studio, partitioned off into several work spaces, a ceramics studio (with a skutt electric kiln, an electric wheel, equipment for pit firing, and a large outdoor deck), and dark-rooms. The facility also has a large community room, a library, and a kitchen for shared use.

How to Apply

Send a SASE for an application and brochure. Return completed application with a $20 nonrefundable processing fee, a résumé, a statement of intent, three professional references, a SASE for notification, and a sample of your work. Appropriate work samples are ten to twenty slides, black and white prints, sketches, demo tapes, videos, and/or writing samples such as poems, short stories, or excerpts from a novel. Enclose an adequate SASE if you want your samples returned. If you are applying for financial aid, list any writing, computer, administrative, or office skills you may have.

Deadline

Rolling application process. Cottages are assigned on a first-come, first-served basis.

Approximate Cost of a Four-week Residency

$20, plus cost of accommodations, utilities, transportation, meals, materials, and incidentals.

The National Endowment for the Arts   U.S.
INTERNATIONAL PROGRAM   CANADA & MEXICO

The National Endowment for the Arts
International Program
United States/Canada/Mexico Creative Artists Residencies
Nancy Hanks Center, Room 618
1100 Pennsylvania Avenue, N.W.
Washington, D.C. 10506-0001

Attention: Information Management Division/IFR, 8th Floor
(202) 682-5422 or (202) 682-5496 Voice/T.T.

Type of Facility/Award

Residency.

Who Can Apply

Architects, choreographers, composers, creative writers, designers, media artists, playwrights, solo theater artists (including puppeteers, storytellers, and performance artists) who work with original material, visual artists, multidisciplinary artists, or artistic directors of theater and dance companies.

Provisos

Applicants must be citizens or permanent residents of the United States. Administrators, critics, curators, presenters, scholars, and students are not eligible. Candidates are ineligible if they have spent more than three months (in the last ten years) working professionally in the country they wish to visit. In the case of creative writers, applicants must have published (in the last ten years) at least one of the following: twenty poems or pages of poetry in five or more literary journals, five short stories or essays (of creative nonfiction) in two or more literary journals or publications, a book of poems of more than forty-eight pages, a novel, a novella, or a book of creative nonfiction. Candidates must be available for the full two-month session. Proficiency in either Spanish or French is not required, but may be helpful. The host government will provide interpreters, if necessary, for any public demonstrations, workshops, or performances.

Citizens of Canada and Mexico: Please see information in *What They Offer*.

Dates of Operation

Spring Session: May 6 through June 28, 1996. Summer Session: July 1 through August 23, 1996. Fall Session: September 9 through November 1, 1996. Winter Session: January 6 through February 28, 1997. (Dates vary from year to year.)

Location

U.S. applicants must choose either Canada or Mexico. Location in that country to be determined by host country. Canadian and Mexican applicants apply to come to the United States. Location here to be determined by N.E.A.

History

"The National Endowment for the Arts, an independent agency of the Federal Government, was created in 1965 to encourage and assist the nation's cultural resources. The Endowment is advised by the National Council on the Arts, a presidentially appointed body composed of the Chairman of the Endowment and twenty-six distinguished private citizens who are widely recognized for their expertise or interest in the arts. The Council advises the Endowment on policies, programs, and procedures, in addition to making recommendations on grant applications."

What They Offer

Residencies in Canada or Mexico are available for periods of eight weeks. Each award carries a stipend of $2,000. The host government provides round-trip airfare and local transportation, health insurance, room, board, studio space, basic materials, and other miscellaneous costs for selected U.S. artists. The host government will arrange artists' accommodations, usually in moderate hotels or a small apartment buildings. The host government will inform each artist of the location of his or her award approximately two months before the session begins. Artists are generally left to do their own work, except for eight hours each week that should be dedicated to public activities such as workshops, demonstrations, classes, lectures, or collaborations with the host country's civic organizations. Ten residencies are awarded for Canada and ten are awarded for Mexico. In their proposals, artists must show a compelling reason why a visit to either of these countries would be important to their work. The grant is taxable to the recipient.

This is an exchange program. Canada and Mexico will each send ten artists to the United States with similar awards. If you are a Canadian citizen, call or write The International Cultural Relations Bureau of the Department of Foreign Affairs Canada, or The Canada Council. If you are a Mexican citizen, call or write the Consejo Nacional para la Cultura y las Artes, or the Fondo Nacional para Cultura y las Artes (FONCA), or the Instituto Nacional de Bellas Artes (INBA). You may be placed in one of the colonies in this book!

Facility Description
Not applicable in this listing.

How to Apply
Call or write for a booklet on this program. Return original and three copies of completed application with: a brief summary of your proposed activities in Canada or Mexico; a list of any fellowships, prizes, or honors you've received; a statement about why working in Canada or Mexico is important to your work; a description of public activities you could perform as part of your service to your host government; a list of any host organizations you may have identified as being particularly suited to your requirements; a statement about how you might communicate what you learned from this experience upon your return to the U.S.; a history of any previous travel to Canada or Mexico and your plans for language study; a statement regarding disposition of any final reports due from previous Arts Endowments Programs; a statement regarding your standing on delinquent Federal debt; three copies of a résumé; and a sample of your recent work.

Composers: send two copies each of up to two audio cassettes (created within the last three years) cued to a three to five minute section, and two copies of the scores that correspond to the material on the tapes. *Design artists:* send two copies of relevant work samples (two publications or videos, or a maximum of nine slides or photos) and an accompanying descriptive sheet of no more than three pages.

Media artists/visual artists: Send one (VHS) video tape cued to a three to five minute section of work created within the last three years or send nine 35 mm slides (packaged and labeled according to instructions) of work created within the last three years.

Playwrights: send two copies each of excerpts (no longer than ten pages and created in the last five years) of up to two plays/works in English (works in progress are okay) and an accompanying descriptive sheet explaining the context of the excerpt, and also submit three copies of a one-page statement explaining your aesthetic and philosophy of writing for the theater and information about your creative process.

Creative writers: send two copies of a manuscript in English of work created within the last five years (may contain previously published work, unpublished work, or work in progress). Sample should include one of the following: eight typescript, single-column pages of poetry with no more than one poem per page, or one long poem of up to fifteen pages; twenty to thirty pages of short fiction, short stories, or creative nonfiction in double-spaced typescript; or a novel excerpt of twenty to thirty double-spaced, typescript pages. All submissions must be packaged and labeled according to detailed instructions. Creative writers are also required to include proof of eligibility: one clearly reproduced copy of a title page or front cover of a published book or magazine, the copyright page, or other proof of authorship.

Deadline
October 31. (1994 was extended to February 20, 1995, for 1996 residencies.)

Approximate Cost of a Four-week Residency
None.

National Foundation for Advancement in the Arts
CAREER ADVANCEMENT OF VISUAL ARTISTS   FL

The National Foundation for Advancement in the Arts
800 Brickell Avenue, Suite 500
Miami, Florida 33131

Attention: NFAA/CAVA Program
(305) 377-1147

Type of Facility/Award
Residency.

Who Can Apply
Visual artists.

Provisos
This program is for emerging professional visual artists who are citizens or permanent residents of the United States, who are over eighteen and under forty years of age (or who have been practicing professionally from one to five years). Only artists who have been out of educational programs of study for one year before the application deadline are eligible. NFAA does not discriminate based on race, creed, religion, geographical location, sexual orientation, physical disability, language, or sex.

Dates of Operation
July 1 to October 31. (1995 dates.)

Location
Miami Beach, Florida.

History
"Career Advancement of Visual Artists (CAVA) is a national residency program for emerging professional visual artists. It is a program of the National Foundation for

Advancement in the Arts (NFAA), a Miami-based, independent, not-for-profit, non-governmental institution dedicated to the support of young artists."

What They Offer

Each year, CAVA selects three artists in the early stages of their professional careers to participate in the program. Residents spend four months in Miami Beach working on their art. Selected artists are provided with round-trip transportation (within the territories of the United States) to Miami, living quarters, studio space, funds for art supplies, and a stipend of $1,000 per month. Residents interact with invited professionals (critics, curators, art dealers, and senior artists) on an informal basis from time to time during their term. CAVA also organizes an annual exhibition showcasing the work of third year residents. It includes an exhibit brochure that is distributed nationally. They also sponsor an Open Studio event for other Fellows and their work. Residents are encouraged to participate in NFAA-sponsored activities and in community cultural and educational programs. Residencies may be renewed annually for up to three years. Renewals are based on how the artist has both benefited from and contributed to the CAVA program.

Facility Description

The CAVA studios are on the second floor of an air-conditioned building in the Lincoln Road area of Miami Beach. There is an elevator. Studios are approximately 300 square feet and have no equipment (tools, kilns, etc.). "Activities that could be considered a fire hazard are not allowed."

How to Apply

Send a SASE for an application and brochure. Return completed application with a $25 nonrefundable processing fee, a résumé, a brief statement about your work (optional), your alien registration card (if applicable), and a sample of your work. Appropriate samples are ten slides of work completed within the last three years (packaged and labeled according to instructions) accompanied by a descriptive sheet, or one VHS video cassette tape (packaged and labeled according to instructions) cued to a total of ten minutes' playing time containing a minimum of three segments completed within the last three years. The videotape must also be accompanied by a descriptive sheet. If you want your samples returned, enclose an SASE.

Deadline

February 1 (postmarked). Notification on or about May 1.

Approximate Cost of a Four-week Residency

$25, plus meals and incidentals — offset by stipend.

New York Mills Arts Retreat
24 North Main Avenue
P.O. Box 246
New York Mills, Minnesota 56567

Attention: Director
(218) 385-3339, (218) 385-3366 Fax, or E-mail: nymills@uslink.net

Type of Facility/Award

Artist-in-Residence Program.

Who Can Apply

Writers, poets, musicians, artists, photographers.

Provisos

None listed.

Dates of Operation

Open year-round.

Location

The town of New York Mills, Minnesota (population 900) is situated among the 1000 lakes of Otter Tail County and is located along the Continental Divide.

History

The Arts Retreat facility was once a working dairy farm, surrounded by cornfields and cows. Now it's a thriving art center.

What They Offer

The Arts Retreat provides housing for one visiting artist during each residency period at its facility three miles from town. In-town housing options are also available. Residents have unlimited use of studio space. A cash stipend ($400 for one week, $750 for two-weeks, and $1,500 for four weeks) is given upon arrival to help defray the artist's costs for transportation and meals. In return, each artist is asked to spend six hours a week involved with the local community, either by teaching classes or workshops in area schools, or by providing some other mutually beneficial, arts-related experience; they're open to suggestions.

Facility Description

The Talday barn has approximately 1,000 square feet of floor space with fourteen-foot ceilings and a large southern window. The New York Mills Regional Cultural Center has a large studio space with windows along both the south and west walls providing an optimal view of downtown.

How to Apply

Send a SASE for an application and brochure. Return completed application along with your résumé, a description of your work, a condensed description of the purpose of retreat, a Community Outreach plan, a sample of your work, and an adequate SASE if you want your work samples returned. Finalists will are required to submit two letters of recommendation and additional work samples. *Visual artists:* send a minimum of five slides. *Writers:* send minimum five pages. *Musicians:* send a minimum of one cassette or CD. *Filmmakers/videographers:* send a minimum of one cassette.

Deadline

Rolling application process.

Approximate Cost of a Four-week Residency

Transportation, meals, materials, and incidentals — offset by stipend.

NEWBERRY LIBRARY   IL

The Newberry Library
60 West Walton Street
Chicago, Illinois 60610-3380

Attention: Committee on Awards
(312) 943-9090 extension 236

Type of Facility/Award

Fellowship.

Who Can Apply

Postdoctoral scholars, certain college instructors, women of Native American Heritage, and others.

Provisos

Postdoctoral scholars, scholars holding the Ph.D. or equivalent, independent scholars who have demonstrated excellence in their (appropriate to Newberry) field through publications, etc., certain college instructors, women of Native American heritage with at least an undergraduate degree, and others who might benefit from research in the library's holdings. See *What They Offer* below.

Dates of Operation

Each fellowship has its own timeline.

Location

Chicago, Illinois.

History

The Newberry Library was founded in 1887. It is an independent research library; admission is free and it is open to the public. "In addition to developing and caring for its extensive collections, and serving the needs of individual scholars, the Newberry fosters the productive use of its resources by developing educational projects and centers where extended research is conducted by a community of scholars."

What They Offer

The Newberry Library offers research opportunities in the form of fellowships to scholars of various levels. Because each fellowship has its own award criteria, I am listing them by name only. If you are interested in any of these fellowships, please contact the library directly.

National Endowment for the Humanities Fellowships
Lloyd Lewis Fellowships in American History
Monticello College Foundation Fellowship for Women
Short-Term Resident Fellowships for Individual Research
Joint Fellowships with the American Antiquarian Society
American Society for Eighteenth-Century Studies Fellowships
South Central Modern Language Association Fellowships
Resident Fellowships for Unaffiliated Scholars
Arthur Weinberg Fellowship for Independent Scholars
John N. Stern Fellowships for Oberlin College Faculty
Newberry-British Academy Fellowship for Study in Great Britain
D'Arcy McNickle Center for the History of the American Indian Fellowships
Frances C. Allen Fellowships
Hermon Dunlap Smith Center for the History of Cartography Fellowships
President Francesco Cossiga Fellowship
Center for Renaissance Studies Fellowship
Consortium Funds
The Audrey Lumsden-Kouvel Fellowship
Herzog August Bibliothek Wolfenbüttel Fellowship

Facility Description

The library houses more than one and a half-million volumes and five million manuscripts in the humanities. The Newberry's collections concern the civilizations of western Europe and the Americas from the late Middle Ages to the early twentieth century. Bibliographic holdings are extensive and certain special collections are internationally noted.

How to Apply

Send a SASE for their *Fellowships in the Humanities* brochure. Then write for additional information on specific fellowships.

Deadline

Each fellowship has its own deadline.

Approximate Cost of a Four-week Residency

Each fellowship has its own stipend/award provisions.

Nexus Press Residency Program
Contemporary Art Center
535 Means Street, N.W.
Atlanta, Georgia 30318

Attention: JoAnne Paschall, Director
(404) 688-1970 or (404) 577-5856 Fax

Notice: This program was suspended due to the overload of projects at the press related to the 1996 Olympic Games in Atlanta. Call or write for details regarding the "Press Olympiad" or resumption of their residency program.

Type of Facility/Award
Residency.

Who Can Apply
Visual artists and writers.

Provisos
None listed.

Dates of Operation
Open year-round.

Location
Atlanta, Georgia.

History
None provided.

What They Offer
Selected artists will spend thirty days at Nexus Press with full staff assistance, an honorarium of $1,000, a production budget of $2,500, travel expenses of $300, and use of all press equipment (with guidance). "Nexus Press is a nonprofit visual arts press that produces, publishes, and distributes artists' books and publications. We are an offset facility that encourages the alternative use of the print medium."

Facility Description
Facility equipment includes a one-color Heidelberg KORD offset press (press sheet size 18" x 25"), a complete darkroom, a Macintosh IIx computer, and design, plate-making, and hand bindery equipment.

How to Apply
Send a SASE for an application and brochure. Your name will be added to a list. Mailings for residency programs go out each spring. Return completed application

with a proposal — anything from a written statement of intent to a mock-up or book dummy. Also send a résumé, some slides or previous books, if available. Include an adequate SASE if you want your proposal (and supporting materials) returned.

Deadline
May 1.

Approximate Cost of a Four-week Residency
Transportation over $300, housing, meals, and incidentals — offset by honorarium.

NIANGUA COLONY   MO
Niangua Colony
Route 1
Stoutland, Missouri 65567

Notice
There is no phone listed for the Niangua Colony. Mail was returned marked "Forwarding Order Expired." I can only assume the colony has ceased operating.

North Pacific Women Writers Soc.   Vancouver, B.C.
NORTH PACIFIC
WOMEN WRITERS RETREAT   CANADA
North Pacific Women Writers Society
3091 West 15th Avenue
Vancouver, B.C. Canada
V6K 3A5

Attention: North Pacific Women Writers Retreat
(604) 733-6295 or (604) 943-6888

Notice: The North Pacific Women Writers Society sponsored an annual retreat for women writers from 1990 until 1994. Women from all over Canada and some from the United States attended the one-week retreat, which provided room, board, and time to write, for $500 (Canadian). Previously, the retreat was held at the Rockwood Centre in Sechelt, B.C., on British Columbia's Sunshine Coast. Currently, the program is underfinanced and the Society is attempting to locate another retreat location in an effort to reduce costs. If you are interested in this program, please call or write the Society. If you write, be sure to enclose a SASE.

Northwood University
ALDEN B. DOW CREATIVITY
CENTER FELLOWSHIPS   MI

Northwood University
Alden B. Dow Creativity Center
3225 Cook Road
Midland, Michigan 48640-2398

Attention: Carol B. Coppage, Executive Director
(517) 837-4478 or (517) 837-4468

Type of Facility/Award
Fellowship.

Who Can Apply
People working in all disciplines and areas of interest including the arts, sciences, and humanities are invited to apply.

Provisos
Program structure requires the maturity to work independently and live cooperatively. Foreign citizens are invited to apply, provided they can communicate in written and spoken English. The Center is looking for new and innovative ideas that have the potential for impact in their field. No creative area will be overlooked when a project idea may result in a significant advance.

Dates of Operation
Mid-June to mid-August.

Location
The Alden B. Dow Creativity Center is located in the Saginaw Valley area of central Michigan, about 125 miles north of Detroit.

History
Alden B. Dow was born in Midland, Michigan, in 1904, the son of Grace A. and Herbert Henry Dow, founder of the Dow Chemical Company. He studied mechanical engineering and earned a degree in architecture. He studied and worked with Frank Lloyd Wright at Taliesin in Wisconsin. Dow returned to Midland and opened his own architectural offices in a studio/home of his own design. He was commissioned to design many homes, churches, schools, college campuses, business complexes, art and civic centers, and one entire town. Among his many awards and honors, Dow received the 1937 Diplome de Grand Prix for residential architecture, he was a Fellow in the American Institute of Architects, he received an honorary doctorate from Northwood Institute in 1969, and in 1982, he was the first recipient of the Frank Lloyd Wright Creativity Award. In 1983, he was named architect laureate of his home state of Michigan.

The Northwood Institute was founded in 1959 by Drs. Arthur E. Turner and R. Gary Stauffer. With Mr. Dow, they shared a devotion to quality and innovation. In 1978, they founded the Creativity Center to encourage individual creativity and to preserve the work and philosophy of Alden B. Dow.

What They Offer

Four fellowships are awarded annually. Residency term is eight weeks from mid-June to mid-August. Fellowship includes travel to and from Midland for the residency. Expenses for foreign citizens will be covered from their point of entry into the continental U.S. Fellows are encouraged to drive, in order to have a car available. If air travel is elected, some shipping expenses may be assumed by the Center. Residents are housed in large, furnished apartments. Board is provided through a per diem allowance. Weekday lunches are provided at the Creativity Center. A stipend of $750 is provided for each awardee to be used at his or her discretion. This may be applied to the cost of project materials, travel during the summer, or incidental expenses. No at-home expenses are covered. Families and pets cannot be accommodated. Upon completion of the residency, Fellows will make oral presentations of their projects to a selected audience including Creativity Center Board Members, evaluators, Northwood University staff, and invited guests.

Facility Description

Northwood University's Alden B. Dow Creativity Center provides residents with individual apartments in a wooded environment. Each apartment is furnished and has a fully-equipped kitchen. Laundry facilities are available on campus.

How to Apply

Send a SASE for brochure and application guidelines. The Center begins considering applications in the fall of each year. Submit a cover page containing your name, address, and telephone number, and a brief (twenty-five words or less) summary of your project. Also include a $10 nonrefundable application fee, a list of facilities and equipment you would request the Creativity Center to provide, a résumé, three references (with contact information), and any materials that would aid in the evaluation of your project, such as writing samples, slides, tapes, etc. Enclose a SASE adequate for return of your support materials.

Deadline

December 31 (postmarked). Notification by April 1.

Approximate Cost of a Four-week Residency

$10, plus materials and incidentals — offset by stipend.

Eugene O'Neill Theater Center
NATIONAL MUSIC THEATER CONFERENCE   CT

Eugene O'Neill Theater Center
National Music Theater Conference
305 Great Neck Road
Waterford, Connecticut 06385-3825

(203) 443-5378 or (203) 443-9653 Fax

Administration/Applications/Winter Address:
234 West 44th Street, Suite 901
New York, New York 10036-3909

Attention: Paulette Haupt, Artistic Director
(212) 382-2790 or (212) 921-5538 Fax

Type of Facility/Award
Residency.

Who Can Apply
Playwrights, librettists, lyricists, writers, and composers.

Provisos
All applicants must be permanent residents (with visas) of the United States or U.S. citizens. All forms and styles of music theater and opera are accepted, as long as singing plays a dominant role in the play. Any works that have received a fully staged professional production are not eligible. Original and adapted works are eligible. (You must submit Proof of Rights with your application if adapted work is not in the public domain.) Works under option are eligible as long as this is stated in the application. Works of any length, except musical revues, are eligible. Works previously submitted are eligible if they have been revised or if they have one or more new collaborators. If you are selected, you must be in residence for the duration of the conference. New and emerging as well as established creative talents are welcome.

Dates of Operation
August. (Dates vary from year to year.)

Location
Waterford, Connecticut.

History
"The O'Neill Theater Center is solely a developmental theater. We support creative artists by providing an empty stage in which they can explore their visions, take risks not possible with production deadlines, and discuss their work with other professionals in the field of music theater."

What They Offer

Selected applicants will receive round-trip transportation from New York to Connecticut for the conference, room, board, and a modest stipend. Term of the residency is between two and four weeks. In addition, residents benefit from use of and exposure to the O'Neill Center's personnel, facilities, and artistic processes. The Center provides on-going discussions of works-in-progress among residents, the artistic director, directors, and musical directors, and panel discussions with theater professionals. There are public and private rehearsals and readings by a group of equity actors and singers (script in hand) on an empty stage with only a piano as accompaniment. The Center does not encumber any work by creative artists but asks for acknowledgment in printed programs and publicity materials for works developed during the residency period.

Facility Description

None provided.

How to Apply

Send a SASE for an application and brochure. Return completed application with: your $20 nonrefundable application fee; a bound, covered, typewritten draft of the script; two audio cassettes with at least six diverse selections in chronological order to the script (include a sheet that tells where the selections are located in the script); one piano/vocal score or piano/vocal lead sheet for each selection on the tape; a one-page description of the work; a typewritten biography or résumé for each creative artist; a separate cast list including brief character and vocal descriptions; Proof of Rights, if the work is an adaptation not in the public domain; and a SASP or SASE for notification of receipt of application materials. Also include an adequate SASE if you want your materials returned, or you may pick up your materials at the NY office after adjudication. Submit applications between November and February 1. Additional support materials may be requested during the selection process.

Deadline

February 1 (postmarked). Notification in May.

Approximate Cost of a Four-week Residency

$20, plus some transportation and incidentals — offset by stipend.
Note: This listing was drawn from information for the 1993/94 season. Please call the facility to inquire about any program changes. My requests for updated information went unanswered.

Eugene O'Neill Theater Center
NATIONAL PLAYWRIGHTS CONFERENCE CT

(See addresses in previous listing)

Attention: Lloyd Richards, Artistic Director
(212) 382-2790 or (212) 921-5538 Fax

Type of Facility/Award

Opportunity for Playwrights.

Who Can Apply

Playwrights, screenwriters, and scriptwriters.

Provisos

Applicants must be American citizens or permanent residents of the United States. Collaborations are eligible. All full-length plays are eligible. "A long one-act is acceptable, as is a series of short, thematically interrelated one-acts (although the Conference may choose not to work on them all)." No adaptations. All submissions must be previously unproduced and not currently under option, although scripts that have been radically rewritten (spine of the play has been changed) may be considered. Emerging and established talented writers are invited to apply. See details in their brochure or contact the office in New York for clarification on production/developmental issues.

Dates of Operation

The month of July. Dates vary from year to year.

Location

Waterford, Connecticut.

History

1994 was the Conference's thirtieth year. "The National Playwrights Conference is concerned with the growth of talented writers (whether emerging or established) and exercises this commitment by offering them the opportunity to work on their plays together with other talented professional theater and media artists in a non-competitive atmosphere."

What They Offer

Each playwright accepted (they choose ten to fifteen each year) receives a $1,000 stipend, room, board, and transportation to the Conference and Pre-Conference. No provisions (room, board, travel) are made for the playwright's family. Families are not permitted to attend the Pre-Conference. The stipend is paid at the end of the conference and payment is predicated on attendance throughout. All work presented at the Conference will be under option by the Conference from the time of acceptance until six weeks after the end of the Conference.

Each writer is assigned a dramaturge or story editor who assists and advises the playwright during the development of the work. At the Pre-Conference, each playwright reads his or her work aloud to the others. Afterward, they discuss the nature of the work to be done at the Conference. After a short, intensive rehearsal period (at the Conference) stage plays are given two staged readings in front of an audience. "Actors work with script in hand and performances have limited production values: modular sets, minimal lights, essential props, and no costumes. Media playwrights are acquainted with the effects of the camera on their scripts; their material is developed, and the works are read to the assembled Conference and invited observers by a company of actors."

Facility Description

None provided.

How to Apply

Send a SASE for information and application guidelines. Submit one copy of a typed, bound, covered script (and an adequate SASE for its return) with the $10 nonrefundable application fee (for each script). Include as part of the script the number of acts or scenes, time and place, and a list of characters. For each script, you must complete and return one set of catalog cards (two sets are sent to you when you request application guidelines) — be sure to circle the category in which you are submitting. Enclose a one-page (not attached to script) biography, including information on other plays, teleplays, or films you have written, or other literary forms in which you have worked. Also include a #10 SASE for notification of their decision. If you wish acknowledgment that your script was received, include a SASP. (All self-address envelopes/postcards must have stamps affixed — not metered tapes.)

Deadline

December 1 (Scripts are accepted between September 15 and December 1). Notification (by mail) is before the end of April.

Approximate Cost of a Four-week Residency

$10, plus incidentals — offset by stipend.

164

ON THE BOARDS   WA

On the Boards
153 14th Avenue
Seattle, Washington 98122

Attention: Artists Project Grants
(206) 325-7902

Type of Facility/Award
Grant.

Who Can Apply
Visual artists.

Provisos
Individual or teams of collaborative artists (not organizations) who have been residents of Alaska, Oregon, or Washington for at least one year are welcome to apply. Applicants cannot be full-time students, or members of the staff or Board of Directors of On the Boards.

Dates of Operation
Open year-round.

Location
This is a nonresidential grant. No location is provided, but work must take place in Alaska, Oregon, or Washington.

History
"On the Boards is a center for the development and presentation of contemporary performances, launched in 1978 by a group of diverse performing, visual, and media artists seeking to create new work that expands traditional definitions of theater, dance, and music." This grant is part of a national project funded by the National Endowment for the Arts, the Rockefeller Foundation, and the Andy Warhol Foundation for the Visual Arts.

What They Offer
Six to ten grants ranging from $1,000 to $5,000 may be awarded each year "to support the creation of innovative works that challenge traditional artistic disciplines and explore new definitions of art forms or cultural traditions." Emphasis is on work that combines two or more artistic disciplines and challenges standard artistic practices. Applicants cannot receive funds two years in a row. Grant does not fund completed works, research projects, extensive travel, purchase of equipment, newsletters, catalogs, or projects that are primarily educational or part of an ongoing educational program. Grant does not fund projects that end in a purely traditional, single-discipline project, like a book, a painting, a sculpture, a video, an audio recording, or play.

Facility Description

No facility or studio description is provided.

How to Apply

Send a SASE for an application and brochure. Submit one original and nine collated copies of the completed application and budget information forms, plus one copy of each of the following: a résumé or biography of the artist(s) involved (and any past reviews, etc.) and work samples for each of the artists involved in the project. As work samples, send: up to ten slides per artist, labeled according to instructions and accompanied by a descriptive sheet; a $1/2$" video cassette cued to a three to five minute segment per artist and accompanied by a descriptive sheet; an audio cassette or CD cued to a three to five minute segment per artist and accompanied by a descriptive sheet; no more than three pages of a manuscript accompanied by a descriptive sheet (please note if the work is an excerpt and describe the excerpted work); and photographs, sketches, etc., accompanied by a descriptive sheet. Clearly label all samples. Do not send originals of artwork or slides. If you want your samples returned to you, you must enclose an adequate SASE.

Deadline

June 19 (postmarked). June 19 by 5 p.m. if hand-delivered. (1995 date.)

Approximate Cost of a Four-week Residency

Transportation, housing, meals, materials, and incidentals not covered in the grant budget.

OREGON SCHOOL OF ARTS & CRAFTS   OR

Oregon School of Arts & Crafts
8245 Southwest Barnes Road
Portland, Oregon 97225

Attention: Summer Residencies for Mid-Career Artists Program
or Junior Residency Program
(503) 297-5544

Type of Facility/Award

Artist-in-Residence Program.

Who Can Apply

Artists working in book arts, ceramics, drawing, metalsmithing/jewelry, photography (in combination with other media), and furniture-making are invited to apply. There are two programs: one for mid-career artists and one for emerging artists.

Provisos

Summer Residencies for Mid-career Artists: Applicants must be U.S. nationals or permanent residents. This program is for mid-career artists, defined as "an artist with at least five years' experience in the medium and a substantial exhibition record." Applicants from culturally diverse backgrounds are encouraged to apply. *Junior Residency:* Applicants must be U.S. nationals or permanent residents. Preferred applicants will have the MFA or three to five years as a working artist. Minority applicants are encouraged.

Dates of Operation

Mid-Career Residency: Ten weeks in Summer. Junior Residency: Academic semesters (eighteen or nineteen weeks). Dates vary from year to year.

Location

Portland, Oregon.

History

The Oregon School of Arts and Crafts is "a four-year art college offering a Bachelor of Fine Arts in Crafts and a Certificate Program in Crafts for artists working in Book Arts, Ceramics, Drawing, Fibers, Metal, and Wood, as well as coursework in Photography, a year-round Visiting Artists Workshop Program, and residencies for emerging and mid-career artists."

What They Offer

Summer Residencies for Mid-career Artists: Four positions are available each summer — two from the School's (annually appointed arts) faculty and two from off-campus. Selected applicants receive on-campus housing, a $1,200 fellowship, plus up to $500 reimbursement for travel to and from the School, $300 for materials, and up to $100 for shipping their completed work. Studio space is available in the sponsoring department (see "Facility Description" below). In September, the resident's work will be exhibited in the Hoffman Gallery. During the residency, Summer Residents are required to give two public presentations on their work.

Junior Residency: There are two residency periods. The first, for residents working in drawing or wood is from September 11 to January 12. The second, for those working in metalsmithing/jewelry or photography is from January 15 to May 24. (These are 1995/96 dates.) Residents receive a $100 per week stipend, up to $400 reimbursement for travel to and from the School, up to $400 for supplies, and up to $100 for shipping their completed work. Campus housing is provided. Studio space is provided in the sponsoring department. Residents may take workshops on a space-available basis. Work will be exhibited in the Hoffman Gallery as part of their ongoing exhibition.

Facility Description

Drawing residents have the use of a small, private studio in the Fibers Department. They are also welcome to use the Drawing Department's classrooms (as a temporary workspace) when classes are not in session. They have a Drawing Studio (a large open room with two-story windows), or the Fibers Design Studio. Both rooms have large tables and expansive wall areas. Easels and horses, drawing boards, a human skeleton, and a large supply of still-life props are available for artists' use.

The metalsmithing/jewelry studio is arranged into stations with specific functions. Students are provided with a workbench equipped with metalsmithing tools and a flexible shaft. Machine tools include two rolling mills, a metal lathe, horizontal and vertical bandsaws, drill presses, sanders, grinders, a box break, a jig saw, a trim saw, a slab saw, and stonecutting and lapidary machinery. Also available are electroforming and plating equipment, a sandblaster, a spray etcher, photoetching equipment, a steam cleaner, a hydraulic press, casting equipment, including a wax injector, a vulcanizer, a Uni-mat, and five enameling kilns.

The photography facility consists of twelve black and white medium format enlarging stations housed in two group darkrooms, a color darkroom equipped with two medium-format enlargers, a 16" RA-4 color print processor, two black and white film developing rooms, a high-speed RC paper dryer, a 16" x 20" archival print washer, and a 15" x 18" process camera. There is also a finishing area equipped with a 16" x 20" dry-mount press, a rotary paper trimmer, light tables, and a professional grade 40" mat cutter. A small tungsten lighting kit, view camera, and 35 mm outfit are available for checkout.

Furniture-making residents use the spacious Wood Studio (divided into three separate work areas: the bench room for hand-tool work, the machine room for work on stationary tools, and the finishing room — soon to be equipped with a spray booth). Machinery includes two tablesaws, two jointers, two drill presses, a planer, two heavy duty lathes, two bandsaws, a radial arm saw, and equipment for steam bending. The bench room is supplied with all necessary hand tools, including sharpening equipment.

Book arts residents have the use of a private studio in the Fibers building as well as access to the Book Arts studios when classes are not in session. One studio has long tables and excellent natural light, the other contains two etching presses, including a 27" x 48" Griffin, rollup slabs, the ink library, and hand tools for relief printing processes. Letterpress equipment includes two Vandercook presses and several cabinets of type. For bookbinding, there is a board shear, a French standing press, several nipping presses, a guillotine cutter, and hand bookbinding tools. The nearby papermaking studio houses vats, molds and deckles, and a Hollander beater.

The ceramics department has separate areas for wheel throwing, handbuilding, glaze preparation, firing, and clay mixing. Equipment includes sixteen potters wheels, wedging tables, movable ware carts, an extruder, a slab roller, a fully stocked glaze lab, and a spray booth. The kiln room houses two large downdraft, gas-fired kilns and three electric kilns. An outside courtyard contains salt, Alpine updraft, and raku kilns, as well as space for experimental firings.

The Hoffman Gallery schedules monthly exhibitions ranging from traditional to contemporary art and craft.

How to Apply

For either program, send a SASE for an application form and guidelines. Return completed application form, a résumé, an artist's statement; a description of your proposed project; ten slides of your work (packaged and labeled according to instructions); an accompanying slide inventory; and two letters of reference. Include an adequate SASE for return of your work samples.

Deadline
December 1 for Summer Residencies for Mid-career Artists; notification by February 1. April 15 for Junior Residencies; notification by June 1.

Approximate Cost of a Four-week Residency
Meals and incidentals offset by stipend.

Oregon Writers Colony
COLONYHOUSE   OR

Colonyhouse
Rockaway Beach, Oregon

Administration:
Oregon Writers Colony
P.O. Box 15200
Portland, Oregon 97215

Attention: Marlene Howard, Director
(503) 771-0428

Type of Facility/Award
Residency.

Who Can Apply
Writers and other artists.

Provisos
Applicants must be members of the Oregon Writers Colony. Applicants must reside in the state of Oregon.

Dates of Operation
Open year-round.

Location
Rockaway Beach, Oregon (on the Oregon coast).

History
The OWC was started by a group of five writers in 1981 who wanted to have a place on the beach to write.

What They Offer
For a modest usage fee, members of the OWC may use the house on a space-available basis. Members must supply their own food, bed linens, pillows, and blan-

kets. Members are expected to leave the house as clean as they found it (or cleaner). Members must supply their own wood (for the fireplace). There are four bedrooms, two baths, a kitchen, and a gallery. One week a month at the house is designated for "writers only." At other times, the house may be rented out for workshops, conferences, or vacations/getaways.

Membership in the OWC comes in three categories: Regular at $25 per year; Patron at $50 per year; and Angel at $1,000 per year. Colonyhouse usage fees barely cover the cost of maintaining the property. For a list of current usage fees, you must become a member of the group. (See *How To Apply* below for 1993 rates.)

Facility Description

The facility is a four-bedroom house on the Oregon coast. The bedroom in the daylight basement has a double and a hideabed. The bedroom on the main floor has one queen bed. The large upstairs bedroom has two single and two double beds. The west bedroom upstairs has two built-in single beds. The house can easily sleep eight people.

How to Apply

If you are a resident of Oregon and would like to join OWC, send a SASE to the above address. They will send you information on the group and the current usage rates. For your information, rates in 1993 were $150 for a weekend — $350 for a week during October through May, and $275 for a weekend — $450 for a week during June through September. No doubt these fees have gone up, but rates were not included in the information I received from the OWC.

Deadline

Rolling application basis.

Approximate Cost of a Four-week Residency

Annual membership fee, rental fee, transportation, meals, materials, and incidentals. House is not normally available for a full month.

OSSABAW ISLAND PROJECT   GA

The Ossabaw Island Project
P.O. Box 13397
Savannah, Georgia 31406

Attention: Mrs. Ford West, President

Notice: This visual arts project was temporarily suspended. Inquire about possible reopening after 1996. Their postcard of April 1995 stated simply: "No hope now."

The Ox-Bow Summer School of Art
Saugatuck, Michigan
(616) 857-5811

Winter Address/Administration/Applications:
The School of the Art Institute of Chicago
The Ox-Bow Summer School of Art
Division of Continuing Studies and Special Programs
37 South Wabash, Room 707
Chicago, Illinois 60603

Attention: Professional Artists Residency Program
(312) 899-5130

Type of Facility/Award

Artist-in-Residence Program.

Who Can Apply

Professional and practicing visual artists.

Provisos

Professional and practicing artists who wish to work in a secluded, natural environment unencumbered by the outside world are invited to apply. Students are not eligible.

Dates of Operation

June 18 to August 26. (1995 dates.)

Location

Between Lake Michigan and the Kalamazoo River near Saugatuck. The nearest airport is in Grand Rapids. For $30 (each way), someone at Ox-Bow will pick you up at the airport if you notify them at least five days in advance. Greyhound buses serve Saugatuck. Ox-Bow itself provides parking for those who bring their cars.

History

For eighty years, Ox-Bow has hosted many beginning and experienced artists in its unparalleled natural setting. They are a nonprofit artists' colony and summer school founded in 1910, operating now in association with the School of the Art Institute of Chicago. "The mission of Ox-Bow, in keeping with its history, is to sustain a haven for nurturing the creative process, through instruction, example, and community. Ox-Bow provides professional and amateur artists with lifelong learning opportunities, and fosters an appreciation of art in the surrounding community, while preserving the natural environment that has energized Ox-Bow since its founding."

What They Offer

Residencies are for one week only. They start on Sunday afternoon and end on

Saturday morning. No exceptions. Room and board are provided for $336, which must be paid upon arrival. Residents are encouraged to present a slide lecture of their work and to participate in discussions.

Facility Description

Working facilities include a large studio (with northern light) for painting and drawing as well as studios for papermaking, glassblowing, ceramics, and printmaking. There is also an open-air studio for sculpture. The Inn provides dining and housing. The dining hall, a lecture room, the gallery, and two large screened-in porches are located on the first floor. Upstairs are the shared guest rooms and bathrooms with showers. Type of housing for artists-in-residence is not specified.

How to Apply

Send a SASE for an application and brochure. Return application with ten slides of your current work, a letter of intent on use of the residency, and a current résumé.

Deadline

May 15.

Approximate Cost of a Four-week Residency

$336, plus transportation, materials, and incidentals.

Painting Space 122 Inc.
PS 122 PROJECT SPACES   NY

Painting Space 122 Inc.
150 First Avenue
New York, New York 10009

Attention: Director
(212) 228-4150

Type of Facility/Award

Artist-in-Residence Program.

Who Can Apply

Visual artists.

Provisos

None listed.

Dates of Operation

One-year program beginning in September.

Location

New York City.

History

"Painting Space 122 Inc. was founded in 1978 by two local artists in the former Public School 122. The members run and operate the PS 122 Gallery, a not-for-profit, alternative space providing an excellent showcase for emerging artists."

What They Offer

They have two programs that offer reduced-rate studio space. *Project Spaces* offers three studio spaces that rotate on a yearly basis. *PS 122 Mini Project Spaces* offers several short-term project spaces for artists needing studio space for a limited period in order to install a special exhibition. *Project Space* artists are asked to donate small amount of their time each month to help run the organization and gallery.

Facility Description

Two studios are between 250 and 300 square feet; the third is approximately 500 square feet. All studios have good light. Artists have twenty-four hour access. There was no description of the *Mini Project Spaces*. The studios are private, so artists are undisturbed except during the Open House each Spring.

How to Apply

Send a SASE for an application and guidelines. When applications are ready, they will mail one to you. (Forms were not available when I inquired.)

Deadline

Applications are accepted in late February and March. No specific deadline was specified.

Approximate Cost of a Four-week Residency

Transportation, housing, meals, materials, and incidentals.

PALENVILLE INTERARTS COLONY　　　　　　　　NY

Palenville Interarts Colony
P.O. Box 59
Palenville, New York 12463

Administration/Winter address:
2 Bond Street
New York, New York 10012

Attention: Joanna Sherman
(212) 254-4614

Notice: The Colony ceased operation in 1995. No inquiries, please.

PENLAND SCHOOL OF CRAFTS   NC

Penland School of Crafts
Penland, North Carolina 28765-0037

Attention: Dana Moore, Program Director
(704) 765-2359 or (704) 765-7389 Fax

Type of Facility/Award

Artist-in-Residence Program.

Who Can Apply

Visual artists working in sculpture, textiles, photography, jewelry, mixed media, books, paper, drawing, iron, metals, printmaking, wood, glass, or clay who are creating nontraditional studio crafts.

Provisos

Applicants must be professional-level, independent artists. Preference is given to former Penland students, studio assistants, visiting artists, and instructors. If you do not have previous Penland experience, write to let them know of your interest in the program, then plan to spend some time at the school in another capacity.

Dates of Operation

Open year-round.

Location

The Penland School is located in Mitchell County, North Carolina, which is fifty miles north of Asheville.

History

The Residents Program was founded in 1963 by Bill Brown. His hope was that the program would encourage craftspeople to settle in the area. Penland offers classes in books and paper, clay, drawing, glass, iron, metals, photography, printmaking, textiles, and wood. The school is supported by a North Carolina Arts Council grant.

What They Offer

Penland offers residencies of two or three years to artists in all media. Residencies are on a space-available basis. The facilities accommodate seven residents at a time. The school provides unfurnished housing and studio space for $100 per month. The resident is responsible for utility costs, which average $125 to $175 per month. (These are 1995 rates.) Interaction between residents and other school programs is encouraged, including helping to organize occasional group exhibitions of your work. Residents are expected to hold an Open House at their studios once each quarter and to maintain an open door policy toward students and instructors.

Facility Description

Residents live and work at the Sanford Center, adjacent to the school. The building has high ceilings, electricity, and running water. Upstairs studios have wooden floors, limiting their use for certain crafts.

How to Apply

Send a SASE for brochure. Submit your name, address, and telephone number with a nonrefundable application fee of $25 and two letters of recommendation. Include fifteen to twenty slides of your recent work (packaged and labeled according to instructions) with accompanying descriptive sheet, a résumé, a personal statement describing your work and the direction you'd like to take while at Penland, why you want a residency at Penland, and how you plan to support yourself while you are there. Include an adequate SASE for return of your support materials. Also include any personal information (marital status, number of dependents, pets). What will your family do while you are in residency?

Deadline

October 28. Notification by December 1.

Approximate Cost of a Four-week Residency

$25, plus rent and utilities of approximately $250 per month, transportation, meals, materials, and incidentals.

PETERS VALLEY CRAFT CENTER   NJ

Peters Valley Craft Center
19 Kuhn Road
Layton, New Jersey 07851

Attention: Artist-in-Residence Program Coordinator
(201) 948-5200 or (201) 948-0011 Fax

Type of Facility/Award

Artist-in-Residence Program.

Who Can Apply

Professional artists in blacksmithing/metals, ceramics, photography, fine metals, fibers, and woodworking.

Provisos

None listed.

Dates of Operation

Open year-round.

Location

The Craft Center is located in the country on a beautiful and unspoiled site in the Delaware Water Gap National Recreation Area.

History

Peters Valley Craft Center was founded in 1970. Its mission as a "non-profit, educational organization has been to provide opportunities for the development of craft skills and to foster an appreciation of traditional and contemporary crafts."

What They Offer

Very limited program. One craftsperson (from each discipline) is selected for a year-round position at Peters Valley Craft Center. Residencies are from one to four years. When openings are available, the residency program is offered to accomplished professionals who would like the opportunity to manage a studio while earning a living at their craft. Resident receives studio and living accommodations at a nominal monthly rate.

Facility Description

Peters Valley offers a variety of classes (with appropriate equipment and facilities) in each of the following disciplines: *blacksmithing/metals* (including forging, knifemaking, metal sculpture, forged furniture, and engraving), *ceramics* (including techniques for English slipware, raku, earthenware, tile making, and anagama firing), *fibers* (including basketry, weaving, looming, quilts, silk painting, beadwork, book and papermaking), *fine metals* (including filigree jewelry making, enameling, casting, die-forming, chasing and repoussé, stonesetting, metal textures, metalsmithing, and embellishment), *photography* (including sunpriting, ilfochrome classic printing, black and white, color landscapes, infrared, pinhole photography, composition, darkroom tutorials, and multiple images), and *woodworking* (including volutes and "C" scrolls, veneers and inlays, furniture making, small and large containers, and the making of an acoustic guitar).

How to Apply

Send a SASE for their brochure, which describes the facility and program in detail and advises those interested in residencies to call or write for additional information.

Deadline

Rolling application basis.

Approximate Cost of a Four-week Residency

Transportation, reduced-rate housing and studio space, meals, materials, and incidentals — offset by wage.

PEWABIC POTTERY   MI

Pewabic Pottery
Pewabic Society, Inc.
10125 East Jefferson Avenue
Detroit, Michigan 48214

Attention: Artist-in-Residence Program
(313) 822-0954

Type of Facility/Award
Artist-in-Residence Program.

Who Can Apply
Ceramic artists.

Provisos
None listed.

Dates of Operation
Open year-round.

Location
Detroit, Michigan.

History
"The program is based on the belief that an exchange of ideas and knowledge will encourage the creativity of the residents as well as others working at the Pottery." They provide a supportive environment where artists can pursue their creative goals.

What They Offer
Pewabic Pottery offers a twelve-month residency for a fee of $100 per month. Included are studio space, clay, glazes, firing, and access to kilns and equipment. A resource committee of professionals periodically reviews studio work in progress and offers critical guidance. Residents work at the Pottery at least sixteen hours each week. Work may include teaching, gallery or design work, or work in tile and vessel production. Payment for this work is $7 per hour. Residents are expected to allocate at least twenty-four hours each week to individual studio time. The residency culminates with an exhibit of work at Pewabic Pottery and at area galleries.

Facility Description
Studios are located in a historic firehouse equipped with tables, a slab roller, electric kilns, and storage. Gas, wood, and soda kilns are available at the main building.

How to Apply
Send a SASE for brochure. Submit a résumé, twenty slides (and an adequate SASE for their return), a letter of intent stating your personal goals and interest in the

program, and two letters of recommendation (sent directly to the Pottery by their authors).

Deadline
April 30.

Approximate Cost of a Four-week Residency
Transportation, housing, meals, and incidentals — offset by wage.

Phillips Exeter Academy
GEORGE BENNETT FELLOWSHIP   NH

Phillips Exeter Academy
20 Main Street
Exeter, New Hampshire 03833

Attention: Dean of Faculties Office
(603) 772-4311 or (603) 778-9563 Fax

Type of Facility/Award
Fellowship.

Who Can Apply
Writers, with preference given to fiction writers. Nonfiction writers will be considered only if their work is intended for a general audience in expectation of a career as a professional writer.

Provisos
The writer must already have a writing project in the works that he or she needs time to complete. The Fellow shall be in residence while school is in session. Encouragement from a publisher is not a requirement. The Fellowship is meant to free the writer from the obligations of accepting a publisher's advance with its inevitable restrictions. There are no requirements as to sex, age, or marital status of the applicants. Quality and originality of the work are the main considerations.

Dates of Operation
Academic year (September to June).

Location
Exeter, New Hampshire.

History
"The manuscripts are the primary basis for the selection of the Fellow, and each manuscript will receive the careful attention of the selection committee, made up of members of the Academy English Department. We are genuine in our desire to select the most promising candidate, and we are always conscious that the Fellowship is for a writer at the beginning of his or her career and that much of the material we receive is necessarily unfinished."

What They Offer

The George Bennett Fellowship provides housing (furnished, if necessary), meals (at the Academy's dining hall) for the writer and his or her family (while school is in session), and a stipend of $5,000. Term of the residency is one academic year (September to June). Only one Fellowship is awarded annually. The writer must live in Exeter and make his or her self and talents available in an "informal and unofficial way" to students interested in writing, and more specifically, to students in English classes, and to members of student literary organizations. The writer will not be required to teach any classes, will not be asked to coach athletics or dramatics or debating, and will not be an adviser to any Academy organization. This is not a faculty position. The nature of the association between the writer and the Academy will be determined by the writer's own interests and good will, not by Academy demand. It is the hope of the Academy that the partially completed manuscript will be completed during the tenure of the Fellowship and subsequently submitted to a publisher.

Facility Description

This is a private school campus, but on-campus housing is not provided. Writer chooses his/her own housing within Academy guidelines.

How to Apply

Send a SASE for an application and guidelines. Return the completed application with a statement on why the Fellowship would be appropriate to your situation, a description of your partially completed project and your plan for its completion, a sample of the work (fifty typed pages of prose, or if poetry, send at least twenty poems), and $5 for return postage and handling of your manuscript. The two references listed on the application will only be contacted if you make it to the final stage of the competition.

Deadline

December 1 (postmarked). Notification on or about March 15.

Approximate Cost of a Four-week Residency

$5, plus transportation, materials, and incidentals — offset by stipend.

Pilchuck Glass School
Stanwood campus: (May through September)
1201 316th Street N.W.
Stanwood, Washington 98292-9600

(360) 445-3111, (360) 445-5515 Fax, or (360) 445-9941 Pay phone

Seattle office: (September to May)
315 Second Avenue South
Seattle, Washington 98104-2618

Attention: Emerging Artists-in-Residence Program
(206) 621-8422, (206) 621-0713 Fax, or (206) 517-1351 Event reservation line.

Type of Facility/Award
Residency.

Who Can Apply
Glass and other visual artists.

Provisos
Artists with prior achievement in glass and other visual arts media.

Dates of Operation
Mid-September through mid-November.

Location
Stanwood, Washington — one hour north of Seattle.

History
In 1971, artist Dale Chihuly and patrons Anne Gould Hauberg and John H. Hauberg founded the school. Pilchuck is now a leading model of education in the visual arts. Both glass blowing as a studio art and the broader contemporary interest in glass as a medium have evolved in part because of Pilchuck. Pilchuck supports experimentation, investigation, team work, and personal growth. Pilchuck also "nurtures artists at all stages of their careers; the school values artistic pursuits and the people who engage in them, and rejoices in international friendships."

What They Offer
The Emerging Artists-in-Residence program is an eight-week program for five or six artists at a time that includes living accommodations, studio space, and a $1,000 stipend. The brochure does not indicate if meals are provided for the EAiR's (call to confirm before applying). Artists have access to many Pilchuck studios and equipment including: the glass plate printmaking shop; plaster studios; fusing, slumping, and pâte-de-verre kilns; and such cold working equipment as sandblasters, Vibralaps, lathes, and saws. The flat shop and hot shop are not available to EAiR's.

Pilchuck also has a *Professional Artists-in-Residency* program with the same application requirements as the EAiR program. This program is for from a few days to a week or more and is open to experienced professional artists seeking to extend their education and experimentation on a proposal basis. Two or three artists will be invited to participate in this program and will be responsible for funding their own projects. During the summer months, Pilchuck offers several classes/workshops by professional artists on a variety of visual arts topics.

Many full and partial scholarships are available for students. Also, some students receive grants from their employers, artists' associations, or a government agencies. Information on scholarships, financial aid, and other awards is in the brochure.

Facility Description

Pilchuck is nestled in the hillside meadows overlooking Puget Sound. The fifty-acre wooded site is set in the middle of a 15,000-acre tree farm, providing isolation from the influence of commerce and urban centers and allowing a community of artists to focus on art. All students, faculty, and staff live and work on the campus. The award-winning architecture of the buildings is evident in the lodge, with its massive wood posts, great stone hearth, and three levels of decks overlooking the islands of Puget Sound. The lodge houses the dining room, kitchen, library, projection equipment, and printmaking studio and is located at the heart of the campus. The campus gallery is a showcase for exhibitions and installations. Other buildings/shops include:

Hot shop: casting tables and equipment, four color pot-furnace, pick-up and color ovens, eight top-loading annealers, five glassblowing stations, six glory holes, four front-loading annealers, and two 1500-lb. continuous melt furnaces.

Studio building: nine electric kilns, four flexible shaft tools, gas flash kiln, glass routers, light tables, plaster-mold making room, small test kilns, wax burn-out kiln, wax steamers, and a wood-cutting band saw.

Cold working studio: carbide band saw, diamond chop saw, diamond cut-off saw, diamond slab saw, sandblasting room, four engraving lathes with copper and diamond wheels, three silicone carbide flattening wheels, Maja diamond flattening/beveling machine, three Vibralaps, two glass-cutting lathes, water-feed drill press, and three wet belt sanders.

Flat glass studio: electric flash kiln, three computer-controlled annealers, flame working torches, four small slumping or enameling kilns, gas and compressed air, and neon fabricating equipment.

Wood and metal shop: band saw, belt sanders, compressed air, drill press, joiner, lathes, radial arm saw, table saw, and welding equipment (stick, tig, mig).

How to Apply

Send a SASE for an application and brochure. Return completed application and a $25 nonrefundable application fee with the following support materials: ten slides and two slide scripts (at least five slides should show work in glass); a brief proposal describing your objectives and intentions for the residency in aesthetic, technical, and conceptual terms; a current résumé; two recommendations from persons familiar with your work and character; and an SASE for return of your slides.

Deadline
March 1.

Approximate Cost of a Four-week Residency
$25, plus transportation, materials, and incidentals — offset by stipend.

THE PLAYWRIGHTS' CENTER   MN

The Playwrights' Center
2301 Franklin Avenue East
Minneapolis, Minnesota 55406-1099

Attention: Director of Fellowships and Awards
(612) 332-7481 or (612) 332-6037 Fax

Type of Facility/Award
Fellowships/Grants. Opportunity for playwrights.

Who Can Apply
Playwrights and screenwriters.

Provisos
All applicants must be U.S. citizens. For some of the awards listed below, applicants must also be residents of Minnesota.

Dates of Operation
Open year-round.

Location
Minneapolis, Minnesota.

History
"Since 1971 the Playwrights' Center has fueled the contemporary theater by providing services that support the development and public appreciation of playwrights and playwriting. The Center is committed to artistic excellence; diversity of aesthetic, culture, age, and gender; playwright leadership in governance; advocacy of playwrights' work; and freedom of expression."

What They Offer
The Center offers a number of fellowships, grants, and/or opportunities for playwrights and screenwriters. Here are several:

The Jerome Fellowships: The Center annually awards five emerging American playwrights fellowships of $7,000 each. Fellows spend a year in residence developing their skills through readings, workshops, and developmental programs.

Many Voices: This program serves writers from the African-American and Latino/Chicano communities with culturally focused playwriting roundtables, multicultural collaboration grants, and residencies.

The McKnight Advancement Grants: Minnesota playwrights may apply for these $8,500 grants (three are awarded annually), which are intended to significantly advance the recipients' art and careers. Winners are allowed access to the Center's developmental programs. In exchange, they must participate in the Center's Educational Outreach program.

The McKnight Fellowships: Each year, two American playwrights whose work has made a significant impact on contemporary theater are each awarded $10,000. Additionally, Fellows spend a month in residence at the Center participating in its developmental programs and contributing to the Center's Educational Outreach program.

PlayLabs offers thirty to forty hours each of intensive workshop time to developing four or more unproduced, unpublished scripts by Americans. Playwrights refine their scripts with the help of professional directors, dramaturges, and actors. Each play receives a public reading followed by an optional audience discussion.

The McKnight Screenwriting Fellowships: Five $5,000 fellowships are awarded each year to Minnesota screenwriters.

Jones One-Act Commissions: Six commission awards of $250 each are awarded each year for the creation of a new one-act theater piece. Playwrights are given a public reading of their plays followed by an optional audience discussion.

Detailed information on each of these programs can be obtained by sending a SASE to the Center during the months specified below.

Facility Description
Theater Center.

How to Apply
Send a SASE for an application form and brochure. Applications for *The Jerome Fellowships* are available each year in July. *Many Voices* applications for grants and residencies are available each year in July. *The McKnight Advancement Grants* applications are available each year in December. Applications for *The McKnight Fellowships* are available each year in November. *PlayLabs* applications are available each year in October. Application availability for *The McKnight Screenwriting Fellowships* was not specified in their brochure; write or call the Center if you'd like to apply for this program. *Jones One-Act Commissions* inquiries are accepted throughout the year, but are preferred between March 1 and June 1.

Unfortunately, the deadline for my book did not coincide with most of the above application periods, so you'll have to call or write the Center at the specified times for detailed information.

Deadline

Various.

Approximate Cost of a Four-week Residency

Transportation, housing, meals, materials, and incidentals — some offset by fellowship or grant cash awards.

POETRY SOCIETY OF AMERICA   NY

Poetry Society of America
15 Gramercy Park
New York, New York 10003

Attention: George Bogin Memorial Award
(212) 254-9628

Notice: The George Bogin Memorial Award used to include a one-month residency at the Virginia Center for the Creative Arts. As of May 1995, the residency was no longer part of the award. If you are interested in other programs/awards provided by the Poetry Society of America, send a SASE for their brochure.

Princeton University
ALFRED HODDER FELLOWSHIP   NJ

The Council of the Humanities
122 East Pyne
Princeton University
Princeton, New Jersey 08544

Attention: Alfred Hodder Fellowship Director
(609) 258-4717 or (609) 258-2783 Fax

Type of Facility/Award

Fellowship.

Who Can Apply

Humanists.

Provisos

Humanists "with more than ordinary learning" and "much more than ordinary intellectual and literary gifts." Preference is given to candidates outside of academia. Candidates for the Ph.D. degree are ineligible. The Council seeks humanists in the early stages of their careers who have demonstrated exceptional promise but may not yet enjoy widespread recognition. The fellowship is designed to identify and nurture extraordinary potential rather than to honor distinguished achievement.

Dates of Operation

Academic year.

Location

Princeton, New Jersey.

History

"The Council of the Humanities was founded in 1953 to foster teaching and research in the humanities. Given the broad scope of its mission, the Council serves as a locus for many endeavors that bring together faculty, students, and distinguished visitors from many fields. Each year, the Council invites more than thirty guests for visits ranging from a day to a year. It is the home of a wide array of interdisciplinary courses and programs, including those in the Creative Arts."

The Hodder Fellowship was endowed by Mary MacKall Gwinn Hodder in honor of her husband, Alfred, who became an attorney at age twenty-three without any formal undergraduate education. He then went on to earn a Ph.D. in philosophy at Harvard University (in two years) and accepted a position at Bryn Mawr College, where he met his wife in 1898. They were married in 1904, but Alfred died three years later in 1907. Upon her death, she left her papers to Princeton and endowed the Charles John Morris Gwinn and Alfred Hodder Memorial Fund in honor of her father and her husband. The list of fellowship recipients since 1944 is very impressive.

What They Offer

The award carries a stipend of $41,000 (1995–96) so that the Fellow can undertake a significant new project in "studious leisure." The Hodder Fellow spends an academic year in residence at Princeton, pursuing an independent project.

Facility Description

University campus. No mention of on-campus housing.

How to Apply

Send a SASE for brochure. Then submit a résumé, a sample of previous work (ten-page maximum, not returnable), a project proposal of two to three pages, and a SASE for acknowledgment. Letters of recommendation are not required.

Deadline

November 15 (postmarked). Appointment is made in February.

Approximate Cost of a Four-week Residency

Transportation, housing, meals, materials, and incidentals — offset by stipend.

Pudding House Bed & Breakfast for Writers
60 N. Main Street
Johnstown, Ohio 43031

Attention: Jennifer Bosveld, Director
(614) 967-6060

Type of Facility/Award

Retreat.

Who Can Apply

Writers, poets, musicians, artists, therapists, and teachers.

Provisos

None listed.

Dates of Operation

Open year-round.

Location

Pudding House is twenty miles northeast of downtown Columbus and Ohio State University, and fourteen miles southeast of I-71 on State Route 37 at its crossroads with U.S. 62.

History

Pudding House Bed and Breakfast is the home of poet Jennifer Bosveld, who publishes *Pudding Magazine,* an international journal of applied poetry, and sponsors many writing and publishing workshops throughout the year.

What They Offer

Rooms are equipped with a desk. Writers have access to an electronic typewriter and all the paper they can use while at the house. Rooms are $65 per night, including breakfast. Writers receive a twenty-percent discount. If you are interested in long stays (weekly or monthly), call to negotiate an even better rate. Each guest has kitchen privileges. Reservation and deposit are required. Pudding House requires a fourteen-day cancellation notice for refunds (less a ten-percent fee).

Facility Description

Pudding House is a stately, twelve-room home one block from Johnstown's old town hall, public library, post office, restaurants, laundromat, drugstore, and other conveniences. Two blocks away is a community park. The house is fifteen minutes from Denison University in Granville and Otterbein College in Westerville, seven minutes from Morris Woods State Nature Preserve, and ten minutes from Hoover Reservoir (for boating and fishing). The house is on two bike paths. Antiques are abundant in Sunbury, Granville, and New Albany, all within about twelve minutes.

Johnstown also has a large antique mall and Jennifer and Jim are antique dealers. Pudding House has a twenty-four hour writer's workshop (and a wonderful library) on the premises, where you can type, work on revisions and submissions, research, read, and purchase books and writer's supplies.

How to Apply
No application process. Call for reservations. First-come, first-served.

Deadline
None.

Approximate Cost of a Four-week Residency
$1,456, plus lunch, dinner, transportation, and incidentals ($1,456 is based on the daily rate; a discount for weekly or monthly stays is available).

Radcliffe College
MARY INGRAHAM BUNTING FELLOWSHIP   MA

Radcliffe College
34 Concord Avenue
Cambridge, Massachusetts 02138

Attention: Administrator — Bunting Fellowship Program
(617) 495-8212

Type of Facility/Award
Fellowship.

Who Can Apply
Scholars, creative writers, visual or performing artists.

Provisos
The Institute seeks applications from women scholars in any field who have held a doctorate or appropriate final degree at least two years prior to appointment. Women creative writers and visual or performing artists with a significant record of accomplishment and professional experience, i.e., publications, solo or group shows, are also invited to apply. Bunting Fellows may not simultaneously hold another major fellowship that provides more than $20,000.

Dates of Operation
Mid-September to mid-August each year (dates vary).

Location
Boston area.

History
The Mary Ingraham Bunting Institute of Radcliffe College was founded in 1960. It is a multidisciplinary research center with programs designed to support women

of exceptional promise and demonstrated accomplishment who wish to pursue independent work in academic and professional fields and in the creative arts.

What They Offer

The Institute may annually award six to ten awards of $33,000. Office or studio space, auditing privileges, and access to libraries and most other resources of Radcliffe College and Harvard University are provided. Fellows are expected to present their work-in-progress at public colloquia, performances, or exhibitions.

The *Affiliation Program* offers ten to twenty women office space and the same resources as the Bunting Fellowship Program, but without stipend. (Women holding or seeking other funded awards are invited to apply.) Appointments can be made for the Fall or Spring Semesters or for both.

Facility Description

Radcliffe College campus.

How to Apply

Send a SASE (after June 1) for an application and brochure. Return completed application and other specified materials before deadline.

Deadline

January 15 (postmarked) for Affiliate Program. October 15 (postmarked) for Bunting Fellowship Program. November 15 (postmarked) for Visual Arts applications (both programs).

Approximate Cost of a Four-week Residency

Transportation, housing, meals, materials, and incidentals — offset by stipend. No stipend for Affiliate Program.

RAGDALE FOUNDATION   IL

Ragdale Foundation
1260 North Green Bay Road
Lake Forest, Illinois 60045

Attention: Michael Wilkerson, Director
(708) 234-1063 or (708) 234-1075 Fax

Type of Facility/Award

Residency.

Who Can Apply

Writers, composers, visual artists, and sometimes other disciplines.

Provisos

None listed.

Dates of Operation

January 2 to April 30. May 16 to December 15.

Location

Thirty miles north of Chicago near Lake Michigan, Ragdale is accessible from O'Hare International Airport by bus or limousine service, and by rail through Chicago with a transfer to the Metra commuter line to Lake Forest.

History

Ragdale is on the National Register of Historic Places. The house and Barnhouse were designed and built in 1897 by Howard Van Doren Shaw, a leader in American Arts and Crafts architecture. The family, artists themselves, established a haven for artists by creating an outdoor theater on the grounds and staging productions for the enjoyment of their friends and the community. In 1976, Shaw's granddaughter, Alice Ryerson Hayes, created the Ragdale Foundation; in 1980, the Foundation, formally incorporated and tax-exempt, bought back the barn and expanded Ragdale to accommodate twelve residents.

What They Offer

Ragdale offers residencies of two weeks, four weeks, six weeks, or eight weeks. Residencies begin on either the first or sixteenth of each month and end on the fifteenth or the last day of each month. The Ragdale House can accommodate twelve artists at a time. Six nights a week, a well-prepared, wholesome evening meal is served to residents. Breakfast and lunch supplies are stocked in communal kitchens, allowing

Ragdale, the main house. (Photo courtesy of the Ragdale Foundation.)

residents to set their own schedules. There is a residency fee of $15 a day. Some full and partial fee-waivers (based solely on need) are available. The Foundation also sponsors readings, concerts, workshops, art exhibitions, and seminars in poetry and fiction writing. Additionally, there are two fellowships offered: The *Frances Shaw Fellowship* for women writers whose serious work began after the age of fifty-five, and the *Pan-African Fellowship*, part of the U.S./Africa Project. Separate brochures are available for these programs. Send a SASE if you are interested.

Facility Description

There are five comfortable rooms for writers in the Ragdale House. In the Barnhouse, there are three rooms for writers and two rooms for visual artists. Both houses have large kitchens and living rooms for community use, informal libraries, and laundry facilities. The Friend's Studio can accommodate two additional visual artists or one visual artist and one composer. All studios have plenty of working space and skylights. The beautifully landscaped property overlooks a nature preserve.

How to Apply

Send a SASE for an application and brochure. Ask for information on fee-waivers and special programs if you are interested. Return completed application with your $20 nonrefundable application fee and the names and addresses of three references. Also include the following. *Writers:* four copies of a description of your proposed project (no longer than 250 words), four copies of a work sample (one short story, essay, chapter of a novel, ten poems, or one act from a play or script) representative of the genre in which you intend to work, and one copy of a current résumé or vita. Manuscripts should include a cover sheet with your name, address, and title of the work submitted. Do not include a SASE — manuscripts will not be returned. *Visual artists:* one copy of a description of your proposed project (no longer than 250 words) indicating if you have any special studio or equipment needs, one set of ten slides (packaged and labeled according to instructions) accompanied by a descriptive sheet, one copy of a current résumé or vita, and a SASE. *Composers:* three copies of a description of your proposed project (no longer than 250 words) indicating if you have any special studio or equipment needs, two tapes and two scores of one recent composition, one copy of a current résumé or vita, and a SASE. *Other disciplines:* Ragdale has limited space for performance artists, filmmakers, and choreographers. Call for details on applying in these disciplines.

Deadline

January 15 for residencies from May 16 to December 15. June 1 for residencies from January 2 to April 30. Late applications are considered if space is available.

Approximate Cost of a Four-week Residency

$440, plus transportation, materials, and incidentals. Full and partial fee-waivers may be available. Full fellowships (with specific provisos) may be available by separate application.

REAL ART WAYS   CT

Real Art Ways
94 Allyn Street
Hartford, Connecticut 06103-1402

Attention: Media Residency Program
(203) 525-5521

Notice: The above telephone number has been disconnected. Mail to the above address was returned marked "Forward Expired" indicating the program has ceased operations.

MILDRED I. REID WRITERS COLONY   NH

Mildred I. Reid Writers Colony
146 Penacook Road
Contoocook, New Hampshire 03229

Attention: Mildred I. Reid
(603) 746-3625

Notice: The Mildred I. Reid Writer's Colony closed in 1991 after forty years of service. No inquiries, please.

ROCKY MOUNTAIN NATIONAL PARK   CO

Rocky Mountain National Park
Artist-in-Residence Program
Estes Park, Colorado 80517

Attention: Coordinator
(303) 586-1224, (303) 586-1399, or (303) 586-1256 Fax

Type of Facility/Award
Artist-in-Residence Program.

Who Can Apply
All artists, including literary, visual, and performing artists. Housing is not fully accessible for those with disabilities. Call for information.

Provisos
Applicants are expected to be on a professional level.

Dates of Operation
Mid-May through mid-September.

Location
Rocky Mountain National Park.

History

"Currently used as the 'home' of Rocky Mountain National Park's Artist-in-Residence program, the rustic cabin on the hill overlooking Moraine Park was the summer retreat of William Allen White from 1912 to 1943. A nationally recognized journalist and editor of the *Emporia Gazette* (Kansas), the spirit of this Pulitzer Prize-winning author lives on with the contemporary artists who work in his cabin today."

What They Offer

From mid-May to mid-September, the Park Service offers the use of the William Allen White cabin for periods of two weeks. Artists are allowed to pursue their particular art form while surrounded by the inspiring landscape of the Park. In return, artists are asked to donate to the park's collection a piece of work representative of their style and their stay. Works will be displayed on a rotating schedule for public viewing. Artists are also strongly encouraged to participate in an offering such as a demonstration, a talk, an exploratory hike, or a performance. This activity is expected to consume only a few hours of the artist's stay. Eight or nine finalists will be chosen each year, based solely on merit.

Facility Description

The cabin has a living/dining area with high-beamed ceilings and a large fireplace. There is one bedroom, a bath, and a small kitchen. There is no central heat. The cabin is fully furnished, including linens and kitchenware, but some artists choose to bring some of their own belongings with them. The cabin is not fully accessible for those with disabilities. Call the program coordinator to discuss individual needs.

How to Apply

Send a SASE for a brochure and application guidelines. Submit four copies of a one to two page résumé and summary of your creative works, four copies of a brief statement stating what you hope to achieve from your residency, and a sample of your recent work. *Visual artists:* send six slides. *Musicians and composers:* send a cassette recording. *Dancers and other performing artists:* send a ¹/₂" VHS video tape. *Writers and journalists:* send no more than six pages of a manuscript excerpt, a short story, an article, or poetry. Enclose an adequate SASE for return of your work sample. Applications are only accepted between November 1 and the deadline. Deadline dates may vary slightly from year to year.

Deadline

January 16 (postmarked). Notification on or before March 10. (1995 dates.)

Approximate Cost of a Four-week Residency

Transportation, meals, materials, and incidentals.

Rocky Mountain Women's Institute
Associates Program
7150 Montview Boulevard
Denver, Colorado 80220

Attention: Bonnie F. McCune, Executive Director
(303) 871-6923

Type of Facility/Award

Artist-in-Residence Program.

Who Can Apply

Literary artists, media artists (film/video), performing artists, visual artists, and scholars pursuing independent study.

Provisos

Applicants must be permanent Denver-area residents within commuting distance of the Institute. Students enrolled in a degree granting program are not eligible.

Dates of Operation

Associateships run from September 1 through August 31.

Location

Denver, Colorado.

History

"Founded in 1976 to promote the intellectual and artistic accomplishments of women, the Rocky Mountain Women's Institute fosters the creation of a community of artists, writers, and scholars." The Institute has served over 130 Associates.

What They Offer

Seven individuals each year are provided with an office or studio space, a $1,000 stipend, and other support services for the completion of a creative project. Artistic merit, project feasibility, and group diversity are the primary selection criteria. Associates must attend biweekly meetings with fellow Associates and participate in Institute events.

Facility Description

None provided.

How to Apply

Send a SASE for an application and brochure. Return completed application, a proposal of the work you intend to do at the Institute (either work in progress or a new project), a list of prior achievements or experience in the area of your proposed project, and a statement of your need and desire to work in a women-oriented, cross-disciplinary environment. The Institute will specify appropriate work samples when you send for your application. Requests for applications are accepted after January 1st each year, until the deadline of March 15.

Deadline
March 15.

Approximate Cost of a Four-week Residency
Transportation, housing, meals, some materials, and incidentals — offset by stipend.

ROSWELL MUSEUM AND ART CENTER NM

Roswell Museum and Art Center Foundation
100 West 11th Street
Roswell, New Mexico 88201

Attention: Stephen Fleming, Artist-in-Residence Program Director
(505) 622-6037 AIR program, (505) 624-6744 Museum, or (505) 624-6765 Fax

Type of Facility/Award
Residency/Grant.

Who Can Apply
Artists involved in painting, drawing, sculpture, printmaking, and other fine arts media are invited to apply.

Provisos
The Center does not accept performance artists or production crafts artists. Foreign applicants will be considered.

Dates of Operation
Open year-round.

Location
At an elevation of 3560 feet, Roswell is a high plains community of 47,000. Albuquerque and Santa Fe are each approximately 200 miles away. Roswell is served by bus or by Mesa Airlines commuter service.

History
The Center's program was established in 1967 to provide professional studio artists with the opportunity to concentrate on their work in a supportive, communal environment. "The Artist-in-Residence Program serves as a contemporary counterpoint to the traditional arts of the Southwest, reinforces the Program's interest in strengthening the vitality of art in New Mexico, and has been a catalyst in broadening community understanding of modern art."

What They Offer

Each artist accepted into the program is provided with a separate rent-free/utilities-free house and a studio. The house can accommodate a single person or a family. Residencies are from six months to one year. Residents receive a stipend of $500 per month, plus $100 per month for each dependent living with them. Residents must supply their own art materials and pay their own telephone bill. Pets are allowed only under extreme circumstances and will be considered with specific provisions on a case-by-case basis before the residency begins.

Facility Description

The studios measure approximately 25' x 25' x 12'. They are well-lighted, open spaces convertible to the artist's requirements (within reason). The printmaking facility is a small, fully operational lithographic/etching studio. Residents' housing is a complex of six houses and nine studios on five acres. Buildings are close to one another. Houses are partially furnished with major furniture items, appliances, and utensils. Vacuum cleaners and laundry facilities are available for shared use.

How to Apply

Send a SASE for an application and brochure. Beginning in 1996, each applicant will be required to pay a nonrefundable $10 application fee. Return completed application, your statement of intent, and no more than fifteen 35 mm slides (packaged and labeled according to instructions) of at least ten works completed within the past two years. Slides must be accompanied by a descriptive sheet. Sculptors may submit up to twenty slides to allow for alternate views. Installation artists should show the widest range of their most recent works. Also include no more than ten pages of additional support materials, including a résumé, copies of reviews, and any other information helpful to the selection committee. Be sure to enclose an adequate SASE if you want your materials returned. Do not submit letters of recommendation. References are listed on the application and will be contacted if necessary by the Art Center. Because of storage limitations, applications are accepted only during the months of June and December, with deadline for submittal at the end of each of those months.

Deadline

End of June. End of December. Dates vary from year to year.

Approximate Cost of a Four-week Residency

$10, plus transportation, meals, materials, and incidentals — offset by stipend.

Saskatchewan Writers Guild   Regina, Saskatchewan
WRITER/ARTISTS
COLONIES AND RETREATS   CANADA

Saskatchewan Writers Guild
P.O. Box 3986
Regina, Saskatchewan S4P 3R9
Canada

Attention: Saskatchewan Writer/Artists Colonies and Retreats
(306) 757-6310 or (306) 565-8554

Type of Facility/Award
Residency.

Who Can Apply
Writers and artists.

Provisos
Writers and artists from around the world are invited to apply, but preference is given to residents of Saskatchewan.

Dates of Operation
St. Peter's Abbey Colony has one two-week winter session in February and a series of sessions in July and August. They also host year-round retreats. *Emma Lake Colony* has one two-week session in August. *Riverhurst Colony* has one two-week session in September. Dates vary from year to year.

Location
St. Peter's Abbey is located just outside the village of Muenster. *Emma Lake* is only a few miles from the town of Christopher Lake, approximately twenty-five miles north of Prince Albert. *The Riverhurst Colony* is held at the Mainstay Inn near Riverhurst about a mile from Lake Diefenbaker.

History
"The Saskatchewan Colonies were established in 1979 to provide a place where writers could write free from distraction. The colonies were soon expanded to include visual artists. Not only is the uninterrupted working time invaluable, but conversation after hours provides a stimulating exchange of ideas. The individual retreats make the program more flexible in response to the needs of writers."

What They Offer
Colonies in this context are two-week sessions at either St. Peter's Abbey, Emma Lake, or Riverhurst. For $100 (Canadian) per week, residents are provided with private rooms and three meals a day. Visual artists are provided with studio space as well. The program at *St. Peter's* lasts for six weeks. The colony can accommodate

eight residents per week. Selected residents may stay as long as they like. *St. Peter's* also has a year-round retreat program. Selected artists may stay for a period of no more than one month. Only three residents at a time can be accommodated. Application procedures for the retreat are the same as for the colonies, but applications are accepted on a rolling basis and preferably at least four weeks in advance of your requested dates, if space is available. Plan ahead. Cost of the retreat is not specified. The *Emma Lake Colony* has only one two-week session in the summer each year. The *Riverhurst Colony* has only one two-week session in September. The Guild also offers the Gertrude Story Scholarship for a fiction writer or poet whose writing has an obvious Saskatchewan setting. The scholarship is in the amount of $200 (Canadian), which will be applied to the cost of the colony. If interested, you must apply as directed below and indicate your interest in the scholarship. If you win, $200 of your prepaid fee will be refunded. Deadline for the scholarship is April 15.

Facility Description

St. Peter's Abbey is a Benedictine Abbey. Guests are accommodated in private rooms in a former convent on Abbey grounds or in Severin Hall. Meals are homegrown and served in the college facility. Studio space for visual artists is provided. The setting is serene and timeless, promoting both work and relaxation. *Emma Lake* is located in a forest region. Accommodations include separate cabins or single rooms in a one-story building. Artists share a large studio space. Meals are served in the dining room of a centrally located building, which also has a lounge. The *Riverhurst Colony* is held at the Mainstay Inn. This colony is ideal for applicants interested in an isolated setting. The hotel, with a vast prairie view, is situated between two deep forested coulees about a mile from the sandy beaches of Lake Diefenbaker.

How to Apply

Send a SASE for brochure. Submit ten typewritten pages of a manuscript or ten slides of artwork (packaged and labeled according to instructions), a description of your proposed project, names of two references who are familiar with your work, the length of stay and preferred dates, and a brief résumé of past work, including publications and exhibitions. Applications received after the deadline are considered on a space available basis. A check for $100 per week of requested time must accompany your application.

Deadline

January 1 for St. Peter's winter colony. April 15 for St. Peter's summer colony and Emma Lake summer colony. April 15 for the Gertrude Story Scholarship. July 1 for Riverhurst. Rolling application process for St. Peter's year-round retreat.

Approximate Cost of a Four-week Residency

$400 (Canadian), plus transportation, materials, and incidentals.

SCULPTURE SPACE NY

Sculpture Space Inc.
12 Gates Street
Utica, New York 13502

Attention: Sylvia de Swaan, Executive Director or Jonathan Kirk, Studio Manager
(315) 724-8381

Type of Facility/Award

Artist-in-Residence Program.

Who Can Apply

Professional artists and sculptors.

Provisos

Sculpture Space can accommodate a great variety of projects both in terms of materials and scale. They are willing to discuss each case individually and look at the definition of sculpture in its broadest possible sense. They have no geographic or stylistic restrictions.

Dates of Operation

Open year-round.

Location

The Sculpture space is located in downtown Utica, New York.

Jeanne Flanagan, work-in-progress at Sculpture Space, 1993. (Photo © Sylvia de Swaan.)

History

Sculpture Space, in a former steel fabricating shop, incorporated as a nonprofit arts organization in 1975. It is funded by the New York State Council on the Arts, the National Endowment for the Arts, Oneida County, foundation grants, and private donations. Sculpture Space is a member of the National Association of Artists Organizations, the New York State Arts and Cultural Coalition, and the National Alliance of Artists Communities. "Sculpture Space fosters experimentation and encourages new work that covers the full spectrum of contemporary sculptural concerns."

What They Offer

Sculpture Space has two artist-in-residence programs: funded and non-funded. The funded program is designed to support professional artists by providing free use of a professionally equipped studio facility, access to industrial resources, and a support system to promote the development and presentation of sculptural projects. Artists accepted to work at Sculpture Space are given a key to the studio and are free to use the facility at any time, seven days a week. The Studio Manager is available to assist artists with an introductory orientation, to act as a liaison with suppliers, and to advise on technical problems. Artists are responsible for their own materials, specialized tools, fees for work done outside the premises, and for an assistant should they require one. Through their resources and contacts, Sculpture Space is able to help artists keep their expenses to a minimum. Residents spend an average of $1,000 per month. If you would like to be considered for a funded residency, you must apply by December 15. They award a limited number of $2,000 stipends for a two-month work stay. Funded residents are chosen by Sculpture Space's Review Com-

John Monti, work-in-progress at Sculpture Space, 1993. (Photo © Sylvia de Swaan.)

mittee with the assistance of a rotating guest panelist. Primary criteria for selection are quality, originality, and potential for growth. They do not guarantee housing, but they try to find accommodations for the artists in the homes of Board Members and volunteers, when possible. However, motels and the YMCA are located within walking distance of the studio. In exchange for time spent at Sculpture Space, they ask that each artist contribute on some level to help support and promote the organization. There are several options that can be discussed on an individual basis. Artists are advised to bring their own hand tools. A list of equipment available for artists' use will be mailed to you with your brochure and application form. Residents must provide their own transportation to the facility. Non-funded residencies offer the same benefits as funded residencies, except there is no stipend to cover costs. Inquire for specifics if you are interested.

Facility Description

Sculpture Space is proximate to scrap yards, light industry, and fabrication shops. The facility consists of 5,500 square feet of open space, and one 400-square-foot private studio for special projects. The space is outfitted with concrete floors, a two-ton system of traveling hoists, and extra wide overhead doors. The building is surrounded by three-quarters of an acre of land that can supplement indoor studio space in the summer. They have an outdoor work pad with a 50-foot monorail and hoist. Depending upon the scale of the work, Sculpture Space can accommodate four artists at one time. The list of equipment available for artists' use is huge and includes hand tools (air and electric), steel, wood, and other miscellaneous tools and industrial equipment.

How to Apply

Send a SASE for an application and brochure. Applications should consist of not more than ten slides (labeled according to instructions) and a corresponding slide narrative with title, date, dimensions, and medium. Include a SASE for return of your materials. In addition, Sculpture Space would like a brief project description (half-page), a current résumé, and the names of some references. A personal visit is advisable before application.

Deadline

December 15 deadline for panel-selected, funded residencies. Rolling application process for non-funded residencies. Notification within three months.

Approximate Cost of a Four-week Residency

$1,000 (average amount spent by artists), plus transportation, meals, incidentals, and possibly housing (they try to accommodate artists in private homes). Limited stipends of $2,000 for two-month stays are available by application.

MARIE WALSH SHARPE ART FOUNDATION CO/NY

The Marie Walsh Sharpe Art Foundation
711 North Tejon Street, Suite B
Colorado Springs, Colorado 80903

Attention: Kim M. Taylor, Administrative Assistant
(719) 635-3220

Studio space located at:
443 Greenwich, Tribeca
New York, New York

Type of Facility/Award
Artist-in-Residence Program.

Who Can Apply
Visual artists.

Provisos
Visual Artists twenty-one years of age and older who are U.S. citizens or permanent U.S. residents. Students will not be considered.

Dates of Operation
Spaces available after September 1, 1996 for a period of one year.

Location
443 Greenwich Street, Tribeca, Manhattan, New York City, New York. (No zip code or telephone number for the New York location were provided in flyer.)

History
The Foundation was established by Marie Walsh Sharpe in 1985 to benefit visual artists. Twenty-six visual artists met in November of 1988 to discuss the needs of artists today. An Artists Advisory Committee was formed out of this meeting. The AAC developed two programs: *The Space Program* (as outlined herein), and a national toll-free information hotline (in cooperation with The American Council for the Arts) for visual artists, which began on October 1, 1990. This referral service provides artists with information on programs and services available to them.

What They Offer
The Space Program provides non-living studio space, rent-free, for the making of new art. No stipend, equipment, or materials are provided.

Facility Description
There are fourteen studios available ranging from 450 to 500 square feet. Ceilings are eleven feet tall.

How to Apply

Send a SASE for information and application guidelines. Proposal should include eight 35 mm slides (no glass slides) of recent work (labeled according to instructions) with accompanying description sheet, a résumé, a brief statement (no more than one page) indicating why studio space is needed, other support materials only if necessary, and an adequate SASE for return of your slides. No videos, please.

Deadline

January 31, 1996. Notification by the end of March 1996.

Approximate Cost of a Four-week Residency

Transportation, housing, meals, materials, and incidentals.

SHENANDOAH INTERNATIONAL PLAYWRIGHTS RETREAT VA

Shenandoah International Playwrights Retreat
Pennyroyal Farm
Route 5, Box 167-F
Staunton, Virginia 24401

Attention: Robert Graham Small, Director
(703) 248-1868

Type of Facility/Award

Residency.

Who Can Apply

Writers for the stage and screen.

Provisos

None listed.

Dates of Operation

August.

Location

Virginia's Shenandoah Valley.

History

"At once a safe haven away from pressures and distractions of everyday life, and a stimulating, challenging environment for creative exploration, the Retreat has already nurtured the work of writers from thirty-eight states, sixteen countries, and six continents."

What They Offer

Ten playwrights (six representing cultures and nationalities from various regions of the world and four Americans) are selected each year to work and live in fellowship with a multicultural company of theatre artists. Room, board, and transportation are provided. The writers work in close and intensive collaboration with dramaturges, directors, and the acting company. "What occurs is a simultaneous on-the-feet/on-the-page exploration of each play, culminating in a staged reading before an audience of invited professionals and advocates. After several weeks of development, translation, and adaptation, Shenandoah's company of artists travel to New York City for performances of each writer's new play in a Festival of New Works for a New World."

Facility Description

The Pennyroyal Farm was built in 1808. It is the headquarters of ShenanArts, and the home of the Shenandoah International Playwrights Retreat. The farm has been a gathering place for theatre performance and fellowship for nearly fifty years.

How to Apply

Send a SASE for a brochure and guidelines. Submit two typed and bound copies of a draft of your proposed project (and an adequate SASE for their return), a personal statement and/or bio of your background as a writer, and a SASP for acknowledgment of receipt of your materials.

Deadline

March 1. Notification in early June.

Approximate Cost of a Four-week Residency

No cost except incidentals.

Siena College
INTERNATIONAL PLAYWRIGHT'S COMPETITION   NY

Siena College
Department of Fine Arts, Theatre Program
515 Loudon Road
Loudonville, New York 12211-1462

Attention: International Playwrights Competition
(518) 783-2300

Type of Facility/Award

Opportunity for Playwrights.

Who Can Apply

Playwrights.

Provisos

Scripts must be full-length, original, unpublished, unproduced, and free of royalty and copyright restrictions. No musicals. Plays that have had staged readings are acceptable, but not plays that have had workshop productions. Plays must require a unit set or minimal changes, be suitable for undergraduate performers, and require a cast of three to ten actors.

Dates of Operation
Spring.

Location
The college is located just north of Albany, New York.

History
"Siena College is a private undergraduate college of more than 2,700 full-time students founded by the Franciscan friars in 1937." Previous winners include *Territorial Rights* by Kerry Kennedy, *The Boston Boy* by Tomm Doyle, and *Killgarden* by Thomas Hinton.

What They Offer
The winning playwright will receive an honorarium of $2,000 and full production of the play by Siena College's Theatre Program in the Spring as part of its Theatre Series. Living expenses and transportation to and from the college (maximum $1,000) will be awarded to the winning playwright for a four- to six-week residency so he or she can participate in the rehearsal and design process, public discussions, and the academic life of the Siena community.

Facility Description
Siena College has a 310-seat black box theater.

How to Apply
Send a SASE for an application and brochure. Return completed application with your typed, bound script and a business-sized SASE. Include an adequate SASE if you want your script returned. If you send more than one script, include an adequate return SASE for each. Entries will only be accepted between February 1 and June 30. If you are a finalist, you will be asked to submit a copy of your educational and professional credentials, three letters of reference, and a documented production history of the submitted script.

Deadline
June 30 (received). Notification no later than September 30. (These are 1994 dates.)

Approximate Cost of a Four-week Residency
Transportation, housing, meals, and incidentals — offset by stipend and honorarium.

Sitka Center for Art and Ecology
Neskowin Coast Foundation
P.O. Box 65
Otis, Oregon 97368

Attention: Sitka Residency
(503) 994-5485

Type of Facility/Award

Artist-in-Residence Program.

Who Can Apply

Visual artists, naturalists, writers, and musicians.

Provisos

This program is designed for artists and naturalists who have earned a BA, BS, BFA or an MA, MS, MFA, or PhD degree, or for those who have equivalent professional experience. If you have had a residency at a nonprofit arts institution within the last two years, you are not eligible to apply. Preference is given to those doing research on the Oregon coast environment.

Dates of Operation

Fall (October 1 to January 15). Spring (February 1 to May 21).

Location

The Center is just north of Lincoln City on the Oregon coast. Located at Cascade Head Ranch, which is part of the Cascade Head National Scenic Research Area, the Center borders a Nature Conservancy Preserve, the Siuslaw National Experimental Forest, and the Salmon River Estuary. The Center is situated within a National Scenic Research area and a United Nations Biosphere Reserve.

History

Founded in 1970, the Neskowin Coast Foundation strives "to promote interest in and opportunity to study various forms of art and music and the ecology of the central Oregon coast." The Center was built in 1971. "Its unique geographic location and high caliber of instruction in the arts and natural sciences create an inspiring atmosphere for the educational, scientific, and artistic experience." Sitka offers year-round workshops in natural sciences and arts — book arts, botanical illustration, ceramics, ecology, fibers, drawing and painting, printmaking, and other media. Workshops are open to people of all ages and levels of experience. In addition to weekend workshops and week-long classes, the Center hosts a selection of evening events (lectures, slide shows, and films), summer workshops, and two open houses to bring the community together. "The Sitka Center fills a need on the central Oregon coast, offering the only program in the coastal environment combining fine arts, craft, and natural science, in a setting that inspires inquiry and discovery for all ages."

What They Offer

There are three categories: *Emerging Artist/Naturalist, Mid-Career Artist/Naturalist,* or *Artist/Naturalist on Sabbatical.* Residencies are for four months during the Fall or Spring. Shorter residencies may be available by arrangement. There is no stipend. The Center provides living accommodations and studio space in exchange for twenty hours per month of community service on behalf of Sitka. Residents are encouraged to hold an open studio or community outreach program at Sitka one day per month during the residency, or to present workshops. In January and May, Sitka hosts an exhibition of artists' works. Sitka charges a fee of twenty percent of the sales price for work produced and sold while at Sitka.

Facility Description

The Center is semi-isolated. The Boyden studio, which is the main workspace, is approximately 1,500 square feet. It can be shared by two residents. There is a Gallery Studio, which is 550 square feet, and a new studio of approximately 800 square feet, which may be used in coordination with printmaking and ongoing workshop activities. Residents live in the Morley House or in Russ's Treehouse. Both are self-contained and are equipped with a sleeping loft, a kitchen, and a bathroom.

How to Apply

Send a SASE for an application and brochure. Return completed application form with a description of your project, the names of three references, a résumé, two letters of recommendation, and samples of your work (with an adequate SASE for their return). Appropriate work samples would include slides, a written manuscript, a thesis, or a copy of a published work.

Deadline

June 20.

Approximate Cost of a Four-week Residency

Transportation, meals, materials, and incidentals.

SKOWHEGAN SCHOOL OF PAINTING AND SCULPTURE ME

Skowhegan School of Painting and Sculpture
Skowhegan, Maine
(207) 474-9345

Information/brochures/registration:
Skowhegan School of Painting and Sculpture
200 Park Avenue South, Suite 1116
New York, New York 10003-1503

Attention: Summer Residency Program for Advanced Visual Artists
(212) 529-0505

Type of Facility/Award
Residency.

Who Can Apply
Advanced visual artists (painting, sculpture, fresco, installation, and performance artists). Art school students are welcome to apply.

Provisos
Artists may attend Skowhegan only once. No artists under nineteen years of age. Foreign students will be considered if they are proficient in English and can secure appropriate visa. Skowhegan does not discriminate on the basis of racial or ethnic origins, sex or sexual orientation, religious affiliation, or handicapped status.

Dates of Operation
Mid-June to mid-August.

Location
Skowhegan is located in the heavily forested lake district of Central Maine.

History
Skowhegan was founded in 1946 by artists for artists. The intense nine-week summer residency program allows sixty-five talented artists to produce their art in a communal, rural environment of great natural beauty. The session does not offer structured classes. "Instead, it provides an extended and concentrated period of independent work, done with the critical assistance and camaraderie of resident and visiting artists." Since no artist is allowed to return, it is a once-in-a-lifetime experience. One out of four attendees goes on to become a practicing artist.

What They Offer
Skowhegan is a nine-week summer session where artists work independently (on projects of their choice), receiving weekly visits by a panel of rotating professional artists (brochure lists many well-known professionals) who offer one-on-one critiques of works-in-progress. No structured workshops are offered — just ample time to work without limitations. Risk-taking is encouraged. The program is recognized and accepted for credit by most art schools and universities around the country. Some financial assistance is available. The *Matching School Fellowship Program* offers one full-tuition fellowship to the student with the highest ranking in the selection process who is enrolled in a participating school. Other full and partial tuition waivers are available based on need. In addition to slide shows and lectures offered by the current staff of art professionals, there is an archive of slides and tapes (left by previous professionals who have taught at Skowhegan) available for private or group viewing. Fees include tuition of $4,900 for the entire nine-week session, an activities fee of $15, and an application fee of $30. Each artist is provided with living quarters, all meals, and studio space. Artists must provide their own blankets, sheets, and towels. This is one of few schools to provide instruction in fresco. All attending artists are encouraged to experiment in fresco. No pets allowed.

Facility Description

Set on 300 heavily forested acres, Skowhegan is comprised of four large houses and a cottage situated on the edge of a large, loon lake. Each artists usually shares a room with one or two other artists. Bath facilities are also shared. The Robert Lehman Library has over 15,000 art books, catalogs, and bound magazines, as well as historical information on Maine and the environment. Studios are surrounded by woods and rolling cow pastures. All facilities, including the Common House, are open twenty-four hours a day for everyone's use. The lake offers excellent swimming, and sometimes artists organize special events like volleyball games, poetry readings, costume balls, or other social or sports events.

There is a machine shop and a darkroom. Equipment is provided for working in wood, metal, clay, terra cotta, and wax. There is an assortment of power tools, as well as a pneumatic hammer and gas/arc and MIG welding equipment. There is a small art supply store on campus.

How to Apply

Send a SASE for an application and brochure. Return completed "Form A for Admission" with a $30 nonrefundable application fee. "Form A" asks for two references, a list of professional schools and/or colleges attended, and your activities since then. Return completed "Form B" (simultaneously) if you are requesting financial assistance or a fellowship. All artists must submit twelve 35 mm slides labeled according to instructions and accompanied by a descriptive sheet. Do not submit video tapes. The $30 fee covers the cost of returning these application materials to you. If accepted, you will need to provide a doctor's certificate and two photographs.

Deadline

February 10 (postmarked) for forms A & B. March 3 (postmarked) for evidence of need. Notification in early April. (1995 dates.)

Approximate Cost of a Four-week Residency

$4,945, plus transportation, some materials, and incidentals. Fellowships/financial assistance available. (Amount quoted is for the nine-week session — 1995 rates.)

SLEEPING BEAR DUNES NATIONAL LAKESHORE   MI

Sleeping Bear Dunes National Lakeshore
P.O. Box 277
9922 Front Street (Highway M-72)
Empire, Michigan 49630

Attention: Neil Bullington
(616) 326-5134 or (616) 326-5382 Fax

Type of Facility/Award

Artist-in-Residence Program.

Who Can Apply

All visual artists.

Provisos

The program is for American artists. The artist should be in good health, self-sufficient, and expect to work closely with the park staff to achieve the goals of the program. Selections are made without regard to race, religion, sex, marital status, age, or national origin.

Dates of Operation

First session: last three weeks of September. Second session: first three weeks of October. (1995 dates.)

Location

Located in the northwest corner of Michigan's lower peninsula, Sleeping Dunes National Lakeshore stretches fifty-seven kilometers along Lake Michigan's eastern coastline between the towns of Frankfort and Leland. Traverse City is just forty kilometers to the east.

History

"Artists have had a long-standing influence on the formation, expansion, and direction of our National Parks. Painting landscapes of the American West, artists publicized many of the natural wonders of a land little known to Eastern residents. This body of work helped to stimulate the establishment of many of our National Parks and to foster a continuing appreciation of them." Artists today continue this process, translating the Parks' purpose as "places of pleasure and preservation into images that bring other people new insights, enjoyment, and understanding."

What They Offer

The program offers rent-free use of either a campsite in one of the developed mainland campgrounds, or a park house located in the vicinity of the village of Empire. Two three-week blocks of time are offered: the last three weeks of September or the first three weeks of October. Limited reimbursement for mileage and other out-of-pocket expenses during your park stay may be available. In return, the Park asks the artist to donate a piece of artwork produced during the residency, and to contribute to the advancement of the Park's mission by sharing their knowledge with the public by leading a talk, demonstration, or workshop. Residents should bring their own personal gear, food, and art or photo supplies.

Facility Description

Living accommodations (depending upon availability) are provided in a modern house with adjacent garage in or near Empire. The house has a stove, a refrigerator, and cooking/eating utensils. There is a rustic outbuilding that serves as a studio. The Platte River Campground is in the southern half of the Park and provides a modern environment. It has paved roads and parking, electrical hookups, running water, flush toilets, and coin-operated hot showers. The D. H. Day Campground is in the northern half of the Park near Glen Haven and provides a more primitive environment. It has unpaved roads and sites, cold water outlets, and vault toilets.

The region is hilly with massive coastal plateaus, sand dunes, and numerous clear lakes. There are quiet, tree-lined streams, imposing beech-maple forests, and rugged bluffs towering as high as 140 meters above Lake Michigan. "Because Sleeping Bear Dunes National Lakeshore offers so many varied cultural and natural resources, it offers an ideal location for creative endeavor."

How to Apply

Send a SASE for a brochure and application guidelines. Send your résumé, a summary of your creative work, eight slides of your recent work (and an adequate SASE for their return) accompanied by a descriptive sheet, a statement of what you hope to gain from a residency at Sleeping Bear Dunes National Lakeshore, a specific explanation of how you propose to assist the Lakeshore to further its mission, the period of residency you'd prefer, and the accommodations you'd prefer.

Deadline

May 13. Notification in early June. (1995 dates.)

Approximate Cost of a Four-week Residency

Transportation, meals, materials, and incidentals. (Limited reimbursement for mileage and other out-of-pocket expenses may be available.)

Smithsonian Institution
RENWICK GALLERY   DC

Renwick Gallery
Smithsonian Institution, MRC-107
Washington, D.C. 20560

Attention: Director, James Renwick Fellowship in American Crafts
(202) 357-2531

Type of Facility/Award

Fellowship.

Who Can Apply

Scholars.

Provisos

Applicants must be graduate, masters, predoctoral, or postdoctoral students knowledgeable in the history of twentieth-century American art, craft, or design. The Gallery is most interested in "research proposals concentrating on post-1930 craft developments or their historical antecedents."

Dates of Operation

Open year-round.

Location
Washington, D.C.

History
This award is funded by the National Museum of American Art and the James Renwick Alliance.

What They Offer
The Gallery offers research residencies of from three to twelve months at the Renwick Gallery. Residency is supported by a cash award (amount not specified).

Facility Description
None provided.

How to Apply
Send a SASE for an application and brochure. Follow instructions provided with those materials.

Deadline
Unknown.

Approximate Cost of a Four-week Residency
Transportation, housing, meals, materials, and incidentals — offset by fellowship.

SOAPSTONE   OR

Soapstone
622 SE 29th Avenue
Portland, Oregon 97214

Attention: Judith Barrington, Director
(503) 236-9862

Type of Facility/Award
Residency.

Who Can Apply
Writers.

Provisos
At present, residency awards are limited to women writers from the state of Oregon. Serious women writers from a wide diversity of cultures and backgrounds are invited to apply.

Dates of Operation
Soapstone is scheduled to open in 1996. It will operate six months of each year. Write for updated information.

Location

One and one-half hours from Portland in Oregon's Coast Range.

History

Soapstone was conceived as a place for women writers to find the peace and support they need to work on their projects. Directors Judith Barrington and Ruth Gundle (also directors of The Flight of the Mind writers' conference) have spent years raising funds for this project so that women, whose lives generally make it impossible for them to go away and concentrate on their writing, can put their own needs above those of others and do so. "The practical support and validation offered by an organization devoted to women's writing is essential to the creation of work that embodies the powerful truths of women's lives."

What They Offer

Two writers at a time, each with her own private sleeping and work spaces. They share a kitchen with a wood cookstove and a living room with a wood-burning stove for heat. The cabin has electricity. The septic system and a bathroom were scheduled for installation in 1995. Residency terms are from one week to one month. The future vision is to build additional studios in order to accommodate more writers. Tax-deductible donations to this worthwhile project are gratefully accepted. The directors have already raised first-stage funding. They are currently seeking an additional $50,000, as well as donations of skilled and unskilled labor, materials, and professional assistance of various kinds. If you have particular skills you can offer, please contact them. Although acceptance into the program constitutes a fellowship, those who can afford to contribute to the cost of their stay are encouraged to do so. (Since at the time of publication, the retreat had not yet opened, the scope of the entire offering had not been fully defined.)

Facility Description

A twenty-four-acre expanse of densely forested alder, hemlock, cedar, maple, and fir, Soapstone is home to a variety of wildlife, including deer, elk, and beaver. There is nearly a mile of creek running through the property. In the winter, the salmon-spawning creek swells to a thirty-foot wide river. In the summer, it sports two fishing holes. The sound of water coursing through a series of rapids can be heard year round from anywhere on the property. The original cabin was built by a Portland artist and architect. The interior, with its series of lofts soaring up to the treetops, is beautifully finished in white pine, and topped by a cube-shaped study with bubble windows on four sides overlooking the creek. In 1992, the cabin was restored to good condition in preparation for expansion (to provide additional sleeping and work spaces).

How to Apply

Send a SASE for an application form and brochure. Return completed application along with samples of your writing and information about your proposed project. Friends or writing partners may apply together.

Deadline

Not yet defined.

Approximate Cost of a Four-week Residency

Unknown at time of publication. Be prepared to pay for transportation, meals, materials, and incidentals. Donations toward housing would be much appreciated.

SONTERRA CONDOMINIUMS   NM

Sonterra Condominiums
206 Siler Road
Box 5244
Taos, New Mexico 87571

Attention: Sharon Fredericks, Owner
(505) 758-7989

Type of Facility/Award

Retreat.

Who Can Apply

Anyone.

Provisos

None listed.

Dates of Operation

Open year-round.

Location

Residential area of Taos, four blocks from the historic Taos Plaza. Taos offers breathtaking scenery, over eighty art galleries, unusual historic sites (including the Taos Pueblo), and premier skiing.

History

None provided.

What They Offer

Ten one-bedroom condominiums are available on a daily, weekly, or monthly basis. Rates for two guests are as listed below. Additional guests are $10 each (maximum four). Children are considered guests. Taxes are additional. Maid service is available for an additional fee. These 1995 rates are subject to change. Call for current rates.

Dates	Daily	Monthly
April 10–30 Nov. 1–22	$49/$59	$675/$750
May 1–June 30	$59/$69	$800/$900

Dates	Daily	Monthly
July 1–Oct. 31 Nov. 23–Dec. 15 Jan. 3–31 Mar. 26–Apr. 9	$69/$79	$1,000/$1,100
Dec. 16–Jan. 2	$99/$109	No monthly

Facility Description

Each unit under 450 square foot is individually furnished in the warm southwestern style; some have traditional kiva fireplaces. The bedroom opens onto a private patio. The bathroom has a shower only, and access is through the bedroom. Units are not air-conditioned. Amenities include a generously equipped kitchen, color cable television, and a guest laundry. Surrounded by an adobe wall and latilla fence, the condominiums face an inner courtyard with a graceful Mexican fountain and flower gardens. No pets allowed. Also available are the Wild Rose Casita, the Columbine Casita, and a 2100-square-foot main house, all located on a six-acre compound near the mouth of the Valdez Valley. Call for rates on these facilities.

How to Apply

Call or write for reservations. First-come, first-served.

Deadline

None.

Approximate Cost of a Four-week Residency

$675 to $1,100, plus transportation, meals, materials, and incidentals.

Southern Oregon State College
WALDEN RESIDENCY   OR

Southern Oregon State College
Extended Campus Programs
The Walden Residency
Ashland, Oregon 97520

Attention: Celeste Stevens
(503) 552-6331 or (503) 552-6047 Fax

Type of Facility/Award

Residency.

Who Can Apply

Writers (fiction, creative nonfiction, poets, playwrights, essayists, and all other creative writers).

Provisos

Applicants must be residents of the state of Oregon and must be nonsmokers.

Dates of Operation

March through August. (Dates vary from year to year.)

Location

Ten minutes from Gold Hill, Oregon, and forty minutes from Ashland.

History

This award, offered since 1987, is sponsored by a private citizen.

What They Offer

The residency is for three to six weeks. Housing in the cabin is provided and there is no charge for utilities. Partial board is provided (specific details were unavailable). All residents must do their own cooking and keep the cabin in good order. In exchange, residents are asked to acknowledge the assistance of the Walden Fellowship in any publications resulting from their work at the cabin.

Facility Description

The residency provides a fully furnished cabin (suitable for one working writer) on a quiet and beautiful mountain farm in southern Oregon. The cabin sits on a meadow surrounded by forest. There is a phone nearby.

How to Apply

Send a SASE for an application and brochure. Return completed application, a project proposal, a list of your recent publications (if any), your choice of dates, and three copies (original and two copies) of a sample of your writing (from within the last five years). Appropriate samples would be eight to ten poems or no more than thirty pages of prose. Samples should be representative of the genre in which you intend to write during the residency. Be sure to enclose an adequate SASE if you want your writing sample returned. Enclose an additional SASE if you would like to be notified of the winners.

Deadline

November 30 (postmarked). Notification by mid-December.

Approximate Cost of a four-week Residency

Transportation, some meals, materials, and incidentals.

Stanford University
CREATIVE WRITING FELLOWSHIPS   CA

Stanford Writing Program
Creative Writing Fellowships
Stanford University
Stanford, California 94305-2087

Attention: Program Coordinator
(No telephone number given)

Type of Facility/Award
Fellowship.

Who Can Apply
Writers of all schools, e.g., naturalism, realism, new formalism, modernism, and post-modernism.

Provisos
No degree is required for admission. No degree is awarded. When reviewing the writer's portfolio, the program is looking for potential for growth and the ability to contribute to and benefit from their writing workshops. No fellowships are offered for work in drama or in nonfiction prose.

Dates of Operation
Academic year.

Location
Stanford University is located just south of San Francisco, California.

History
The program has been in existence for over forty years. Ten of the fellowships are named for Wallace Stegner, founder of the Stanford Writing Program. The other ten are named for: Karen O. Brownstein, Truman Capote, Harriet Doerr, Elsie P. Ettinger, Scott Clarkson Kovas, Jean Lane, Joan Lane, Edith R. Mirrielees, Richard P. Scowcroft, and Sheila and Walter Weisman.

What They Offer
"Each year, the program awards at least twenty fellowships — ten in poetry and ten in fiction. Fellowships are awarded for two years, depending upon satisfactory performance. The terms of the fellows are staggered so that there are five new poetry fellows and five new fiction fellows each year." Fellowships include a living stipend of $13,000 and workshop tuition of nearly $5,000. Total for the two years is approximately $36,000. Stipend is paid in equal installments at the end of each month of the academic year. Fellows must register for and participate in the writing workshop. Members read and criticize each other's work. They also participate in various events sponsored by the program and occasionally serve as judges for undergradu-

ate writing prizes. Winners of fellowships will receive an official application form by April 15, which must be filled out and returned with all required credentials, such as college transcripts (although possession of a college degree is not a consideration in evaluating candidate's suitability for the program).

Facility Description

University campus. Brochure does not mention on-campus housing provisions.

How to Apply

Send a SASE for an application and brochure. Return completed application with a $25 processing fee, a statement briefly explaining your writing plans and what the fellowship would contribute to them, two letters of recommendation, and a manuscript. Poetry: send a small group of poems (ten to fifteen pages). Fiction: send no more than 9,000 words — either two stories (three if they are very short) or up to forty pages of a novel. Fiction manuscripts must be typed and double spaced. Also complete and return the mailing labels that come with your application packet.

Deadline

No later than the first working day after January 1 of the year in which the fellowship is to begin. Applicants will be notified by early April.

Approximate Cost of a Four-week Residency

$25, plus transportation, housing, meals, materials, and incidentals — offset by stipend.

STUDIO MUSEUM IN HARLEM   NY

The Studio Museum in Harlem
144 West 125th Street
New York, New York 10027

Attention: Artists-in-Residence Program Coordinator
(212) 864-4500

Type of Facility/Award

Artist-in-Residence Program.

Who Can Apply

Visual artists.

Provisos

Emerging African-American artists, and other artists from Africa and the African Diaspora, including sculptors, painters, printmakers, photographers, fiber artists are encouraged to apply.

Dates of Operation

Open year-round.

Location

New York City.

History

"The Studio Museum in Harlem is a fine arts museum whose mission is the study, documentation, collection, preservation, and exhibition of the art and artifacts of Black America and the African Diaspora." For more than a quarter of a century, the museum has supported an artists-in-residence program whose consistent avoidance of stylistic or theoretical straitjacketing has been a lesson to other museum programs. The list of past participants is impressive.

What They Offer

Three emerging artists per year are awarded studio space and a fellowship (amount not specified) for a period of twelve months. Artists have access to museum facilities during designated hours, but must spend a minimum of twenty hours per week working in their studio. An exhibition of the artists' work will be presented toward the end of the residency in the Museum's galleries. Resident artists must also conduct two public workshops or presentations during their year in residence and may occasionally be asked to meet with museum visitors.

Facility Description

Art studios/gallery.

How to Apply

Send a SASE for an application form and brochure. Return completed application with a résumé, two letters of recommendation, catalog cuts, reviews, slides, or other support materials.

Deadline

May 26.

Approximate Cost of a Four-week Residency

Transportation, housing, meals, materials, and incidentals — offset by fellowship.

THE SYVENNA FOUNDATION   TX

The Syvenna Foundation
Route 1, Box 193
Linden, Texas 75563

Attention: Barbara Carroll, Associate Director
(903) 835-8252

Notice: The Syvenna Foundation discontinued its residency program for women writers in May of 1994. The above telephone number is disconnected. No inquiries, please.

THEATER AT LIME KILN   VA

Theater at Lime Kiln
14 South Randolph Street
Lexington, Virginia 24450

Attention: Eleanor Connor, Community Liaison/Dramaturge
(No telephone number given)

Type of Facility/Award

Opportunity for playwrights.

Who Can Apply

Playwrights.

Provisos

Playwrights whose (submitted) material is limited geographically to Appalachia
(Virginia, Western North Carolina, West Virginia, Eastern Kentucky, and Eastern
Tennessee) are invited to apply. Plays with music are encouraged.

Dates of Operation

Summer.

Location

Facility is an outdoor theater set in the ruins of an abandoned lime quarry and kiln
outside Lexington, Virginia.

History

"Founded in 1983, Lime Kiln has built a body of work steeped in the heritage and
culture of the Southern mountains. We have produced ten world premieres in ten
years. By presenting works of theater reflective of the indigenous stories and music of
the region, we seek to foster a better understanding of our past, present, and future."

What They Offer

Cash prize of $1,000 and a staged reading for first-place winner. Cash prize of $500
and a staged reading for second-place winner. There is a possibility of full production for winning scripts. The funding for this award is provided by a grant from the
Lila Wallace-Readers Digest Fund's Theaters for New Audiences Fund.

Facility Description

Set in an abandoned lime quarry, the lovely outdoor theater has stone ruins as a
stage and a star-studded sky as a roof. During the summer, actors and musicians
provide audiences with a unique entertainment experience where stone masons
previously plied their trade and red-hot kilns burned with the making of lime.

How to Apply

Send a SASE for an application and brochure. Return completed application with
a securely bound and legible script (no television or film scripts), a biography of the

author, history of the play, and a short synopsis. Title page of the script must show name, address, and telephone number of author. Only one submission per author is allowed. The play must be previously unpublished or unproduced (developmental workshops okay). Enclose a SASP if you want receipt of your script acknowledged. No rewrites or revisions will be accepted after submission.

Deadline

Submissions accepted between August 1 and September 30. (1994 dates.)

Approximate Cost of a Four-week Residency

Transportation, housing, meals, and incidentals — offset by cash award.

JAMES THURBER RESIDENCY PROGRAM   OH

The Thurber House
77 Jefferson Avenue
Columbus, Ohio 42315

Attention: Michael J. Rosen, Literary Director
(614) 464-1032 or (614) 228-7445 Fax

Type of Facility/Award

Artist-in-Residence.

Who Can Apply

Poets, playwrights, and journalists.

Provisos

Poets: must have published at least one book with a major publisher and should possess some experience in teaching. *Playwrights:* should have had at least one play published and/or produced by a significant company and must show some aptitude for teaching. *Journalists:* should have experience in reporting, feature writing, reviewing, or other areas of journalism, as well as significant publications. Experience as a teacher or writing coach is helpful.

Dates of Operation

Poets: Autumn 1996 or Winter 1997. Playwrights: Winter or Spring 1997. Journalists: Summer and Autumn 1996 or Spring or Summer 1997. Call or write for succeeding years' dates.

Location

The Thurber House is within walking distance of downtown Columbus, Ohio.

History

James Thurber's boyhood home, The Thurber House, was opened as a literary center in 1984. It is unique in its combination of historic preservation of Thurber archives, literary programming, bookstore, children's writing academy, and writer's residencies. Since 1984, more than a dozen residents have spent time living and working at the house. The center also sponsors a lecture series called Evenings With Authors. In the summer they sponsor Literary Picnics.

What They Offer

Award includes housing (and work space) in a furnished, third-floor apartment of the Thurber House and a stipend of $5,000 for the academic quarter. Each writer will have limited responsibilities as follows: *Poets* will teach a writing class in the Creative Writing Program at Ohio State University (two afternoons each week), and will offer one public reading, and a short workshop for writers in the community. *Playwrights* will teach one class in playwriting in the Theatre Department at Ohio State University (two afternoons each week), and will have one play considered for a public reading, mounting, or production by the school's Theatre Department. *Journalists* will teach at the Ohio State University School of Journalism (one afternoon each week) and will act as the writing coach for reporters at *The Columbus Dispatch* approximately eight hours each week.

Facility Description

The Thurber House is listed on the National Register of Historic Places. It is a "faithfully restored version of a nineteen-teens dwelling for a family of modest means. Mission oak furniture, oiled pine flooring, beveled glass windows, and lace curtains characterize this home."

How to Apply

Send a SASE for a brochure and submittal guidelines. Then send a letter of interest with your curriculum vitae to the Literary Director any time before December 15. A field of writers will be selected in each genre to complete an official application form and to send writing samples. Selected writers will be brought to Columbus for an interview. Final choices will be announced in March.

Deadline

December 15 (postmarked) for letter of interest. January 1 for application and samples (if requested). Notification in March.

Approximate Cost of a Four-week Residency

Transportation, meals, materials, and incidentals — offset by stipend.

THE UCROSS FOUNDATION   WY

The Ucross Foundation Residency Program
2836 U. S. Highway 14 — 16 East
Clearmont, Wyoming 82835

Attention: Elizabeth Guheen, Executive Director
(307) 737-2291

Type of Facility/Award

Residency.

Who Can Apply

Painters, poets, sculptors, photographers, printmakers, composers, authors, play-wrights, storytellers, filmmakers, video, and interdisciplinary artists.

Provisos

Ucross accepts applications from artists in all creative disciplines and areas of interest provided the project has significance in its field. Quality of work is the primary consideration.

Dates of Operation

Open year-round.

Location

The Colony is located "at the confluence of Piney, Clear, and Coal Creeks in Ucross, Wyoming." The retreat is twenty-seven miles southeast of Sheridan in the rugged foothills of the Big Horn Mountains. Sheridan is served by commuter airlines via Denver, Colorado. By car, Ucross is located at the point where U.S. Highways 14 and 16 intersect, seventeen miles north of Buffalo, Wyoming.

History

"The Ucross Foundations was established to promote the fullest development of human potential by supporting a range of activities and independent research appropriate to the setting and its resources and facilities. Upon incorporation as a non-profit organization on June 1, 1981, the primary objectives included the restoration of the historic Clear Fork headquarters of the Pratt and Ferris Cattle Company (the complex of buildings known as Big Red and built in 1882), the promotion of the preservation of other historical sites in the area through education and conferences, and the provision of facilities and program activities for an artists-in-residence project. The Ucross Foundation Residency Program opened its doors in 1983."

What They Offer

Approximately sixty residents are selected each year. The Foundation provides eight residents (four writers and four visual artists at a time) with studio space, living accommodations, meals, and time to concentrate on their work. Residency terms are from two to eight weeks. Meals are prepared by a professional kitchen staff and served in the School House dining room. Residents must provide their own transportation to the Colony. Collaborators must apply separately. While there is no charge for a residency, the Ucross Foundation depends on both public and private support to continue to provide an optimum retreat environment.

Facility Description

The site is 22,000 acres of High Plains landscape, with a complex of buildings known as Big Red. The largest building is the Big Red Barn, which houses four studios, a gallery, and a conference area. A printmaking facility is included and a small maintenance fee is charged for its use. Additional studios are located at the Kocur Writers' Retreat along the bank of Clear Creek north of Big Red. The Clearmont Depot provides private living quarters as well as laundry facilities. All studios have natural light, running water, and private entrances. The Ucross School House has private bedrooms, laundry facilities, and living and dining areas. The facility is handicapped-accessible.

How to Apply

Send a SASE for an application form and brochure. Return four copies of each of the following: the completed Ucross Information Form (one copy must be the original); a résumé; a description of your intended project; three letters of personal reference (two from authorities in your field); and a sample of your recent work. Include a SASE adequate for return of your materials. Appropriate work samples vary by category of art. *Writers, scholars, and scientists:* send ten pages of poetry or twenty pages of other work (work must be recent — published or unpublished). *Musicians and composers:* send a cassette, record, or other audio form of work. *Visual artists:* send a representative selection of ten to fifteen slides of your recent work (packaged and labeled according to instructions) with an accompanying descriptive sheet. Submit one work sample and four full sets of all other materials. If you would like notification that your application and materials were received, please include a SASP.

Deadline

October 1 for February to early June. March 1 for early August to early December. Notification in eight weeks.

Approximate Cost of a Four-week Residency

Transportation, materials, and incidentals.

United States Institute of Peace
JENNINGS RANDOLPH FELLOWSHIPS   DC

United States Institute of Peace
1550 M Street, N.W., Suite 700
Washington, D. C. 20005-1708

Attention: Jennings Randolph Program for International Peace
(202) 457-1700 Institute, (202) 429-3886 Program, or (202) 429-6063 Fax

Type of Facility/Award
Fellowships.

Who Can Apply
Doctoral students are eligible for the Peace Scholar Award.

Scholars, diplomats, public leaders, and professionals may compete for the Distinguished Fellow Award.

Provisos
The Peace Scholar Fellowship is intended for outstanding students enrolled in a recognized doctoral program in a U.S. university. All course work and examinations (not the dissertation) must be completed before the beginning of the Fellowship term. Peace Scholar awards may not be deferred or combined with any major award or fellowship unless approved in advance by the Institute.

The Distinguished Fellow is available for scholars, diplomats, public leaders, and professionals who have achieved exceptional international stature and recognition by virtue of their extraordinary academic or practical contributions to one or more fields. There is no specific degree-requirement for this award, but applicants typically will have completed at least an undergraduate degree.

The Institute welcomes applications from citizens of all nations and all walks of life. Women and members of minority groups are especially encouraged to apply. Also scholars and researchers, educators of students and citizens, and those who are practitioners in international security, peacemaking, and public affairs.

Dates of Operation
Fellowships are for one year each beginning in September.

Location
The Peace Scholar works at his or her own university. The Distinguished Fellow spends his or her year in residence at the Institute.

History
"The Jennings Randolph Program for International Peace enables outstanding scholars, practitioners, and students to focus their learning, practical experience, leadership abilities, and communication skills on a broad variety of issues concerning

conflict and peace. It achieves this goal through providing fellowship support for individual research and education projects proposed by the fellowship candidate and through arranging program-wide activities designed to promote mutual learning, collegiality, and wider dissemination of the fellows' work. Named for the former United States Senator from West Virginia, whose efforts over four decades helped to establish the Institute, the Jennings Randolph Program has awarded 142 fellowships since it began in 1987." (1994/95.)

What They Offer

For 1995/96 there are two different fellowships offered:

The Peace Scholar is for a doctoral student researching and writing his or her dissertation at their home university and carries a stipend of $14,000.

The Distinguished Fellow spends a year in residence at the Institute participating in Institute-sponsored conferences, outreach activities, and the collegial life of the Institute. The stipend for this fellowship is based on the recipient's salary for the preceding twelve months, but cannot exceed the GS-15/10 level of the federal pay scale, which for 1994 was $86,589 per year. It is expected the Fellow will devote his or her full attention to completing his or her project within the agreed-upon time. This award also provides contributions toward health insurance (if needed), use of an office and a Macintosh word processor, research assistance, and, subject to availability of funds, appropriate levels and kinds of assistance to complete the fellowship project. Additionally, the Institute provides one round trip to Washington, D.C., at the beginning and end of the fellowship period for the Fellow and dependents who reside with the Fellow during the entire fellowship period.

Facility Description

Federal office building.

How to Apply

Send a 9" x 12" SASE with $1.21 in postage for an application and brochure. It is recommended you thoroughly familiarize yourself with the Institute and the Program before applying. For Peace Scholars: return completed application, a description of your proposed dissertation work, a letter of support from your primary dissertation adviser, graduate transcripts, and two current letters of reference. For Distinguished Fellows: return completed application, a résumé, a description of your proposed project, a writing sample, and three letters of reference.

Deadline

December 1 for the Peace Scholar Award. October 16 for the Distinguished Fellow Award. (1995 dates.)

Approximate Cost of a Four-week Residency

Housing, meals, some materials, and incidentals — offset by stipend.

University of Arizona
POETRY CENTER
AZ

The University of Arizona
Poetry Center
1216 N. Cherry Avenue
Tucson, Arizona 85719

Attention: Residency Program
(602) 321-7760

Type of Facility/Award
Residency.

Who Can Apply
Writers.

Provisos
The University of Arizona Poetry Center is looking for writers who, at the time of submission, have not published more than one full-length work (self-published works and chapbooks are excepted). Unpublished writers are encouraged to apply.

Dates of Operation
Summer (dates are negotiable).

Location
University of Arizona campus.

History
None provided.

What They Offer
A one-month residency for an individual writer. Dates are negotiable.

Facility Description
The recipient is housed in a historic adobe guest cottage two blocks from the University of Arizona campus and two houses away from the Poetry Center.

How to Apply
Send a SASE for guidelines. Then send a letter with name, address, phone, and titles of submitted work, along with three copies of no more than ten pages of poetry or twenty pages of prose and a SASE for their reply. Manuscripts are not returned.

Deadline
Send materials between February 15 and March 15. Winner notified by May 1.

Approximate Cost of a Four-week Residency
Transportation, meals, materials, and incidentals.

University of California at Los Angeles
CENTER FOR 17ᵀᴴ AND 18ᵀᴴ
CENTURY STUDIES   CA

University of California at Los Angeles (UCLA)
Center for 17th and 18th Century Studies

For Ahmanson/Getty fellowships contact:
William Andrews Clark Memorial Library
395 Dodd Hall, UCLA
405 Hilgard Avenue
Los Angeles, California 90024-1404

Attention: Fellowship Coordinator
(310) 206-8552 or (310) 206-8577 Fax

For all other fellowships, contact:
William Andrews Clark Memorial Library
2520 Cimarron Street
Los Angeles, California 90018-2098

Attention: Fellowship Coordinator
(213) 735-7605 or (213) 731-8617 Fax

Type of Facility/Award
Fellowship.

Who Can Apply
Scholars.

Provisos
Scholars with Ph.D. degree who might benefit from research in the extensive holdings of the William Andrews Clark Memorial Library are invited to apply.

Dates of Operation
Academic quarters.

Location
Los Angeles, California.

History
"The Center for the 17th and 18th Century Studies, an organized research unit of the University of California, provides a forum for the discussion of central issues in the study of the 17th and 18th centuries, facilitates research and publication, supports scholarship, and encourages the creation of interdisciplinary, cross-cultural programs that advance the understanding of this important period. The William Andrews Clark Memorial Library, which is administered by the Center, is known for its collections on 17th and 18th century Britain, Oscar Wilde and the 1890's, the history of printing, and certain aspects of the American West."

What They Offer

The University offers various fellowship programs. *The Ahmanson/Getty Postdoctoral Residential Fellowship*, which is theme-based (theme changes annually), carries a stipend of $9,200 per quarter. Award is for two or three academic quarters. *The Clark Short-Term Fellowship* is a residential award for one to three months and carries a stipend of $1,500 per month. *The ASECS/Clark Fellowship* is for one-month resident fellowships and carries a stipend of $1,500. *The Predoctoral Fellowship*, which is a three-month resident fellowship, carries a stipend of $4,500.

Facility Description

University campus library.

How to Apply

Send a SASE for brochure and application materials. Then respond as directed for specific fellowships.

Deadline

March 15.

Approximate Cost of a Four-week Residency

Transportation, housing, meals, materials, and incidentals — offset by stipend.

University of Nebraska
GREAT PLATTE RIVER PLAYWRIGHTS FESTIVAL   NE

University of Nebraska
Great Platte River Playwrights Festival
UNK Theatre
Kearney, Nebraska 68849

Attention: Director
(308) 234-8406

Type of Facility/Award

Opportunity for playwrights.

Who Can Apply

Playwrights.

Provisos

None listed.

Dates of Operation

Annual competition.

Location

University of Nebraska campus, Kearney, Nebraska.

History
None provided.

What They Offer
Winners of the competition receive cash awards of $500 for first place, $300 for second place, and $200 for third place. In addition, winners have their plays developed and produced by the University. Winning playwrights also receive travel expenses and housing on the University campus while the play is in production.

Facility Description
University campus.

How to Apply
Send a SASE for application guidelines. Then send two copies of an original, unpublished play (or play in progress) on any subject (although Great Plains themes are encouraged) for entry in one of the following categories: (1) *Adult* — drama or comedy, (2) *Musical* — drama or comedy (include tape), (3) *Historical* — drama or comedy, and (4) *Native American* — drama or comedy. You may submit more than one entry. If you want your manuscript (and tape, if applicable) returned, you must enclose an adequate SASE.

Deadline
April 1.

Approximate Cost of a Four-week Residency
Meals and incidentals.

University of New Mexico
D. H. LAWRENCE FELLOWSHIP   NM

University of New Mexico
D. H. Lawrence Fellowship
Department of English Language and Literature
Humanities Building 217
Albuquerque, New Mexico 87131-1106

Attention: Scott P. Sanders, Chair, D. H. Lawrence Fellowship Committee
(505) 277-6347

Notice: This program was suspended by the University of New Mexico for expansion of the facilities at the D.H. Lawrence Ranch north of Taos. The program is being revised to incorporate increased and more diverse uses of the Ranch as a conference center, an artists' retreat, and a place of learning, creativity, and contemplation in areas both in and out of the arts. Watch for announcement of the reinstatement of the fellowship in the appropriate literary listings. Reinstatement should occur within two to three years. (3/95.) The information listed below is outdated, but shows the structure of the fellowship in 1991/92.

Type of Facility/Award
Residency.

Who Can Apply
Poets, fiction writers, and dramatists.

Provisos
Applicants must work in English.

Dates of Operation
June to August.

Location
Sagre de Cristo Mountains near Taos, New Mexico.

History
Established 1958.

What They Offer
One fellowship. Includes June to August residency and a $700 stipend. Families are welcome.

Facility Description
Resident is housed in a four-room house at the D. H. Lawrence Ranch.

How to Apply
Send a SASE for an application form and brochure. Return completed application, a work sample, a résumé, and a project description.

Deadline
January 31.

Approximate cost of a Four-week Residency
Transportation, meals, materials, and incidentals — offset by stipend.

University of Texas at Austin
THE DOBIE PAISANO FELLOWSHIPS   TX

Office of Graduate Studies
University of Texas at Austin
Main Building 101, Mail Code 10400
Austin, Texas 78712

Attention: Audrey N. Slate, Ph.D., Director of the Dobie Paisano Project
(512) 471-7213, (512) 471-7620 Fax, or GSANS@UTXDP.DP.UTEXAS.EDU

Type of Facility/Award
Residency.

Who Can Apply
Writers.

Provisos
The program is offered exclusively to writers who are native Texans, writers living in Texas, writers who have previously lived in Texas for two or more years, or writers whose lives and published works have been substantially identified with the State of Texas or whose published works focused on a Texas subject. (For native, current, and past Texas residents, there is no restriction on subject matter.)

Dates of Operation
February 1 to July 31. August 1 to January 31.

Location
The late J. Frank Dobie's ranch "Paisano" is located just west of Austin, Texas.

History
More than fifty writers and artists have won the fellowship since it was established in 1967. The Texas Institute of Letters and the University of Texas at Austin offer two residencies each year to stimulate the creative endeavor by making it possible for a person to work without distractions. One is the *Ralph A. Johnston Memorial Fellowship*, the other is the *Jesse H. Jones Writing Fellowship*.

What They Offer
The University of Texas Office of Graduate Studies selects two people each year to spend four to six months in residence at the Paisano ranch. Residencies take place either February through July or August through January. Residents live in a house on J. Frank Dobie's 265-acre ranch. Each award carries a stipend of $1,200 per month to offset living expenses. Families are welcome.

Facility Description
The house is simply but adequately furnished. All utilities and maintenance are provided by the University of Texas at Austin.

How to Apply

Send a SASE for an application and brochure. Mark the outside of the envelope "Dobie Paisano Application — 1996" (or appropriate year). Applications are mailed out in October. With the application fee of $10, return in triplicate the completed application, an outline of your project, and examples of your work.

Deadline

January 28. (1994 date. May vary slightly from year to year.)

Approximate Cost of a Four-week Residency

$10, plus transportation, meals, materials, and incidentals — offset by stipend.

University of Wisconsin
WISCONSIN INSTITUTE FOR CREATIVE WRITING   WI

Wisconsin Institute for Creative Writing
Department of English
University of Wisconsin
Madison, Wisconsin 53706

Attention: Director
(No telephone provided.)

Type of Facility/Award

Fellowship.

Who Can Apply

Writers.

Provisos

Poets and fictions-writers who have completed an MA, MFA, or equivalent degree in creative writing and who are working on a first book of poetry or fiction are invited to apply.

Dates of Operation

Academic year (August 15 to May 15).

Location

Madison, Wisconsin.

History

None given.

What They Offer

Time, space, and an intellectual environment, plus a fellowship in the amount of $17,000 for the academic year. Two awards are given annually. Fellows must teach one introductory creative writing workshop per semester and give one public reading from their work-in-progress. Fellows may also participate in other University English Department programs.

Facility Description
University campus.

How to Apply
Send a SASE for brochure. Submit a résumé, two letters of recommendation, one story of up to thirty pages in length (typed, double-spaced, and stapled) or ten pages of poetry (typed, single-spaced, and stapled), and one manuscript cover sheet including the applicant's name, address, telephone, social security number, and titles of works submitted. The applicant's name must not appear on any page of the manuscript except the cover sheet. Letters of recommendation may arrive under separate cover, but must be received in February. Include a #10 SASE for results.

Deadline
Applications are accepted throughout the month of February. Notification May 1.

Approximate Cost of a Four-week Residency
Transportation, housing, meals, materials, and incidentals — offset by fellowship.

THE URBAN INSTITUTE OF CONTEMPORARY ART   MI

The Urban Institute of Contemporary Art
88 Monroe Avenue N.W.
Grand Rapids, Michigan 49503

Attention: Marjorie Kuipers, Executive Director
(616) 454-7000 or (616) 454-7013

Notice: The Urban Institute of Contemporary Arts is currently inhabiting an interim facility with space limitations. They have scaled back many of their programs for lack of space. In 1997, they will move to their permanent home. At that time, they will be offering their full program to Artists-in-Residence, once again.

Type of Facility/Award
Artist-in-Residence Program.

Who Can Apply
Visual artists of all types, filmmakers, musicians, dancers, performance artists, writers, and interdisciplinary artists.

Provisos
None listed.

Dates of Operation
Open year-round.

Location

Grand Rapids, Michigan. The center used to be located on Race Street N.E. It is now temporarily located on Monroe Avenue N.W., where it will stay until the permanent facility is available in 1997. Contact for new address at the end of 1996.

History

"The Urban Institute for Contemporary Arts is dedicated to the development of a vital cultural community by generating and supporting innovative thought and creative activity."

What They Offer

The UICA Artist-in-Residence program is currently scaled back to only one award due to space limitations. In 1997, their full program (four AIR's) will be operational. The Institute provides artists with free studio space for two years. In return, the artists are expected to interact with the organization and with the community. "Visual artists are expected to exhibit, writers to read, filmmakers to screen, and musicians to perform." They also encourage gallery talks, workshops, etc.

Facility Description

None provided.

How to Apply

There are no positions available for 1996. If you are interested in applying for 1997/98, call the center. They are restructuring the program and may change their application procedures. Be sure to send a SASE if you request information by mail.

Deadline

None provided.

Approximate Cost of a Four-week Residency

Transportation, housing, meals, materials, and incidentals.

VALLECITOS RETREAT   NM

Vallecitos Retreat
P.O. Box 226
Vallecitos, New Mexico 87581

Attention: Elizabeth Esquer and Gina Covina, Directors
(505) 582-4226

Notice: The Vallecitos subsidized program is suspended until further notice. Call for current information.

Type of Facility/Award

Retreat.

Who Can Apply

Writers and artists or anyone seeking time and space for creative expression, a contemplative vacation, or a place to use as a home base while exploring northern New Mexico.

Dates of Operation

Open year-round.

Location

The retreat is located seventy miles north of Santa Fe, New Mexico. Ojo Caliente Hot Springs is a half-hour away and Taos is one hour away. The valley is surrounded by Carson National Forest. The Rio Vallecitos runs through the center.

History

The Retreat was established in 1990 by artists/writers Liz Esquer and Gina Covina. They received sponsoring support from the Santa Fe Council for the Arts and hoped to convert to nonprofit status so they could offer funded and/or work-exchange residencies in the future.

What They Offer

Vallecitos Retreat offers private rooms (big enough to also serve as studios) in an old adobe house for writers and visual artists. From June through September, breakfast and dinner are provided for an additional charge. 1993 rates were: Private room for one person: $30 per night/$160 per week. Private room for two people: $46 per night/$235 per week. There is a minimum stay of two nights. The monthly rate October through May is: $400 (one person); $600 (two people). The retreat is available for groups of up to ten people. Reservations are required. A deposit of one-half of the total amount is due when the reservation is made (or within one week of a phone reservation). Personal checks are accepted, but not credit cards. The balance is due upon arrival.

Facility Description

Vallecitos Retreat is a spacious adobe house surrounded by garden, orchard, and pasture, in a quiet northern New Mexico mountain valley. Some rooms are set up especially for visual artists. Natural lighting is excellent. Rooms are furnished with desks and comfortable chairs as well as double or queen beds. They can accommodate computers, looms, easels, and other tools brought by guests. All rooms have great views; all but one have doors leading directly to the garden or to the long covered porch. The bathrooms, kitchen, living room, and library are shared. The large kitchen is fully equipped with appliances — from wood cook stove to microwave.

How to Apply

There is no application process. Call to see if the program is operational or if they're accepting guests. If so, send a SASE for brochure, or call for reservations. Vallecitos is booked on a first-come, first-served basis.

Deadline

None.

Approximate cost of a Four-week Residency

$640, plus transportation, meals, materials, and incidentals during months June through September. $400, plus transportation, meals, materials, and incidentals during months October through May.

VERMONT STUDIO CENTER   VT

Vermont Studio Center
Box 613
Johnson, Vermont 05656

Attention: VSC Writing Program
(802) 635-2727 or (802) 635-2730 Fax

Notice: The Vermont Studio Center also has a residency program for Visual Artists. Unfortunately, specific details on that program were not included in the materials mailed to me by the Center. Please write (and enclose a SASE) or call for information on the Center's Visual Artists' Studio and Residency Programs. The program described below is for writers only.

Type of Facility/Award

Residency.

Who Can Apply

Writers, also Visual Artists (see Notice above).

Provisos

Established mid-career and emerging writers are invited to apply.

Dates of Operation

Open year-round.

Location

The Center is located in Johnson, Vermont, just twenty minutes from major hiking and ski areas. The drive from New York City is six and a half hours, from Boston, three and a half hours, from Montreal, two hours.

History

Founded by artists in 1984, "the Vermont Studio Center is the ideal creative community dedicated to supporting emerging and mid-career writers and artists. VSC provides the distraction-free time and space necessary to work, with the added inspiration of, and interaction with, the country's finest writers and artists."

What They Offer

Residencies at the Vermont Studio Center provide room, board, and uninterrupted time for work. Interaction with other artists at the Center is up to each individual. Four residencies per month are available year-round. Each writer is provided with a large private room (that also serves as a studio) with a large writing table and a reading lamp. Rooms are in individual houses in the village. Bathrooms are shared. Bed linens, pillows, blankets, and towels are provided. All meals are provided (and prepared by a celebrated gourmet chef!). Special diets cannot be accommodated. Fees are $750 for a two-week session or $1,400 for a four-week session. These fees are inclusive. Financial assistance of up to fifty percent is available on a work-exchange basis predicated on documented need (a copy of your tax return must be submitted with application). A limited number of full fellowships are also available. Additionally, if you schedule your residency in tandem with one of the Center's Writing Studio Sessions, the fee for two weeks is $600, instead of $750.

Note: "Two-thirds of the writers and artists who participate at VSC each year receive some form of financial assistance, so do not assume that you are ineligible. Apply early so your eligibility can be determined."

Facility Description

The Center is on the banks of the Gihon River. There are eighteen historic buildings on the site, all within walking distance of each other. There are studios, a lecture hall, dining facilities, a gallery, an art supply store, a lounge, offices, and residences. Nearby Johnson State College (a fifteen-minute walk) has a library, racquetball and tennis courts, a swimming pool, weight and aerobic rooms, and cross country ski and hiking trails. All are available for use by participants in VSC's program. Housing is provided in several Victorian homes in the village of Johnson.

How to Apply

Send a SASE for an application and brochure, indicating whether you want the brochure for writers or that for visual artists. Return completed application with a $25 nonrefundable application fee, a résumé, the names and addresses of three references (who are familiar with you and your work), and a sample of your published or unpublished work. Appropriate samples vary by category of art. *Poets:* five pages. *Fiction and nonfiction writers:* ten pages. *Playwrights and screenwriters:* ten pages. Additional writing samples may be requested during the selection process.

Deadline

October 15, if applying for full fellowship. Rolling application process for paid and work-exchange residencies. Notification within two weeks of receipt of application.

Approximate Cost of a Four-week Residency

$1,425, plus transportation, materials, and incidentals. Fifty-percent fee reduction for work-exchange program. A limited number of full fellowships available.

VILLA MONTALVO CENTER FOR THE ARTS   CA

Villa Montalvo Center for the Arts
15400 Montalvo Road
P.O. Box 158
Saratoga, California 95071-0158

Attention: Lori A. Wood, Artist Residency Coordinator
(408) 741-3421 or (408) 741-5592 Fax

Type of Facility/Award

Residency.

Who Can Apply

All artists and writers.

Provisos

"Anyone may apply who has completed formal training or the equivalent and is seriously engaged in the production of art." Established and emerging artists may apply. Couples must apply and will be considered separately. Accommodations for couples are limited. Prior residents must wait one year before reapplying.

Dates of Operation

October through March, with a few summer residencies.

Location

Villa Montalvo is located in the foothills of the Santa Cruz Mountains, about an hour's drive south of San Francisco, and a half-hour's drive from Santa Cruz. The small city of Saratoga is about a mile and a half from the Center, and Los Gatos is about four miles. Both have interesting specialty shops, pharmacies, restaurants, hardware stores, markets, and gas stations. The closest airport is in San Jose, which is about a half-hour's drive.

History

Villa Montalvo, a 19-room Mediterranean-style Villa on the National Register of Historic Places, was the home of James D. Phelan, a California politician. The Villa was built in 1912. Phelan invited many of the era's leading writers, musicians, and artists to perform at Montalvo and stay for a while as his guests. Senator Phelan's will stipulated that Montalvo be used as a public park and for the development of the arts. In 1942, the first artist residents were invited to the Villa. From April through October, Montalvo hosts a number of arts-related events that operate independently of the residency program.

What They Offer

Residencies range from one to three months. Villa Montalvo hosts only five residents at a time. Each resident has a furnished private apartment with a well-equipped kitchen, bed and bath linens, and minimal cleaning equipment. Residents are responsible for their own meals, materials, and incidentals. If you work on a computer, it will be necessary to bring a surge protector, since the Villa's electrical system was installed in 1912 and can't handle excessive draw. Four fellowships are awarded by the selection committee during the selection process. All applicants are considered for the fellowships, which are based solely on merit. One fellowship is designated specifically for a woman artist. Artists may be invited to hold open studios or share their work with interested members of the community. "The spring and summer months are most appropriate for artists seeking the lively atmosphere of an arts center, who do not need absolute solitude in order to create, and who enjoy having a wide variety of arts brought to their doorstep. The fall and winter season is most appropriate for artists who prefer a secluded, quiet setting in which to create." Keep this in mind when applying, since the Center's other year-round events and activities may conflict with your purpose. Residents are provided with complimentary tickets to the Center's events, including plays, concerts, dance performances, and readings, workshops, exhibits, and receptions. Because the road to the Villa is steep (one mile up a mountain road) the Center may seem remote, so having a car to use while you're in residence might be helpful. Also, in the past, the Center has sponsored a biennial (deadline in odd-numbered years) poetry competition. Included with first prize is a one-month residency at Villa Montalvo.

Facility Description

Villa Montalvo's grounds are maintained as a public park by Santa Clara County. The 175-acre site includes redwoods and formal gardens. There are four or five miles of hiking trails. The Center has two theaters, a gallery, a public arboretum, and wedding facilities. There are two studio apartments (with pianos) on the second floor of the Villa. Nearby, in the guest house, there are two one-bedroom apartments (with pianos) and one studio apartment with a skylit 20" x 15" artist's studio. There is an artist's barn studio near the Villa; and the Carriage House Theatre has a Baldwin grand piano. The Center has a communal laundry. As of summer 1995, the Center was planning additional housing.

How to Apply

Send a SASE for an application and brochure. Return completed application with a $20 nonrefundable application fee and a professional résumé of nor more than two pages, three letters of recommendation (form provided with application packet), a brief project proposal, and a sample of your recent work. Appropriate work samples vary. *Composers:* send three sets of a cassette tape and a corresponding score (packaged and labeled according to instructions). *Performers:* send three sets of a cassette tape (packaged and labeled according to instructions) cued to a ten minute segment. *Writers:* send seven sets of a writing sample (not to exceed twenty pages) such as poems, chapter(s) from a novel, short stories, essays, or playscripts. Do not put your name on writing samples. *Visual artists:* send five color slides of your recent work (packaged and labeled according to instructions). Be sure to enclose an adequate SASE if you want your samples returned.

Deadline

March 1 for residencies between October through December. September 1 for residencies between January through March.

Approximate Cost of a Four-week Residency

$20, plus transportation, meals, materials, and incidentals.

Note: The information in this listing was taken from brochures and application guidelines for the 1993/94 season. Please call or write the facility to inquire about any program changes. Requests for updated information went unanswered.

VIRGINIA CENTER FOR THE CREATIVE ARTS   VA

Virginia Center for the Creative Arts
Mt. San Angelo, Box VCCA
Sweet Briar, Virginia 24595

Attention: Admissions Committee
(804) 946-7236 or (804) 946-7239 Fax

Type of Facility/Award

Residency.

Who Can Apply

Visual artists, writers, composers.

Provisos

The Center does not discriminate as to race, creed, sex, age, or physical condition. The Charter of the VCCA does not admit craftsmen or writers of scholarly theses.

Studio complex, Virginia Center for the Creative Arts. (Photo by Craig Pleasants.)

Admission criteria is competitive and selective. The Center is looking for people with professional achievement or the promise of achievement.

Dates of Operation

Open year-round.

Location

VCCA is located at Mt. San Angelo, a 450-acre estate in Amherst County, Virginia, approximately 160 miles southwest of Washington, D.C.

History

The Center was established in 1971. It's the only artists' colony in the country affiliated with an institution of higher learning. Therefore, Fellows have the opportunity to enjoy recreational and cultural activities not otherwise found in a rural setting. Fellows are free to swim in the Sweet Briar lake or indoor pool, play tennis, or attend movies, lectures and plays at the College. They can also use the college library. Sweet Briar is a private liberal arts college for women, located a mile and a half from Mt. San Angelo. The college owns the Mt. San Angelo property and leases it to the Virginia Center for the Creative Arts.

What They Offer

Residencies of two weeks to two months are offered to twelve writers, nine visual artists, and three composers (twenty-four artists are in residence at a time). Breakfast and dinner are served in the dining room of the Fellows Residence and lunches are delivered to the studios. Everyone who can is expected to pay his or her fair share. The actual cost of a residency is over $75 per day — the Center suggests a daily fee of $30 per resident. Amounts over $30 per day are considered a contribution to Fellowship funds. Abatements of the $30 fee may be granted when true need is indicated. The standard fee for a residency of two weeks or less is $35 per day. Families cannot be accommodated.

The VCCA also participates in an exchange program with the Tyrone Guthrie Centre in County Monaghan, Ireland. Two VCCA Fellows may work in Ireland for a month, and two TGC Fellows may work at the VCCA for a month. Residencies are fully funded, but artists to pay their own airfare. (See Foreign Colonies in the Appendix for address information on the Tyrone Guthrie Centre.)

Facility Description

VCCA Fellows are provided with private bedrooms in a modern, comfortable residential building. Each has a separate studio in the Studio Barn. There is a darkroom available for photographer's use. The facilities at the Fellows Residence include a library, a dining room, a living room, a game room, and a laundry.

How to Apply

Send a SASE for an application form and brochure. Return two complete sets of the following: the completed application form (which asks for a description of your proposed project, your current employment, two references, and a list of the places and dates of other residencies you may have served), your current curriculum vitae, and samples of your work. Appropriate work samples follow. *Writers:* two copies each of six to ten poems, up to two short stories, the first chapter or first twenty pages of a book, or a script of a complete work. The sample should be representative of the genre in which you wish to work at the Colony. Works-in-progress may be submitted, but should be accompanied by a sample of a finished work. *Visual artists:* two sets of up to six color slides (labeled according to instructions) of recent work with a descriptive sheet listing slides by title, medium, size, and year each work was completed. *Composers:* two sets of up to two scores (include dates completed), and if available, a corresponding cassette (labeled according to instructions) of the work. Also include a $20 nonrefundable application fee and a SASE adequate for return of your work sample. No applications are accepted by fax.

Deadline

May 15 for residencies in September, October, November, and December. September 15 for residencies in January, February, March, and April. January 15 for residencies in May, June, July, and August. Notification within two months after deadline. Late applications will be considered for wait listing and/or cancellations. Applications for the Tyrone Guthrie Centre Exchange Program are due in late November. (Call or write for guidelines if you are interested in this program.)

Approximate Cost of a Four-week Residency

$860, plus transportation, materials, and incidentals.

WATERSHED CENTER FOR THE CERAMIC ARTS   ME

Watershed Center for the Ceramic Arts
RR1, Box 845
Cochran Road
Edgecomb, Maine 04556

Attention: Holly Walker, Director
(207) 882-6075

Type of Facility/Award

Residency.

Who Can Apply

Visual and ceramic artists.

Provisos

Serious artists from all countries are invited to apply. AIA (Artists Invite Artists) groups are welcome (groups of up to seven artists who wish to collaborate or work independently together).

Dates of Operation

Watershed runs four sessions of varying length during the summer. Dates vary from year to year. (1995 sessions began June 8 and ended August 29.)

Location

Watershed is about an hour's drive northeast of Portland, Maine, and three hours from Boston. The Center is set on thirty-two rural acres, both open and wooded, with gently rolling hills. It is surrounded by a neighboring farm, Nature Conservancy land, and the Sheepscot River. There are several lakes in the vicinity and the ocean is just a short drive away.

History

The Watershed Center was originally a waterstruck brick factory. High production costs and insufficient demand necessitated the closing of the factory. Margaret Griggs joined forces with artist George Mason to organize a pilot project to utilize the brick factory site in a new way. The program was a great success. In 1986, the Center became incorporated as a nonprofit organization. Watershed provides residents with a peaceful environment, an informal atmosphere, and undisturbed time to concentrate on their work. Exchange of ideas, collaboration, experimentation, exploration, and self-inquiry are encouraged. "The mission of Watershed Center for the Ceramic Arts is to provide serious artists with time and space to create in clay."

What They Offer

Fourteen artists per session work, eat, and live in the Center's intimate community setting. Watershed can also accommodate "AIA" groups (up to seven artists working together). Four residents per summer (one per session) are fully funded. They are provided with room, board, and studio space free of charge. Eight additional residents are partially funded. Summer assistantships are awarded to applicants in need of financial aid — the residency fee is reduced in exchange for work hours. Fees vary according to session and type of residency. For Sessions I, III, & IV, participants pay $700, Artists Invite Artists pay $500, partially funded artists pay $500, and assistantships pay between $385 and $465 depending on hours worked. For Session II, participants pay $1,050, Artists Invite Artists pay $750, partially funded artists pay $750, and assistantships pay between $560 and $685 depending on hours worked. Fees include meals, housing, and studios. Studio rentals are $300 per month/$150 per month with assistantship. (A meal plan for studio rental residents is available.) A deposit of fifty percent of the total fees is due on notification of acceptance. Remainder is due thirty days prior to arrival. Firing fees are charged per kiln, with the cost split between kiln users. Watershed brick clay is free, other clay and glaze materials are sold by weight at reasonable prices.

Facility Description

The studio is housed in a spacious old brick building. There is plenty of flexible studio space with 16,000 square feet on two floors. Equipment includes two 60-cubic-foot low-fire propane car kilns, a 30-cubic-foot high-fire propane kiln, a 15-

cubic-foot wood kiln, various low- and high-fire electric kilns, potters' wheels, a Soldner clay mixer, and a Walker pug mill. A hillside of local earthenware brick clay is free and abundant. Other stand clay and glaze materials are available for purchase. Studio technicians manage and maintain the studio.

A separate residence building provides dorm housing for residents. A central living area and dining room are the sites for conversation and superb, healthy meals prepared by staff artists.

How to Apply

Send a SASE for an application and brochure. Return completed application with a $20 nonrefundable application fee, six slides of recent work (and an adequate SASE for their return), your résumé, and if you're applying for an assistantship, the addresses and telephone numbers of two references, and a list of work skills. Applications will be reviewed beginning April 15, continuing until all spaces are filled.

Deadline

April 15 for Summer Residency Program. April 24 for fully funded residencies. Award recipients will be notified by May 10.

Approximate Cost of a Four-week Residency

$20, plus transportation, materials, kiln fees, and incidentals for fully funded residencies. $20, plus transportation, tuition, materials, kiln fees, and incidentals for partially funded residencies.

WEYMOUTH CENTER   NC

Weymouth Center
P.O. Box 58
145 W. Pennsylvania Avenue
Southern Pines, North Carolina 28387

Attention: Sam Ragan, Editor and Publisher of *The Pilot* or Laurie Kennedy
(919) 692-6261

Notice: Residencies are limited to writers from North Carolina. I received no responses to repeated attempts (mail and telephone) to obtain program details. If you are interested in this program, please contact the Center directly.

WOODROW WILSON CENTER FOR SCHOLARS   DC

The Woodrow Wilson Center for Scholars
1000 Jefferson Drive S.W.
SI MRC 022
Washington, D.C. 20560

Contact: Fellowships Office
(202) 357-2841, (202) 357-4439 Fax, or TELEX 264729

Type of Facility/Award
Fellowship.

Who Can Apply
Scholars.

Provisos
Applicants from any country are welcome. All applicants are expected to have a command of spoken English. The Center is looking for men and women with outstanding capabilities and experience from a wide variety of backgrounds, including government, the corporate world, and the professions, as well as academia. Applicants working on a degree at the time of application (even if it is to be completed prior to the proposed fellowship year) are not eligible.

"For academic participants, eligibility is limited to the postdoctoral level, and normally it is expected that academic candidates will have demonstrated their scholarly development by publication beyond the Ph.D. dissertation." Non-academic applicants are expected to have an equivalent degree of professional achievement.

"The Center normally does not consider projects that represent essentially the rewriting of doctoral dissertations; the editing of papers and documents; the preparation of textbooks or miscellaneous papers and reviews; anthologies, memoirs, or translations. Because the Center has no laboratory facilities, primary research in the natural sciences is not eligible. However, projects that seek to relate the natural sciences to broader intellectual and social issues are welcomed. Proposals that represent essentially advocacy are not eligible."

Dates of Operation
Academic year (September to May or June). A few fellowships are available for shorter periods (minimum four months).

Location
Washington, D.C.

History
The Center was created by Congress in 1968 as a memorial to the United States' twenty-eighth president, Woodrow Wilson, to foster communication between the world of learning and the world of public affairs. Wilson wrote, "The man who has the time, the discrimination, and the sagacity to collect and comprehend the principal facts, and the man who must act upon them, must draw near to one another and feel that they are engaged in a common enterprise."

The Center encourages diversity of views and free and lively debate among its international company of Fellows. It awards thirty-five residential fellowships annually to a wide range of applicants whose project proposals represent scholarship with a strong emphasis on the humanities and social sciences. They also publish selected meetings and Fellows' research.

What They Offer

Stipends average $46,000 per year, including travel expenses for Fellows, their spouses, and their dependent children, and health insurance. In no case can the Center's stipend exceed $59,000. (Amount is based on the no-gain/no-loss principle of the Fellow's previous year's salary.) The Center encourages applicants to seek supplemental funding such as sabbatical support, other fellowships, or foundation grants, since funding is limited. Each fellow is assigned a round-the-clock study. Professional librarians provide access to the Library of Congress, university and special libraries in the area, and other research facilities. IBM-compatible personal computers or manuscript typing services are available, and each Fellow is assigned a part-time research assistant.

Facility Description

The Center's principal offices are located in the original Smithsonian Institution Building on the Mall in central Washington. The building offers conference rooms, a reference library, and a Fellows' lunchroom. The environment is smoke-free. The Center does not provide, but will help Fellows find appropriate housing.

How to Apply

Send a SASE for an application form and brochure. Return five collated copies of the application, a list of your publications, and your project proposal (not to exceed 2,000 words). Submit one copy of their Financial Information Form. The Center also requests three letters of reference from professionals familiar with you and your work. It is your responsibility to make sure the reference letters (sent directly by referee to the Center) arrive by the deadline.

Deadline

October 1. Notification by March 1.

Approximate Cost of a Four-week Residency

Housing, meals, materials, and incidentals — offset by stipend.

WOLF-PEN WOMEN WRITERS COLONY   KY

Wolf-Pen Women Writers Colony
c/o The American Voice
332 West Broadway
Louisville, Kentucky 40202

Attention: Residency Program
(502) 562-0045

Notice: As of January 1993, the Wolf-Pen Women Writer's Colony was no longer accepting applications. It has regenerated itself as a Kentucky eco-feminist retreat. For the foreseeable future, it will not operate as a residential writer's colony. No inquiries please. (4/93)

WOMEN'S STUDIO WORKSHOP   NY

Women's Studio Workshop
P.O. Box 489
Rosendale, New York 12472

Attention: Fellowship Program
(C : 1) 658-9133

Type of Facility/Award

Various awards available here: Artist-in-Residence Program, Residency, and Grants.

Who Can Apply

Visual artists.

Provisos

Women artists who work in intaglio, water-based screen printing, photography, letterpress, or papermaking.

Dates of Operation

September through June.

Location

Rosendale, New York.

History

The Summer Arts Institute program began in the Binnewater Arts Center in the summer of 1984 by offering sixteen workshops in two months. The 1995 program offers fifty-five workshops, beginning in June and running through October. "We are one of the only artists' spaces especially interested in women's work. We have grown to be one of the largest publishers of hand printed artists' books in the country, but we keep hanging on to our grass roots in order to make every artist who works here come to a new understanding about their work."

What They Offer

The program offers women two- to six-week sessions "designed to provide concentrated, uninterrupted work time for artists to explore new ideas in a dynamic and cooperative community of women artists in a rural environment." Artist pays $200 per week, which includes on-site housing and unlimited studio access. Artists are given a studio orientation, but must be able to work independently. Technical assistance is available for a fee. Materials are the responsibility of the artist. Residencies begin on Mondays and conclude on Sundays.

They also offer two types of book production grants. (1) *The Artists' Book Residency Grant* enables an artist to produce a limited edition bookwork at WSW. The grant provides a stipend of $1,800 for the six-week period, materials up to $450, housing, and access to all studios. Artist will be involved in all aspects of the design and production of their new bookworks. WSW will provide technical advice and, when possible, help with editioning. (2) *The Artists' Book Production Grant* is for artists working off-site. This grant is designed for artists working in their own studios on projects of a smaller scale. Funds cover production costs of up to $750 of new bookworks. It is not for reissue of previously published material and not for partial funding of a larger project.

Facility Description

The Binnewater Arts Center is home to the program's studios and classrooms.

How to Apply

Send a SASE for an application and brochure. For fellowships, return completed application with a project description, type of studio needed (etching, silkscreen, papermaking, letterpress, or darkroom), some history on your studio background and skills, the number of weeks you are requesting, and your preference of dates.

For grants, return completed application with a one-page description of the proposed project — the medium or media to be used to print the book, the number of pages in the proposed book, the page size, edition size (an edition of at least 100 copies is preferred), a structural dummy, and a materials budget — a résumé, six to ten slides, and an adequate SASE if your want your materials returned.

Deadline

July 1 for Fall Fellowships (September 1 through December 15). November 1 for Spring Fellowships (February 1 through June 30).

Approximate Cost of a Four-week Residency

$800, plus transportation, meals, materials, and incidentals for fellowships. For residency grant, transportation, meals, and incidentals — offset by stipend. For production grant, transportation, housing, meals, materials, and incidentals — offset by stipend.

Woodstock Guild
BYRDCLIFFE ARTS COLONY   NY

Woodstock Guild
34 Tinker Street
Woodstock, New York 12498

Attention: Artists' Residency Program
(914) 679-2079

Type of Facility/Award

Residency.

Who Can Apply

Visual artists, writers, and playwrights.

Provisos
None listed.

Dates of Operation
June through September. (Dates vary from year to year.)

Location
Byrdcliffe Arts Colony is a mile and a half from the Woodstock village center. Woodstock is in the Catskill Mountains — ninety miles north of New York City.

History
"The Woodstock Guild, founded in 1940 to promote the study and development of the arts, crafts, literature, drama, and music, was incorporated as a not-for-profit arts organization in 1951 to foster friendship and cooperation among artists in all fields." The Guild inherited the historic Byrdcliffe Arts Colony in 1975, which was founded in 1902 and has been operating as an artists' colony ever since. The Guild also offers concerts, theater, and literary events on a regular basis in both the Byrdcliffe Theater and the Byrdcliffe Barn.

What They Offer
The Colony offers four residency sessions each year between June and September. Session length is one month. Residents staying longer than one session receive a discount on successive (full) sessions. Fees for the sessions are as follows: Session One (June) — $400. Session Two (July) — $500. Session Three (August) — $500. Session Four (September) — $400. Exact session dates vary from year to year. Upon acceptance, a nonrefundable deposit of twenty-five percent of your fee is due. The balance is due approximately three weeks prior to the session date. The Colony can accommodate ten residents at a time. Residents are housed in the Villetta Inn, a spacious lodge. Each is provided with his or her own private room and a private studio. Residents, with use of the Inn's well-appointed community kitchen, must provide their own meals. Limited scholarships are available with documentation of your financial situation (last two years' tax returns, list of savings and holdings, and projection of income and expense for the current year).

Facility Description
Set on the slopes of Mount Guardian, the Byrdcliffe Arts Colony consists of twenty-five buildings on 600 acres. There are hiking trails nearby leading into thousands of acres of Catskill Preserve. The Villetta Inn is a turn-of-the-century mountain lodge with communal living, kitchen, and dining rooms.

How to Apply
Send a SASE for an application and brochure. Return two copies of the completed application with a $5 nonrefundable handling fee, a professional résumé, a list of your requirements (for space, light, water, etc.), a list of your work habits, a description of your proposed project, two letters of reference from authorities in your field who are familiar with you and your work, a sample of your work, and copies of any

reviews, catalogs, articles, etc. Appropriate work samples follow. *Visual artists:* eight to ten slides (packaged and labeled according to instructions). *Literary artists:* no more than twelve pages of poetry, or one chapter or story-length prose piece. Include an adequate SASE if you want your work sample returned.

Deadline

April 15. Late applications may be considered on a space-available basis.

Approximate Cost of a Four-week Residency

$405 to $505, plus transportation, meals, materials, and incidentals depending on session. Limited financial aid is available by application.

Note: This listing was taken from brochures and application guidelines for the 1993/94 season. Please call or write the facility to inquire about any program changes. Requests for updated information went unanswered.

THE HELENE WURLITZER FOUNDATION OF NEW MEXICO   NM

The Helene Wurlitzer Foundation of New Mexico
Box 545
Taos, New Mexico 87571

Attention: Henry A. Sauerwein, Jr., Executive Director
(505) 758-2413

Type of Award

Residency.

Who Can Apply

Writers, visual artists, composers, choreographers, and other creative artists.

Provisos

No interpretive artists.

Dates of Operation

April 1 through September 30.

Location

Taos, New Mexico.

History

Since 1954, the Foundation has provided twelve individual furnished-studio residencies to persons engaged in creative fields in all media.

What They Offer

Residence grants are normally made for three months, but this period is flexible and may be shortened or lengthened if conditions are mutually satisfactory. Residents are provided with rent-free/utility-free housing. There is no stipend for living expenses or supplies. Residents are expected to clean their own houses, do their own laundry, and to purchase, cook, and serve their own meals. Space is limited so the Foundation's bookings for approved residencies run about two years into the future. (At the time I wrote this listing, May 1995, residencies were booked into 1998, so plan ahead for this one.) No spouses. No children.

Facility Description

The Taos houses are furnished, including linens. A deposit of $150 is required against damage to premises, payable prior to the residency, and returnable within a reasonable time after the residency ends. Any amount required for restitution of the property will be deducted from the deposit. Facilities are handicapped-accessible.

How to Apply

Send a SASE for an application and brochure. Return completed application, a few references, a description of your intended project, and some samples of your work (photographs, transparencies, etc.). If you want your work samples returned, please include an adequate SASE. Also include a cover letter stating your choice of residency dates and the length of residency you desire. There is no application fee.

Deadline

Rolling application process. If you do not file an application within six weeks of requesting information, your file will be closed. Still, with residencies booked so far in advance, people's plans change and cancellations make space available.

Approximate Cost of a Four-week Residency

Transportation, meals, materials, and incidentals.

YADDO   NY

Yaddo
P.O. Box 395 (Union Avenue)
Saratoga Springs, New York 12866-0395

Attention: Admissions Committee
(518) 584-0746

Type of Facility/Award

Residency.

Who Can Apply

Writers, visual artists, composers, choreographers, performance artists, photographers, and film and video artists.

Provisos

Yaddo is looking for artists working at the professional level or artists who have professional promise. Artists from anywhere in the world are welcome to apply even if they are not fluent in English. "Yaddo does not discriminate in its programs and activities against anyone on the basis of race, creed, color, religion, national origin, sex, age, sexual orientation, marital status, ancestry, disability, HIV status, or veteran status."

Dates of Operation

Open year-round (except for a short time in September).

Location

Saratoga Springs, New York.

History

The Yaddo mansion was built by Spencer and Katrina Trask in 1893. It was the scene of many famous parties. When their four children died, leaving the Trasks

Studio at Yaddo. (Photo courtesy of Yaddo.)

with no heirs, they formed and endowed the Corporation of Yaddo "to administer a working community of artists in perpetuity." The first group of artists attended Yaddo in 1926. Recently, Yaddo's Board of Directors "reasserted Yaddo's original commitment to aesthetic daring, social egalitarianism, internationalism, and the support of artists at political risk."

What They Offer

Yaddo offers artists residencies of two weeks to two months. The average stay is five weeks. Small groups of collaborators (two or three people) may apply to work together. Yaddo can accommodate thirty-five people concurrently during their "large season" (mid-May through Labor Day) and fifteen people concurrently during their "small season." Each artist is provided with a private bedroom, a private studio, and three meals a day. Breakfast and dinner are communal; lunch is packed for artists to carry away. Linens are provided. Spontaneous and planned sharing of works-in-progress among guests is allowed after "quiet hours" (9 a.m. to 4 p.m. daily). No guests are allowed at dinner or overnight. No pets, except seeing-eye dogs, are allowed. There are no medical facilities and special diets cannot be accommodated. To offset the cost of your stay, a voluntary payment of $20 per day is encouraged.

Facility Description

"Besides the fifty-five room mansion, the chief residence in the summer, there are three smaller houses, as well as studio buildings and a building for administrative offices and maintenance shops. The estate's 400 acres feature four small lakes, a renowned rose garden (the only part of the property open to the public), and large areas of woodland." There are separate studios for "painting and drawing, intaglio printmaking, sculpture and welding, lithography, and photography. Composer's studios are equipped with pianos. Choreographers may request portable mirrors and barres, and the floors of their studios can be covered with marley." Writers are provided with table space. Yaddo has several small libraries (including one of Yaddo authors), laundry facilities, a tennis court, a swimming pool, a pool table, and a ping-pong table. They have bicycles and cross-country skis for residents' use.

How to Apply

Send a SASE for an application and brochure. Return the original and two copies of the completed application with a $20 nonrefundable application fee, two copies of a professional résumé, a brief biographical note, a brief description of your proposed project, some samples of your recent work, two letters of support sent directly by the sponsors, and a SASP to acknowledge receipt of your materials. Collaborators must submit separate application packages, but should indicate they are "collaborating" with others. Appropriate work samples vary by category. *Typescripts:* three copies of no more than thirty pages of either a group of poems, a short story, a one-act play, or a portion of a novel, play, or other work accompanied by a synopsis if necessary. If your work is not in English, send the original and an English translation. Typescripts will not be returned. *Slides:* seven colored slides (packaged and labeled according to instructions). *Music:* two scores and a clearly labeled audio

Cottage at Yaddo. (Photo courtesy of Yaddo.)

cassette of one of them. *VHS video cassettes:* two clearly labeled cassettes cued to a ten-minute segment and accompanied by a written explanation, if necessary. Include an adequate SASE for return of samples, except in the case of typescripts.

Deadline

January 15 for residencies from mid-May through February. August 1 for residencies from late October to May.

Approximate Cost of a Four-week Residency

$580, plus transportation, materials, and incidentals.

THE YARD   MA

The Yard, A Colony for Performing Artists
P.O. Box 405
Chilmark, Massachusetts 02535

(508) 645-9662

Administration and Winter Address:
890 Broadway, 5th Floor
New York, New York 10003

Attention: Artists' Residency Programs
(212) 228-0911

Type of Facility/Award

Artist-in-Residence Program.

Who Can Apply

Choreographers and dancers.

Provisos

There are various application requirements for each program. *Artist-in-the-Schools Program:* choreography candidates for this residency are expected to be performing at a level that would merit a creative residency; teaching experience in a school situation is a plus. *Company Development Session:* choreographers must have formed a company, performed professionally for a minimum of three years, and performed full-length programs of their own work.

Dates of Operation

Various dates during Summer. (Dates vary from year to year.)

Location

Chilmark, Massachusetts is on the island of Martha's Vineyard.

History

The Yard was founded in 1973 by Patricia N. Nanon. Since its founding, over 500 artists have collaborated on more than 100 new works.

What They Offer

The Yard provides "summer residencies at its theater and housing complex in Chilmark. The Yard supports the creation of new works by providing choreographers and dancers with housing, stipends, rehearsal space, technical and administrative staff, an artistic advisor, and the gift of time for concentrated work." They offer several different programs.

Artist-in-the-Schools Program: One teacher/choreographer will be selected for a four-week residency to teach dance/movement in the Martha's Vineyard public schools. The choreographer may bring up to five dancers. The Yard provides housing and the use of a studio for the artist to develop his or her own work. Dancers may also serve as teaching assistants. The *Artist-in-the-Schools* residency requires approximately twenty-eight hours of teaching each week. In addition to housing, the selected artist will receive a $1,000 fee and a $100 transportation allowance. Dancers' fees, other than housing, must be paid by the choreographer. Final candidates must be interviewed by the Yard's selection committee.

The Patricia N. Nanon Residency goes to a choreographer of Nanon's choice (by invitation). This person will develop a new work that will be premiered at The Yard's Barn Theater in Chilmark.

Company Development Session: Two choreographers and their companies (out of the four finalists who auditioned live for the selection committee) will receive housing, studio space, and a project fee of $4,000 to be distributed according to a proposed budget approved by The Yard. (Fees are expected to cover transportation, stipends, and production costs.) The four-week residency is intended to strengthen the bonds between company members. The performance schedule will include a premiere performance at the Barn Theater, and performances of the choreographer's repertoire of other works at special events and outreach programs for the Vineyard community, schools, and senior citizens.

Technical residencies: Positions are sometimes available for Lighting Directors, Carpenters, Technical Directors, etc. Contact The Yard for current openings.

Facility Description

None provided.

How to Apply

Send a SASE for brochure. All applicants should submit a cover letter indicating session(s) for which you are applying; a typed résumé that includes academic and professional training, choreographic, performing, and teaching experience, as well as experience in related fields; one letter of recommendation and the names, addresses and telephone numbers of two additional references (qualified dance professionals familiar with the applicant's work); information about upcoming performances that selection committee members may attend; a sample of your work (video tape); and a SASP for acknowledgment of receipt of your application materials. Enclose an adequate SASE if you want your video returned. *Artist-in-the-Schools Program:* Application should also include: a detailed description of your teaching experience; a discussion of goals for the proposed curriculum; a proposal for the choreographers own work during the residency period; and a ¹/₂" VHS video tape of your most recent work. *Technical residencies:* Submit: a cover letter, a typed résumé, recommendations, and visual materials.

Deadline

December 15 (postmarked) for Artist-in-the-Schools Program and Company Development Session. January 4 for Technical Residencies. Inquire for Patricia N. Nanon Residency. (1993/94 dates.)

Approximate Cost of a Four-week Residency

Meals and incidentals — offset by stipend. Varies by program.

Note: The information in this listing was taken from brochures and application guidelines for the 1993/94 season. Please call the facility to inquire about any program changes. Requests for updated information went unanswered.

YELLOW SPRINGS INSTITUTE   PA

Yellow Springs Institute
1645 Art School Road
Chester Springs, Pennsylvania 19425

Attention: John A. Clauser, Founding Director
(610) 827-9111 or (610) 827-7093 Fax

Notice: "Yellow Springs Institute is not accepting residency applications for 1995–
96. It is currently undergoing a period of institutional transition into a fully multidisciplinary center that will engage all fields (in addition to those that fall within the
performing arts category) in a new type of residency." The information below describes their previous residency program as of 1994.

Type of Facility/Award
Residency.

Who Can Apply
Musicians, dancers, performance artists, interdisciplinary, and other experimental
artists — transitioning to multidisciplinary facility.

Provisos
Artists interested in developing new and experimental work in music, dance, sound
research, performance art, experimental theater, and interdisciplinary forms are invited to apply. Applicants must have a minimum of three year's professional experience. Students are not eligible. Projects being undertaken to satisfy a degree or
educational requirement are not eligible. Applications are invited from professional
artists living in the United States and abroad.

Dates of Operation
May through October.

Location
Yellow Springs Institute is in an historic village thirty miles northwest of Philadelphia.

History
"The Yellow Springs Institute is an international residency center dedicated to supporting the work of creative people. Our mission, to focus society's creative power
to meet the challenges of a changing world, emerges from the belief that the interdependence of individuals, societies, and cultures is the central fact of the information age. As the world prepares to enter the 21st century, we must develop effective
forms of communication among historically divergent communities and interests.
In carrying out our mission, we commission work of innovative artists from around
the world, we animate the creative skills of leaders and executives, and we heighten
the public's awareness of the role of the creative person through public events,
publications, and radio programs."

What They Offer

Note: Currently, Yellow Springs is restructuring its program, which will not be fully defined until late 1996. YSI asked that I describe their previous program for reference, but to advise all interested applicants that the new program may be substantially different.

Previously, the Yellow Springs Institute's Residency Program (two- and three-week Residency Fellowships from May through October) provided new artists and ensembles with the resources necessary to develop new works. The idea was to encourage creation of new work that reflects the spirit of our times, expresses diverse viewpoints, and draws from and bridges a broad range of cultural traditions. They supported individual artists and ensemble work, and enabled collaborations. They offered access to facilities supported by a skilled technical staff, a commission award, housing at the Institute's guest residence Creekwood, prepared meals, documentation (video, audio, and photographic) of works-in-progress, and assistance to help defer travel expenses if traveling more than 300 miles to Yellow Springs. Fellowships were awarded through a peer review process. Two ensembles of up to five members were on-site at one time. During their residencies, artists had an opportunity to meet with artists and students from the Philadelphia area. At the conclusion of the residency, works-in-progress were presented to the public. The opportunity to exchange and reflect has been a vital part of the Yellow Springs experience.

Facility Description

YSI has a fully equipped 200-seat flexible "black-box" theater, a Skirpan lighting control system with 36 dimmers and 150 circuits, forty-five ellipsoidal and Fresnel lighting instruments, a professional 8-track analog and digital audio production studio, VHS video recording and playback, rehearsal and concert grand pianos, and a unique outdoor Earthwork Performance Space, as well as the Creekwood Residence House.

How to Apply

Call or write regarding reinstatement of a residency program before applying. Be sure to enclose a SASE.

Deadline

Rolling application process.

Approximate Cost of a Four-week Residency

No cost except incidentals if you live more than 300 miles from Yellow Springs. If you live within 300 miles of Yellow Springs, add travel expenses as well.

Yosemite National Park
YOSEMITE RENAISSANCE ARTISTS-IN-RESIDENCE   CA

Artists-in-Residence Program
Yosemite Renaissance
Box 100
Yosemite, California 95389

Attention: Bob Woolard
(209) 372-4946 or (209) 372-4024 Fax

Type of Facility/Award
Artist-in-Residence Program.

Who Can Apply
Visual artists.

Provisos

Artists should have established reputations within the art community. Students, Sunday painters, and amateur artists are generally not considered for the Artists-in-Residence program, but are welcome to participate in the group's annual arts competition.

Dates of Operation
Open year-round.

Location

Various locations within Yosemite National Park or directly adjacent are used (according to availability). Yosemite is located in the Sierra Nevada Mountains of central California. It is about a four-hour drive from San Francisco, and about two and a half hours from Fresno.

History

In early 1994, the program was inactive because of National Park Service budget cuts. Previously administered by the curator of the Yosemite Museum, the program is now in the hands of Yosemite Renaissance, a nonprofit organization. In July of 1995, the program was fully revived. Yosemite Renaissance was founded "to encourage amateur and professional artists to re-examine Yosemite in light of twentieth century artistic developments through a series of competitive exhibits; to develop an Artists-in-Residence program to give professional artists time to become more intimately acquainted with Yosemite; and to encourage dialogue between artists through an annual seminar."

What They Offer

Ten to fifteen artists a year will be selected for the AIR program. Free housing for up to one month is provided. No exchange of services is required, but the artist is asked to choose a piece of work resulting from the residency (in consultation with Yosemite Renaissance and the museum curator) to donate to the National Park Service's Yosemite Museum. The Yosemite Gallery hosts an annual exhibition of works by previous artists-in-residence. Yosemite Renaissance exhibits have also traveled to numerous exhibit sites in the San Joaquin Valley and the San Francisco Bay Area.

Facility Description

Artists will be accommodated in a private house in the Yosemite area, usually in Wawona, Yosemite West, or El Portal. House will be fully furnished and equipped. Yosemite Valley was carved by glaciers and is surrounded by steep walls of granite. There are many spectacular waterfalls, rock formations, and meadows to tantalize any artist and all visitors.

How to Apply

Send a SASE for application guidelines. Submit a résumé, ten to forty 35 mm slides of your recent work (packaged in plastic sleeves), and any other support materials that would be helpful to the selection committee. Include an adequate SASE for return of your slides and support materials. (Return may take up to four months.)

Deadline

Rolling application basis.

Approximate Cost of a Four-week Residency

Transportation, meals, materials, and incidentals.

YUCATEC FARM   VA

Yucatec Farm
Williamsville, Virginia 24487

Attention: A. A. McCaig and Donald McCaig, Sole Proprietors
(703) 925-2234

Type of Facility/Award

Retreat.

Who Can Apply

Writers.

Provisos

None listed.

Dates of Operation

Open year-round.

Location

Two miles from Williamsville, Virginia.

History

None provided. Author/owner has talked about the farm on National Public Radio's *All Things Considered.*

What They Offer

Rental consists of a well-insulated board-and-batten cottage with one 16' x 32' room that sleeps four. The cottage has a kitchen, pots and dishes, a wood heating stove (firewood supplied), and a shower. The outside toilet is clean and odorless. The cottage has no television or radio, but you can bring your own. Bring your own bedding and towels, as well as rough clothes. There is a library in the main house from which you may borrow books. The cottage is quiet and private. "In between bouts at the typewriter, you can take walks, swim, watch the deer, or help out on the farm, if you wish. You can eat berries and fruits without washing them, drink from the springs, and in the evening, watch a pair of redtail hawks over the mountain." Cost (same for one to four people) is $100 per week, except during hunting season (mid-October to November 31) when the rates are $150 per week. The owner is an author and suggests you go to the library and check out his book *An American Homeplace* for a better idea of what life at Yucatec is like.

Facility Description

Yucatec is a sheep farm in a river valley between mountains. The nearest neighbor is a mile down-river. Another mile brings you to Williamsville, which has a post office, Bookmobile, church, general store, and sixteen citizens. Grocery shopping is an hour away in Staunton. There's a lodge nearby that serves reasonably-priced, excellent dinners. Forty minutes away is Hot Springs with its fancy shops, restaurants, and the warm springs pools where you can soak for $6.

How to Apply

Call or write for reservations. First-come, first-served.

Deadline

None.

Approximate Cost of a Four-week Residency

$400 to $600 (depending on season), plus transportation, meals, materials, and incidentals.

ZEN MOUNTAIN MONASTERY NY

Zen Mountain Monastery
P.O. Box 197
South Plank Road
Mt. Tremper, New York 12457

Attention: Joy Jimon Hintz, Information Officer
(914) 688-2415 ext. *0 or E-mail: dharmacom@delphi.com

Type of Facility/Award
Retreat.

Who Can Apply
All artists and writers.

Provisos
All artists interested in pursuing their creative work within the context of Zen practice and the daily Zen training schedule.

Dates of Operation
Only winter and summer sessions are open to artists.

Location
The monastery is located on 230 acres of nature preserve in the foothills of the Catskill Mountains. It is two hours north of New York City and just over one hour south of Albany. By car, take the NY Thruway to Exit 19 (Kingston). At the traffic circle, take Rt. 28 West (Pine Hill) for twenty miles to the junction of Rt. 212 on the right. Take 212 about a half-mile to the first four-way intersection; turn left. The monastery gate is on the right a block after the turn. By bus, arrive at Mt. Tremper via Kingston on Adirondack Trailways from the NY metropolitan area. The bus passes within easy walking distance of the monastery building. By plane, Mt. Tremper is easily accessible from any of the NYC, Albany, or Newburgh airports via Adirondack Trailways (from NYC, take the airport limousine to the Port Authority bus station and then follow the directions for the bus).

History
"Zen Mountain Monastery is a monastic training center dedicated to providing authentic and traditional, yet distinctly American Zen training to people of all ages and religious backgrounds. With a resident community of twenty to thirty male and female monastic and lay residents, ZMM offers a wide variety of programs and retreats geared toward both beginning and advanced practitioners."

What They Offer
Retreats for artists include the daily training schedule with free time in the afternoon for personal study. All residency fees include meals, lodging, and all training

costs, and are payable at the beginning of each month spent in residential training. Prices listed (1995) are for accommodations in the main building; add $100 per month for a private cabin, if available. Full-time: $575 per month (includes monthly sesshin and special weekend retreats). Couples: $975 per month. Monastery Guest: $175 per week includes meals, lodging, and instruction, but does not include special programs or retreats. Work Scholarship: sometimes available if payment for residency is not possible. Applicants are asked to spend at least one month in full-time residence before applying for a scholarship.

Facility Description

Residents of one month or more are housed in private or semiprivate rooms, either in the main monastery building or in one of the rustic cabins located on the property. When available, residents may choose to live in a single cabin or in one of the Monastery's A-frames, but the cost for those accommodations is greater. Cabins and A-frames are located in the woods, which are part of the Monastery's 200 acres of forest preserve. Both are equipped with electricity and wood stoves for heat, and during much of the year, there is a nearby bath house with shower and toilet facilities. Living quarters at the monastery are simple and comfortable. Residents are encouraged to bring with them only what is necessary.

How to Apply

Send a SASE for their brochure. If after reading the brochure you are interested in applying, write or call for an application. They are interested in those who have the ability to follow the daily monastic schedule, are sincere, show a willingness to fully engage the training program in all its various aspects, and are willing to make a commitment to the development of the student/teacher training relationship during the time they are in residency.

Deadline

Rolling application basis.

Approximate Cost of a Four-week Residency

$575, plus transportation, materials, and incidentals.

FOREIGN ARTISTS AND WRITERS CENTERS

BELGIUM

RIJKSCENTRUM FRANS MASEREEL
Zaardendijk 20,
2450 Kasterlee, Belgium
Canada

KINGSTON SCHOOL OF WRITING
Summer Workshop
P.O. Box 1061
Kingston, Ontario, K7L 4Y5, Canada
(613) 548-1556

LEIGHTON ARTIST COLONY
The Banff Center
P.O. Box 1020
Banff, Alberta, T0L 0C0, Canada
(403) 762-6216

NATIONAL ENDOWMENT FOR
THE ARTS
International Program (U.S./Canada/
   Mexico)
Room 618 — Nancy Hanks Center
1100 Pennsylvania Avenue
Washington, D.C. 20506-0001
(202) 682-5422

NORTH PACIFIC WOMEN WRITERS
RETREAT
3091 W. 15 Avenue
Vancouver, B.C., V6K 3A5, Canada
(604) 734-9816, 733-6295 or 943-6888

SASKATCHEWAN WRITERS/
ARTISTS COLONIES
Saskatchewan Writers Guild
P.O. Box 3986
Regina, Saskatchewan S4P 3R9, Canada
(306) 757-631

CHINA

COMMITTEE FOR SCHOLARLY
COMMUNICATION WITH CHINA
1055 Thomas Jefferson Street, N.W., Suite
   2013
Washington, D.C. 20007
(202) 337-1250

CZECH REPUBLIC

PRAGUE SUMMER WRITERS
WORKSHOP
P.O. Box 221
110 01 Praha 01
Czech Republic
(42.2) 257.955 (Fax)

U. S. Office:
USC Professional Writing Program
WPH 404
University of Southern California
Los Angeles, CA 90089-4034

DENMARK

COMMISSION FOR EDUCATIONAL
EXCHANGE BETWEEN DENMARK
AND THE U.S.A.
(The Binational Commission [Fulbright]
   Scholarships)
Fiolstraede 10, 2. Floor
DK 1171 Copenhagen K
Denmark

DOMINICAN REPUBLIC

ALTOS DE CHAVON
Apartado Postal 140
LaRomana
Dominican Republic

U.S. Office:
Stephen D. Kaplan
Arts/Education Director
Altos de Chavon
c/o Parson School of Design
2 West 13th Street, Room 707
New York, New York 10011
(212) 229-5370

ENGLAND

READERS THEATRE WORKSHOP IN
LONDON
c/o Bill Adams
Institute for Readers Theatre
P.O. Box 17193
San Diego, CA 92177
(619) 276-1948
(619) 576-7369 FAX

NEWBERRY-BRITISH ACADEMY
FELLOWSHIP FOR STUDY IN
GREAT BRITAIN
Committee on Awards
The Newberry Library
60 West Walton Street
Chicago, Illinois 60610-3380
(312) 943-9090 extension 236

FRANCE

THE CAMARGO FOUNDATION
Cassis 13260
Bouches-du-Rhône
France
16- (42) 01.11.57 or 01.13.11

U.S. Office:
Jane M. Viggiani
64 Main Street
P.O. Box 32
East Haddam, Connecticut 06423
(203) 873-3239

CERCLE CULTUREL DE
ROYAUMONT
95 Asnières-sur-Oise
France

CHÂTEAU DE LA GARENNE-
LEMOT (this address may be incomplete)
FRAC (Fonds Régionaux d'Art
   Contemporain)
Loire Valley,
France

CHÂTEAU DE LESVAULT
Onlay 58370
Villapourçon
France
011-33 86.84.32.91

GUILLY GLAS (Writer's Retreat)
Brittany, France

U.S. Address:
c/o Mark Greenside
6621 Ascot Drive
Oakland, California 94611
(510) 530-4341

INSTITUT DES HAUTES ESTUDES
EN ARTS PLASTIQUES
75 Rue du Temple
75003 Paris
France

INTERNATIONAL JOURNALISTS IN
EUROPE
33, rue du Louvre
75002 Paris
France

THE N.A.L.L. ASSOCIATION
(Nature, Art, and Life League)
(formerly Michael Karolyi Memorial
   Foundation)
LeVieux Mas
232 Boulevard de Lattre
Vence 06140, France

LA NAPOULE ART FOUNDATION
France
U.S. Office:
Attention: Barbara Hancock/Bruno
   Laverdiere
21 W. 68th Street, #1F
New York, New York 10023
(212) 496-1039
(212) 496-1050 Fax

PARIS WRITERS WORKSHOP
WICE 20 bd du Montpamasse
75015, Paris, France
33-1-45.66.75.50
33-1-40.65.96.53 FAX

SUMMER IN FRANCE WORKSHOP
Bettye Givens
HC01 Box 102
Plainview, Texas 79072
(806) 889-3533

GERMANY

AMERICAN COUNCIL ON GER-
MANY
John J. McCloy Fund (Journalists)
14 East 60th Street
New York, New York 10022

BERLIN KÜNSTLERPROGRAM
(Artists-In-Berlin Program)
Bureau Berlin
P.O. Box 12640
Steinplatz 2
1000 Berlin 12, Germany

DEUTSCHER AKADEMICHER
AUSTAUSCHDIENS (DAAD)
Jaegerstrasse 23
D 10117 Berlin
Germany

U.S. Office:
DAAD
(German Academic Exchange Service)
950 Third Avenue
New York, New York 10022

GOETHE-INSTITUT CHICAGO
Berlin Fellowship Award
401 North Michigan Avenue
Chicago, Illinois 6061

INSTITUT FÜR EUROPÄISCHE
GESCHICHTE
Alte Universitätsstrasse 19
D-55116 Mainz
Germany

WORPSWEDE ART COLONY
Attempt inquires via:
c/o Galerie Cohrs-Zirrus
Bergstrasse 33
Worpswede, Germany
or
c/o Grosse Kunstschau
Lindenallee 3
Worpswede, Germany

GREECE (SKYROS ISLAND)

SKYROS CENTER
92 Prince of Wales Road
London NW5 3NE
England
0171 267 4424, 0171 284 3065, or 0171
284 3063 Fax

ICELAND

MINISTRY OF EDUCATION
(grant for study/research in language,
literature, and history of Iceland)
Reykjavik
Iceland

IRELAND

SUMMER WRITING WORKSHOP IN
DUBLIN, IRELAND
Eastern Washington University
Attention: James McAuley
English Department, MS 25
Cheney, Washington 99004-2415
(509) 359-7064

SUMMER POETRY WORKSHOP IN
IRELAND
c/o Billy Collins
Lehman College, Department of English
250 Bedford Park Boulevard West
Bronx, New York 10468
(718) 960-8556

THE TYRONE GUTHRIE CENTRE
Annaghmakerrig
Newbliss
County Monaghan, Ireland
047-54003

ISRAEL

HILAI: THE ISRAELI CENTER FOR
THE CREATIVE ARTS
212 Beni Ethraim Street
Naoz Avis
Tel Aviv, 69985, Israel
or
P.O. Box 53007
Tel Aviv 61530, Israel

MISHKENOT SHA'ANANIM
(PEACEFUL DWELLINGS)
P.O. Box 8215
Jerusalem, 91081, Israel

ITALY

AMERICAN ACADEMY IN ROME
7 East 60th Street
New York, New York 10022-1001
(212) 751-7200

ART WORKSHOP ASSISI ITALY
463 West Street, 1028H
New York, New York 10014
(212) 691-1159

BELLAGIO STUDY AND CONFER-
ENCE CENTER
The Rockefeller Foundation
420 Fifth Avenue
New York, New York 10018-2702
(212) 869-8500

BRITISH SCHOOL AT ROME
Regent's College
Inner Circle
Regent's Park
London NW1 4NS
England

THE HARVARD UNIVERSITY
CENTER FOR ITALIAN RENAIS-
SANCE STUDIES
Villa I Tatti
Via di Vincigliata 26
50135 Firenze FI
Italy

JAPAN

ASIAN CULTURAL COUNCIL
1290 Avenue of the Americas, #3450
New York, New York 10104
(212) 373-4300 or Fax (212) 315-0996

THE JAPAN FOUNDATION
Artists Fellowship Program

For applications from all states east of the
    Rocky Mountains:
New York Office
152 West 57th Street, 39th Floor
New York, New York 10019
(212) 489-0299
(212) 489-0409 FAX

For applications from Alaska, Arizona,
    California, Colorado, Hawaii, Idaho,
    Montana, Nevada, New Mexico,
    Oregon, Utah, Washington, and
    Wyoming:
Los Angeles Office
The Water Garden
2425 West Olympic Blvd, Suite 620E
Santa Monica, California 90404-4034
(310) 449-0027
(310) 449-1127 FAX

MINISTRY OF EDUCATION
Mombusho Scholarships
3-2-2-chome Kasumigaseki, Chiyoda-ku
Tokyo 100
Japan

NATIONAL ENDOWMENT FOR
THE ARTS
International Program
US/Japan Creative Artists' Fellowships
Nancy Hanks Center, Room 618
1100 Pennsylvania Avenue, N.W.
Washington, DC 20506-0001
(212) 682-5451

MEXICO

CAMPO DE ARTISTAS
c/o Jim Vitale
Santa Cruz via El Llano
Nayarit, Mexico
C.P. 63778

U.S. Address:
1202 E. Pike Street, #689
Seattle, WA 98122

NATIONAL ENDOWMENT FOR
THE ARTS
International Program, Room 618
U.S./Canada/Mexico Creative Artists'
    Residencies
Nancy Hanks Center
1100 Pennsylvania Avenue
Washington, D.C. 20506-0001
(202) 682-5422

WRITING RETREAT/CANOE TRIP
(Women only; some men; some kids)
(Sea of Cortez, Baja California, Mexico)
Beverly Antaeus, Director
Hawk, I'm Your Sister
P.O. Box 9109
Santa Fe, New Mexico 87504
(505) 984-2268

LATIN AMERICAS WRITERS
WORKSHOP IN TAXCO, MEXICO
U.S. Office:
P.O. Box 8293
Portland, Oregon 97207-8293

THE NETHERLANDS

EMERSON COLLEGE
European Programs

100 Beacon Street
Boston, Massachusetts 02116
(617) 578-8567
(617) 578-8618 FAX

POLAND

KOSCIUSZKO FOUNDATION
(Scholarships and grants for research and
publication of scholarly books of all types
on Poland and Polish culture)
15 East 65th Street
New York, New York 10021-6595

SCOTLAND

THE INTERNATIONAL RETREAT
FOR WRITERS AT HAWTHORNDEN
CASTLE
Lasswade
Midlothian EH18 1EG
Scotland

SCOTTISH SCULPTURE WORK-
SHOP
1 Main Street
Lumsden, Aberdeenshire
Scotland AB5 4JN
Lumsden 04648 372

SWEDEN

SWEDISH INFORMATION SERVICE
Bicentennial Fund
One Dag Hammarskjold Plaza, 45th Floor
New York, New York 10017

SWITZERLAND

LA MALADIÈRE
CH1530
Payerne, Switzerland
+41 37 61 26 60 or fax 41 37 61 84 14

WALES

BERLLANDERI SCULPTURE
WORKSHOP
Usk Road
Raglan, Gwent NP5 SHR
Wales
44-291-690268

MISCELLANEOUS FOREIGN PROGRAMS

Inquire directly:

AMERICAN COUNCIL OF LEARNED
SOCIETIES
(Fellowships for post-doctoral research in
the humanities as preparation for a book)
228 East 45th Street
New York, New York 10017
(212) 697-1505

AMERICAN-SCANDINAVIAN
FOUNDATION
(Grants for study/research in Denmark,
Finland, Iceland, Norway, and Sweden)
725 Park Avenue
New York, New York 10021

AMERICAN INSTITUTE OF INDIAN
STUDIES
(Doctoral or postdoctoral fellowships for
research in India)
University of Chicago
1130 East 59th Street
Chicago, Illinois 60637

ARCHAEOLOGICAL INSTITUTE OF
AMERICA
675 Commonwealth Avenue
Boston, Massachusetts 12215-1401
(1. The Olivia James Traveling Fellowships
— for travel and study in Greece, Aegean
Islands, Sicily, Southern Italy, Asia
Minor, or Mesopotamia)
(2. The Harriet Pomerance Fellowship —
scholarly project relating to Aegean
Bronze Age archaeology with preference
to those requiring travel to the
Mediterranean)

ARTSLINK
Arts & Media Programs
Citizens Exchange Council
12 West 31st Street, 4th Floor
New York, New York 10001-4415
(212) 643-1985

CENTER FOR INTERNATIONAL
EDUCATION
U. S. Department of Education
Washington, D.C. 20202
(202) 708-7283

COUNCIL FOR INTERNATIONAL
EXCHANGE OF SCHOLARS
(Fulbright Scholar Awards)
3007 Tilden Street, N.W., Suite 5M
Washington, DC 20008-3009
(Telephone numbers vary by country/
  program)

FOUNDATION FOR AMERICAN
MUSICIANS IN EUROPE
British American Arts Association
116 Commercial Street
London, England, EL 6NF
44-71-247-5385

FULBRIGHT TEACHER EXCHANGE
PROGRAM
United States Information Agency
301 4th Street S.W.
Washington, D.C. 20547
(202) 619-4556

INSTITUTE OF INTERNATIONAL
EDUCATION
U. S. Student Programs Division
809 United Nations Plaza
New York, New York 10017
(212) 984-5329

INSTITUTE OF INTERNATIONAL
EDUCATION
U.S. Artists at International Festivals and
  Exhibitions Division
809 United Nations Plaza
New York, New York 10017
(212) 984-5370

INSTITUTE OF CURRENT WORLD
AFFAIRS
The Crane-Rogers Foundation
4 West Wheelock Street
Hanover, New Hampshire 03755

INTER-AMERICAN FOUNDATION
(Graduate fellowship grants for research/
  study in Latin America and Caribbean)
901 North Stuart Street, 10th Floor
Arlington, Virginia 22203

INTERNATIONAL RESEARCH AND
EXCHANGES BOARD (IREX)
1616 H Street
Washington, D.C. 20006
(202) 628-8188

NATIONAL THEATER INSTITUTE
Eugene O'Neill Theater Center
International Programs
Jane H. Percy, Director
305 Great Neck Road
Waterford, Connecticut 06385
(203) 443-7139

ORGANIZATION OF AMERICAN
STATES
320 East 42nd Street
New York, New York 10017

UNIVERSITY AFFILIATIONS
PROGRAM
United States Information Agency
301 4th Street, S.W.
Washington, D.C. 20547
(202) 619-5289

LILA WALLACE-READERS DIGEST
FUND
(See also Institute of International
  Education)

Art International/IIE
Dept. AA
809 U.N. Plaza
New York, New York 10017
(212) 984-5370

APPENDIX A

Facilities Listed by State

ALABAMA
Creekwood Writers Colony, Birmingham

ARIZONA
University of Arizona Poetry Center, Tucson

CALIFORNIA
Academy of Motion Picture Arts & Sciences, Nicholls Fellowships, Beverly Hills

Chesterfield Film Company, Universal City

Walt Disney Studios Fellowships, Burbank

Djerassi Resident Artists Program, Woodside

Dorland Mountain Arts Colony, Temecula

The Exploratorium, San Francisco

Franciscan Canticle Arts Center, Palm Springs

Glenessence, Ridgecrest

Headlands Center for the Arts, Sausalito

Intersection for the Arts, San Francisco

KALA Institute, Berkeley

Stanford University, The Wallace Stegner Creative Writing Fellowships, Stanford

UCLA, The William A. Clark Memorial Library, Los Angeles

Villa Montalvo Artists-in-Residence, Saratoga

Yosemite National Park Artists-in-Residence Program, Yosemite

COLORADO
Anderson Ranch Arts Center, Snowmass Village

Denver Center Theatre Company, Denver

Ladan Reserve, Steamboat Plaza

Rocky Mountain National Park Artists-in-Residence Program, Estes Park

Rocky Mountain Women's Institute, Denver

The Marie Walsh Sharpe Foundation, Colorado Springs

CONNECTICUT
Eugene O'Neill Theater Center, National Music Theater Conference, Waterford

Eugene O'Neill Theater Center, National Playwrights Conference, Waterford

Real Art Ways, Hartford

DISTRICT OF COLUMBIA
Center for the Arts & Religion, Washington, DC

Dumbarton Oaks, Washington, DC

The Fund for New American Plays, Washington, DC

Howard University Press Book Publishing Institute, Washington, DC

Smithsonian Institution, The Renwick Gallery, Washington, DC

United States Institute of Peace, Washington, DC

The Woodrow Wilson International Center for Scholars, Washington, DC

FLORIDA
Atlantic Center for the Arts, New Smyrna Beach

Maitland Art Center, Maitland

National Foundation for Advancement in Arts, CAVA, Miami

GEORGIA
Alternate Roots/Alternate Visions, Atlanta

Hambidge Center, Rabun Gap

Nexus Press, Atlanta
Ossabaw Island Project, Savannah

HAWAII
Kalani Honua, Pahoa, Hawaii

ILLINOIS
The Newberry Library, Chicago
Ragdale Foundation, Lake Forest

INDIANA
Anderson Center for the Arts, Mt. St. Francis
Goshen College, Goshen

KANSAS
Kansas Newman College, Milton Center Fellowships, Wichita

KENTUCKY
Wolf Pen Women Writers Colony, Louisville

MASSACHUSETTS
Cleaveland House Bed and Breakfast, West Tisbury
Contemporary Artists Center, North Adams
Cummington Community of the Arts, Cummington
Fine Arts Work Center in Provincetown, Provincetown
Harvard University, Nieman Foundation Fellowships, Cambridge
Harvard University, Harvard School of Public Health, Boston
Jacob's Pillow, Lee
Medicine Wheel Artists Retreat, Inc., Groton
Nantucket Island School of Design & Art, Nantucket Island
Radcliffe College, Mary Ingraham Bunting Fellowship, Cambridge
The Yard, Chilmark

MARYLAND
Baltimore Clayworks, Baltimore

MAINE
Acadia National Park Artists-in-Residence Program, Bar Harbor
Carina House, Rockland
Maine Retreat, Troy
Skowhegan School of Painting & Sculpture, Skowhegan
Watershed Center for Ceramic Arts, Edgecomb

MICHIGAN
Isle Royale National Park Artists-in-Residence Program, Houghton
Lakeside Art and Culture International, Lakeside
Northwood University, Alden B. Dow Creativity Center Awards, Midland
Ox Bow, Saugatuck
Pewabic Pottery, Detroit
Sleeping Bear Dune National Lakeshore Artists-in-Residence Program, Empire
Urban Institute for Contemporary Art, Grand Rapids

MINNESOTA
The Loft, The Loft-McKnight Awards, Minneapolis
New York Mills Arts Retreat, New York Mills
Playwright's Center, Minneapolis

MISSOURI
ACTS Institute, Lake of the Ozarks
Niangua Colony, Stoutland

MONTANA
The Archie Bray Foundation, Helena
Montana Artists Refuge, Basin

NEBRASKA
Art Farm, Marquette
Bemis Center for Contemporary Arts, Omaha
University of Nebraska, Great Platte River Playwrights Festival, Kearney

NORTH CAROLINA
Penland School, Penland
Weymouth Center, Southern Pines

NEW HAMPSHIRE
The MacDowell Colony, Peterborough
Phillips Exeter Academy, Exeter
The Mildred I. Reid Writers Colony, Contoocook

NEW JERSEY
Creative Glass Center of America, Millville
Experimental Television Center, Ltd., Newark Valley
Peters Valley Craftsmen, Layton
Princeton University, The Alfred Hodder Fellowship, Princeton

NEW MEXICO
Hawk, I'm Your Sister, Santa Fe
Roswell Museum and Art Center, Roswell
Sonterra Condominiums, Taos
University of New Mexico, The D.H. Lawrence Fellowship, San Cristobal
Vallecitos Retreat, Vallecitos
The Helene Wurlitzer Foundation of New Mexico, Taos

NEW YORK
The Edward F. Albee Foundation Inc., The William Flanagan Memorial Creative Persons Center, Montauk
Art Awareness, Lexington
Art/OMI, Omi
Asian-American Arts Center, New York
Blue Mountain Center, Blue Mountain Lake
Center for Exploratory & Perceptual Art, Buffalo
Council on Foreign Relations, New York
The Farm, An Art Colony for Women, Poughkeepsie
Franklin Furnace, New York
Gell Writers Center of the Finger Lakes, Rochester
Harvestworks, Inc., New York

Hastings Center, Journalist-In-Residence Program, Briarcliff Manor
Henry Street Settlement, New York
Institute for Contemporary Art-P.S.1, Long Island
Ledig House International Writers Colony, Ghent
Light Work, Syracuse
Lila Wallace Readers Digest Fund, New York
Millay Colony for the Arts, Austerlitz
My Retreat, South Fallsburg
Painting Space 122, Inc., New York
Palenville Interarts Colony, Palenville
Poetry Society of America, New York
Sculpture Space, Utica
Siena College, Loudonville
Studio Museum in Harlem, New York
Women's Studio Workshop, Rosendale
Woodstock Guild, The Byrdcliffe Arts Colony, Woodstock
Yaddo, Saratoga Springs
Zen Mountain Monastery, Mount Tremper

OHIO
Pudding House Bed and Breakfast for Writers, Johnstown
Thurber House Residencies, Columbus

OREGON
Gull Haven Lodge, Florence
Lord Leebrick Theater Company, Northwest Playwrights Series, Eugene
Oregon School of Arts & Crafts, Portland
Oregon Writers Colony, The Colonyhouse, Rockaway Beach
Sitka Center for Art & Ecology, Otis
Soapstone, Portland
Southern Oregon State College, The Walden Residency, Ashland/Gold Hill

PENNSYLVANIA
Brandywine Workshop, Philadelphia
Bucknell Seminar for Younger Poets, Lewisburg

Chester Springs Studios, Chester Springs

Clay Studio, Philadelphia

Fabric Workshop, Philadelphia

Mattress Factory, Pittsburgh

Moravian Pottery and Tile Works,
Doylestown

Yellowsprings Institute, Chester Springs

Tennessee:

Arrowmont School of Arts & Crafts,
Gatlinburg

TEXAS

Glassell School of Art, Houston

Syvenna Foundation, Linden

University of Texas, The Dobie Paisano
Fellowship, Austin

VIRGINIA

Dorset Colony House, Dorset

Lynchburg College, The Richard H.
Thornton Residency, Lynchburg

George Mason University, Institute for
Humane Studies Fellowship, Fairfax

George Mason University, Institute for
Humane Studies Nonresidential
Fellowship, Fairfax

Mill Mountain Theater, Roanoke

Shenandoah Playwrights Retreat, Staunton

Theater at Lime Kiln, Lexington

Virginia Center for the Creative Arts,
Sweet Briar

Yucatec Farm, Williamsville

VERMONT

Adamant Program, Adamant

Carving Studio and Sculpture Center,
West Rutland

Vermont Studio Colony, Johnson

WASHINGTON

Centrum Artist-in-Residence, Port
Townsend

Hedgebrook, Langley

On the Boards, Seattle

Pilchuck Glass School, Seattle/Stanwood

WISCONSIN

Apostle Islands National Park Artists-in-
Residence Program, Bayfield

Blue Shores, Sturgeon Bay

The Guest House at New Light Studio's,
Beloit

The John Michael Kohler Arts Center,
Sheboygan

University of Wisconsin, Institute for
Creative Writing, Madison

WYOMING

Ucross Foundation, Ucross

CANADA

Banff Centre, Leighton Residencies, Banff,
Alberta

Banff Centre, Playwrights' Colony, Banff,
Alberta

Banff Centre, Writing Studio, Banff,
Alberta

National Endowment for the Arts, U.S./
Canada/Mexico Creative Artists'
Residencies Exchange, Washington,
DC.

North Pacific Women Writers Retreat,
Vancouver, B.C.

Saskatchewan Writers Guild, St. Peters
Abbey & Emma Lake, Regina, Alberta

Appendix B

Facilities for Writers Only
(including researchers and scholars)

Academy of Motion Picture Arts & Sciences — Nicholls Fellowship

Banff Centre Playwright's Colony

Banff Center Writing Studio

Bucknell Seminar for Younger Poets

Chesterfield Film Company Fellowship

Cleaveland House Bed & Breakfast

Council on Foreign Relations

Denver Center Theater Company

Walt Disney Studios Fellowship

Fund for New American Plays

Gell Writers Center of the Finger Lakes

Glenessence

Goshen College

Harvard University — Nieman Foundation Fellowship

Harvard University — School of Public Health Fellowship

Hastings Center Journalist-in-Residence

Hedgebrook

Intersection for the Arts

Kansas Newman College — Milton Center Fellowships

Ledig House International Writers Colony

The Loft/Loft-McKnight Awards

Lord Leebrick Theater Company/ Northwest Plays Series

Lynchburg College — The Richard H. Thornton Residency

George Mason University/Institute for Humane Studies

Mill Mountain Theater

My Retreat

North Pacific Women Writers Retreat

Eugene O'Neill Theater Center/National Playwrights Conference

Oregon Writers Colony/Colonyhouse

Phillips Exeter Academy

Playwright's Center

Poetry Society of America

Princeton University/Alfred Hodder Fellowship

Shenandoah Playwrights Retreat

Siena College/International Playwrights Competition

Smithsonian Institution/Renwick Gallery

Soapstone

Southern Oregon State College/Walden Residency

Stanford University/Creative Writing Fellowships

Theater at Lime Kiln

Thurber House Residencies

United States Institute of Peace/Jennings Randolph Fellowships

University of Arizona/Poetry Center

University of California/William Andrews Clark Memorial Library

University of Nebraska/Great Platte River Playwrights Festival

University of New Mexico/D. H. Lawrence Fellowship

University of Texas at Austin/Dobie Paisano Fellowship

University of Wisconsin/Institute of Creative Writing

Weymouth Center

Woodrow Wilson Center for Scholars

Yucatec Farm

APPENDIX C

Facilities for Artists Only
(including performance and stage artists)

Anderson Ranch Arts Center
Arrowmont School of Arts & Crafts
Art Awareness
Art Farm
Art/OMI
Asian-American Arts Center
Baltimore Clayworks
Bemis Center for Contemporary Arts
Brandywine Workshop
The Archie Bray Foundation
Carina House
Carving Studio & Sculpture Center
Center for Exploratory and Perceptual Art
Center for the Arts and Religion
Chester Springs Studios
Clay Studio
Contemporary Artists Center
Creative Glass Center of America
Exploratorium
Fabric Workshop
Franciscan Canticle Arts Center
Franklin Furnace
Glassell School of Art
Henry Street Settlement
Institute for Contemporary Art — PS1
Jacob's Pillow
Kala Institute
John Michael Kohler Arts Center
Ladan Reserve
Light Work
Mattress Factory
Medicine Wheel Artists Retreat, Inc.
Moravian Pottery and Tile Works

National Foundation for Advancement in
the Arts/CAVA
On the Boards
Oregon School of Arts and Crafts
Ox Box Summer School of Art
Painting Space 122, Inc.
Penland School
Peters Valley Craftsmen
Pewabic Pottery
Pilchuck Glass School
Roswell Museum and Art Center
Sculpture Space
The Marie Walsh Sharpe Art Foundation/
The Space Program
Skowhegan School of Painting and
Sculpture
Sleeping Bear Dunes National Lakeshore
Studio Museum in Harlem
Watershed Center for the Ceramic Arts
Women's Studio Workshop
The Yard
Yellowsprings Institute
Yosemite National Park/Yosemite
Renaissance

APPENDIX D

Facilities for Multiple Disciplines

Acadia National Park

Adamant Community Cultural Foundation/Adamant Program

The Edward F. Albee Foundation/Flanagan Memorial Creative Persons Center

Alternate Roots/Alternate Visions

Mary Anderson Center for the Arts

Apostle Islands National Park

Atlantic Center for the Arts

Banff Center/Leighton Studios

Blue Mountain Center

Blue Shores

Centrum Artist-in-Residence

Djerassi Resident Artists Program

Dorland Mountain Arts Colony

Dorset Colony House

Dumbarton Oaks

Experimental Television Center, Ltd.

The Farm — An Art Colony for Women

Fine Arts Work Center in Provincetown

Guest House at New Light Studios

Gull Haven Lodge

Hambidge Center

Harvestworks, Inc.

Hawk, I'm Your Sister

Headlands Center for the Arts

Howard University Press Book Publishing Institute

Isle Royale National Park

Kalani Honua

Lakeside Art and Culture International

Lila Wallace Readers Digest Fund

MacDowell Colony

Maine Retreat

Millay Colony for the Arts

Montana Artists Refuge

Nantucket Island School of Design & the Arts

National Endowment for the Arts/U.S.-Canada-Mexico Exchange

New York Mills Arts Retreat

Newberry Library

Nexus Press

Northwood University/Alden B. Dow Creativity Center Fellowships

Eugene O'Neill Theater Center/National Music Theater Conference

Pudding House Bed & Breakfast for Writers (and others)

Radcliffe College/Mary Ingraham Bunting Fellowship

Ragdale Foundation

Rocky Mountain National Park

Rocky Mountain Women's Institute

Saskatchewan Writers Guild

Sitka Center for Art and Ecology

Sonterra Condominiums

Ucross Foundation

Urban Institute of Contemporary Art

Vallecitos Retreat

Vermont Studio Colony

Villa Montalvo Artists-in-Residence

Virginia Center for the Creative Arts

Woodstock Guild/Byrdcliffe Arts Colony

Helene Wurlitzer Foundation of New Mexico

Yaddo

Zen Mountain Monastery

Index

Notice Regarding Arts Organizations

The criteria for inclusion in this directory was simple —those who provided artists with the opportunity to accomplish something they could not otherwise accomplish in their everyday lives because of (1) funds, (2) space, (3) or time (or any combination of the three) were included. It's clear to me that there are many organizations out there who meet this criteria, but I couldn't find them all. I searched high and low, sending out more than 500 requests for information.

If you know of an organization that should be included in any (possible) updates to this directory, please send the information to:

> Gail Hellund Bowler
> P.O. Box 1056
> Edmonds, Washington 98020

Thank you for buying this book. I hope it serves you well.

About the Author

Gail Hellund Bowler is an award-winning fiction writer. She is an avid supporter of the arts, volunteering much of her time in support of community arts organizations. In 1995, she chaired the Edmonds Arts Commission's 10th annual *Write on the Sound* writers' conference. Gail is a member of Mystery Writers of America, the Pacific Northwest Writers Conference, the (Seattle) Artists' Trust, and the Hedgebrook Writers Alumnae Association.

Originally a native of San Francisco, Gail spent the late sixties and most of the seventies working for some of the Bay Area's most famous rock bands including *Jefferson Airplane, Grateful Dead,* and *The Doobie Brothers*. She now leads a quiet life in Edmonds, Washington, with her husband Michael and two cats.